A SHORT HISTORY OF THE STATE IN CANADA

A Short History of the State in Canada tells the story of how institutions of modern government developed in Canada. The story begins with traditions of Indigenous governance, whose statelessness perplexed early European explorers and philosophers. Those Indigenous traditions grew increasingly entangled with the early colonial institutions imported into Canada from France and Britain. Over the next two centuries, fierce warfare continually shattered, rebuilt, and shattered anew the hybrid and precarious instruments of law and governance that Indigenous people sustained and that settlers and officials introduced. After the War of 1812, military exigencies gave way to liberal state institutions that gradually extended across the continent as the modern nation state took form. During the twentieth century, the story changed yet again, as the liberal state became the democratic, social welfare state that we see today.

Throughout, E.A. Heaman sustains a dialogue between the idea of the state and the practical experiments and experiences that occurred in Canada, examining both successes and failures. This concise, elegant survey goes beyond policy to examine political cultures. It incorporates recent international and Canadian writing on the state, including discussions of modern American anti-statism and its influence on recent Canadian history. *A Short History of the State in Canada* is an invaluable historical introduction for anyone interested in past or present Canadian political institutions.

(Themes in Canadian History)

E.A. HEAMAN is an associate professor in the Department of History and Classical Studies at McGill University.

THEMES IN CANADIAN HISTORY

Editors: Craig Heron and Colin Coates

E.A. HEAMAN

A Short History of the State in Canada

UNIVERSITY OF TORONTO PRESS
Toronto Buffalo London

© University of Toronto Press 2015
Toronto Buffalo London
www.utppublishing.com
Printed in the U.S.A.

ISBN 978-1-4426-3707-8 (cloth)   ISBN 978-1-4426-2868-7 (paper)

♾ Printed on acid-free, 100% post-consumer recycled paper
with vegetable-based inks

Library and Archives Canada Cataloguing in Publication

Heaman, Elsbeth, 1964–. Author
A short history of the state in Canada / E.A. Heaman.

(Themes in Canadian history)
Includes bibliographical references and index.
ISBN 978-1-4426-3707-8 (bound).   ISBN 978-1-4426-2868-7 (paperback)

1. Canada – Politics and government – Historiography.   2. Canada –
Social conditions – Historiography.   3. Political culture – Canada –
Historiography.   I. Title.   II. Series: Themes in Canadian history

JA84.C3H42 2015   320.0971   C2015-903302-0

University of Toronto Press acknowledges the financial assistance to its
publishing program of the Canada Council for the Arts and the Ontario
Arts Council, an agency of the Government of Ontario.

Canada Council   Conseil des Arts
for the Arts   du Canada

ONTARIO ARTS COUNCIL
CONSEIL DES ARTS DE L'ONTARIO
an Ontario government agency
un organisme du gouvernement de l'Ontario

Funded by the   Financé par le
Government   gouvernement
of Canada   du Canada

"L'état, c'est moi."
– Attributed to Louis XIV (1638–1715);
probably apocryphal

"A Civil Society or State is a number of proprietors of land within certain limits, united by compact or mutual agreement, for making laws and appointing persons to execute these laws for their common benefit."
– Declaration by a Pennsylvanian in 1775,
quoted in Chilton Williamson, *American Suffrage from Property to Democracy 1760–1860*
(Princeton: Princeton University Press, 1960), 6

"Capitalism is king ... The real government of our nineteenth century civilization is not the parliamentary or administrative bodies in the name of which laws are promulgated. It is the industrial and business and social organization which governs by its iron laws that need no popular assent, and cannot, as matters stand, be affected by the vote of those upon whom they press hardly."
– Phillips Thompson, *The Politics of Labor*
(New York, 1887), 98

"À qui l'état? À nous l'état!"
– Slogan, Quebec's Maple Spring, 2012

Contents

Acknowledgments

A book of this sort rests upon the work of other scholars. I have tried to do justice to the extraordinary vitality of historical scholarship about Canada. The brushstrokes are, however, very broad. This book is a map, not a monograph, and its highest aspiration is to encourage further reading in the subject.

Colin Coates commissioned this book and read it carefully and repeatedly – he's a terrific editor and colleague and a benefactor of Canadian history, as is Len Husband at University of Toronto Press, who encouraged this project from the beginning and steered it through. Thanks also to Lisa Jemison and Stephen Shapiro at the Press, and to copyeditors Beth McAuley and Barbara Kamienski. The anonymous referee's report was extraordinarily generous and thoughtful. I'm also very grateful to friends who read over the manuscript and gave advice: David Edgerton, Don Fyson, Don Nerbas, and Shirley Tillotson; and at McGill, Colin Grittner, Max Hamon, Dan Rueck, Glenn Walker, John A. Hall, and Michael Maxwell. The book also bears the impress of four years spent teaching on the undergraduate survey in Canadian studies, where I could make sweeping transhistorical claims and enjoy hearing corrective guest lectures by Canadianists from across the Faculty of Arts. Thanks to those lecturers and, above all, to Antonia Maioni,

Nathalie Cooke, and Christopher Manfredi for that rewarding experience. Thanks also to the students who challenged me at every turn and forced me to up my game.

Funding for the primary research underlying this book came from the Fonds de Recherche Société et Culture of the Province of Quebec and the Social Sciences and Humanities Research Council of Canada.

I would be remiss if I did not thank the many caregivers, public and private, who afforded me the opportunity to work. Finally, thanks to Neela, Liam, and Shaun, for forbearance, unswerving confidence, and all the love and laughter.

A SHORT HISTORY OF THE STATE IN CANADA

Introduction

There is no such thing as the state in Canada, and this is a book about it. There was not "a" Canadian state through history but, rather, a chained series of institutions, across the various territories constituting contemporary Canada, that people recognized as the state at any given time. Stripped down, the state consisted of a series of office-holding individuals who took certain actions in the name of the Crown but who drew upon a complex material and cultural infrastructure that predisposed other people to accept their claims and enactments. Taken together, particular officers could constitute a reigning government, but the phrase "the state" also refers to the institutions that remained more or less in place when the particular officers made way for others. Boundaries were malleable and sometimes frangible. Some individuals were very obviously servants of the state, universally recognized as such; others were not so widely recognized, because their identities were concealed or their claims spurious. Likewise, some deeds very evidently had some sort of official government warrant, while with others it was hard to tell one way or the other. State-serving actions were never perfectly distinguishable from other kinds of deeds. Rules governing the distinction altered over time, across space, and across social divides. Behaviour accepted as officially warranted in one jurisdiction might epitomize self-interested corruption in another. The quality of the state also inhered in the material infrastructure that these officials used to perform their duties: the gleaming marble corridors of courthouses and parliaments, the dank stone walls of prisons, the bread distributed, the guns fired, the nooses swinging. The state was nothing if it was not a striking material presence, but the quality of the state as it was dispersed through society – the difference between the loaf of bread that was a state instrument and the loaf of bread that was not – came down to one's perception of the relationship between that loaf and the social order as a whole. One of the prominent features of our story is the way in which the state has become increasingly embroiled in the whole life of society, so that very few loaves of bread in Canada today do not have some quality of the state about them.

There were always a few hard-wired qualities of the state that the actual state had to live up to, lest its status as a state fall into question. I have followed sociologist Michael Mann's definition, which insists on the specialized differentiation of offices, centrality of political relations over a given territory, and a formal monopoly on rule making and violence. Canadian state institutions were never uncontested on any of these grounds. Canada was stateless before Europeans came, and much of it remained virtually or entirely stateless long after their arrival. Centrality has required credulity: the "willing suspension of disbelief" that the poet Samuel Taylor Coleridge described in 1817 as necessary for the enjoyment of fiction. Much of Canada's recent political history has been driven by disputes about whether decentralization has been so extensive as to amount to the creation of new states in all but name and detail.

What follows amounts to a history of contestations around the most prominent aspects of the state throughout Canadian history. Those contestations reflect historical conditions under which expectations of the state were formed and crystallized. Scholars of Canadian history enjoy a privileged comparative perspective, because Canada reflected four distinct historical and cultural influences. First, the Indigenous peoples of North America, whose apparent liberty and flagrant statelessness irrevocably marked Enlightenment theorizing about the state as well as providing immigrants with an enhanced repertoire of resistance to centralized authority. Second, a lasting French tradition of statism that Louis XIV and his minister, Jean-Baptiste Colbert, inaugurated during the heyday of New France. Third, British laissez-faire practices formulated in the late eighteenth and early nineteenth centuries from the experience of an expanding commercial empire centred on the Atlantic Ocean; liberal principles provided a broad philosophical and political framework shared by people who designated themselves as Conservative (Tory) and Liberal (Grit) politicians. Fourth, the American example of the mid-nineteenth century, when corporations and local governments collaborated to promote large infrastructural and transportation projects, before the resultant crises and corruption prompted a new anti-statism that also migrated into Canada. All of these influences, which entered Canada both as widely read theories and as practical policies, coupled with conditions in Canada, worked to create distinctly Canadian approaches to and perceptions of the modern state. Sometimes these influences converged; other times, distinct cultures of governance created entrenched divisions – most conspicuously, in recent times, in the battle between small-state Albertans and social-welfare Quebecers for Ottawa's soul.

It is impossible to explain distinct states and statisms without reference to historical specificity and local cultures. Contextualizing the state in society is as old as the study of the state, and it has yielded much scholarly fruit. But the pendulum swung too far: the state was reduced to a mere arena for clashing social classes and interests, lacking any autonomous role, and the study of the state reduced to "dry and dusty legal-formalist studies" of constitutionalism.[1] In recent years, scholars have called for a return to the state and insisted on the state's role in shaping social relationships and defining objects of politics and governance. Take, for example, the perplexities of the mid-nineteenth century, when Canadian sheriffs, judges, and civilians regularly had to decide whether to yield up to Canadian or American authorities such people of contested legal and political status as escaped slaves or Confederate bank robbers, often mobilizing very local definitions of "the state" in the process. Such questions persist in new forms around migrant labour, for example, or transnational adoptions. Some negotiations were makeshift, quietly conducted with minimal state apparatus, while others ponderously wended their way through courts and privy councils – but all were profoundly shaped by overlapping conceptions of law, authority, and borders that influenced outcomes as surely as the economic and diplomatic interests at stake. This synthesis tries to sail between the Scylla of reification and the Charybdis of dissolution, locating the state in the ways it was mobilized historically in the territories that constitute modern Canada.

1

In the Absence of the State

The people who inhabited North America for thousands of years before the Europeans came were stateless. European travellers, coming from monarchical states, were incredulous that these people had neither laws nor states. They did have leadership, but it was not institutionalized either physically in institutions or chronologically with clear lines of succession. The observation was made again and again by explorers, missionaries, royal officials, and political theorists back in Europe. In Acadia in 1612, Jesuit Pierre Biard reflected of the Mi'kmaq that "their authority is most precarious, if, indeed, that may be called authority to which obedience is in no wise obligatory. The Indians follow them through the persuasion of example or of custom, or of ties of kindred and alliance; sometimes even through a certain authority of power, no doubt." Paul Le Jeune, who observed the Wendat or Huron people, wrote in 1634, "They have no true religion nor knowledge of the virtues, neither public authority nor government, neither Kingdom nor Republic, nor sciences." In the 1690s, describing inhabitants of the Gaspé Peninsula, Recollet Chrestien LeClerq remarked "they have neither police, nor taxes, nor office, nor commandment which is absolute (for they obey, as we have said, only their head men and chiefs in so far as it pleases them)."[1]

Early observers could see physical evidence of leadership, but they couldn't work out how it operated. Political leaders were identifiable by such markers as clothing, paint, or jewellery. We know little of Beothuk politics, but we learn from André Thevet that a sixteenth-century Newfoundland war leader was dressed in fine skins and feathers and was carried on the shoulders ahead of his fighting men so that these could see him and obey his orders. If explorers could not see leadership by such crude tokens, then they might not acknowledge it at all. Traders and missionaries worked harder to understand, but they still found it very difficult to grasp the mechanisms of consensual authority that they found in the New World.

Justice, too, defied their understanding. Marc Lescarbot, himself a lawyer, observed of the peoples of Acadia at the turn of the seventeenth century, "As to justice, they have not any law, neither divine nor human, but that which Nature teacheth them – that one must not offend another."[2] The situation was summed up pithily: "*ni roi, ni loi, ni foi*" – neither king, nor law, nor faith. In the late sixteenth century, Michel de Montaigne, who read up on North America and even went to see some "Brazilians" on display in France, wrote an influential essay that situated these peoples in philosophic context:

I should tell Plato, that it is a nation wherein there is no manner of traffic, no knowledge of letters, no science of numbers, no name of magistrate or political superiority; no use of service, riches or poverty, no contracts, no successions, no dividends, no properties, no employments, but those of leisure, no respect of kindred, but common, no clothing, no agriculture, no metal, no use of corn or wine; the very words that signify lying, treachery, dissimulation, avarice, envy, detraction, pardon, never heard of. How much would he find his imaginary republic short of his perfection?[3]

This was poetic licence; so too were William Shakespeare's musings, a few years later, in *The Tempest*, as to whether the new land could sustain a commonwealth with no "treason, felony ... no name of magistrate." But neither was near the scale of licence that Jean-Jacques Rousseau took in his eighteenth-century treatise on the "noble savage." Rousseau sought to idealize society before private property and the state existed, but his savage lived a wholly isolated life – a condition that patently did not describe Amerindians but was widely taken to do so.

Europeans were perplexed and fascinated. Their governments existed as massed physical objects, in some of the stateliest buildings in their respective countries. They also existed as intricate systems of written laws: making and enforcing the rules was one of the most important activities of the early modern state. But, however well they behaved at home, many Europeans committed appalling crimes in their earliest dealings with North Americans. At the turn of the sixteenth century, the Portuguese Corte-Real brothers kidnapped dozens of people from Newfoundland and Labrador; in the 1530s France's Jacques Cartier kidnapped about a dozen inhabitants of Stadacona, or Quebec, returning only two of them alive; in the 1570s the English explorer Sir Martin Frobisher kidnapped several Inuit from the Canadian Arctic; in 1609 the first contact the Iroquois had with the French was when Samuel de Champlain shot at them; and so on. From an Aboriginal perspective, over the centuries of contact, Europeans seemed to be the ones without laws. This view was incorporated into contact narratives. In 1930, one storyteller in the southern Okanagan, Suszen, described how God created two worlds, one for white people and one for Indians: "He took away one land from the top and put it to one side for the Indians-to-be. God took the laws with the Indian land and left the other land without laws. Then God built an ocean to separate these lands: one land was for the Indians, another for the white people. Indians did not need books because they knew things in their minds that they learned from the creatures."[4]

It is difficult to map European writing onto Indigenous political forms: such mapping is always a translation and always an injustice, especially when projected onto a continuous Indigenous present across space and time. Indigenous peoples of Canada had many different political forms and many different ways of sustaining those forms. Some were matrilineal, some patrilineal; some were highly mobile, others more settled. They were always in a process of adaptation, never merely static, for that is the way of human institutions. This chapter draws upon ethnohistory and the observations of Europeans to convey patterns of governance and diplomacy among different peoples across Canada during the early modern period. It also writes these experiences and observations into European history, recording the perplexities that Indigenous freedom created for European philosophers and for officials tasked with managing frontier diplomacy. Those early modern perplexities cast a long historical shadow over subsequent expectations and understandings of the state in Canada.

To say that the Indigenous peoples of Canada had no state is not, of course, to declare them ungoverned. Early modern observers equated the state with governance, but scholars have carefully disentangled them. Lawfulness did exist among all the Indigenous peoples of what is now Canada. Law meant the traditional way of doing things: resolving blood feuds for example, or determining the succession of a chieftaincy, or allocating hunting resources. These laws were – like the fabled British constitution – unwritten. They were often recounted at the beginning of important meetings, sometimes with the use of such mnemonic devices as wampum (woven belts of shell beads) or carved sticks. For the Six Nations, the Great Law was that given by the founder of the Iroquois or Haudenosaunee Confederacy, Deganawidah, sometime around the mid-fifteenth century. Haudenosaunee politics were largely local until the emergence of the confederacy. This political innovation facilitated the formation of durable and effective alliances, enabling member nations to settle disputes, prevent raids from escalating into wars, and band together for mutual defence. It achieved this without imposing any sort of common governance or laws, to the amazement of Europeans. Confederacy political relationships remained locally determined and non-coercive, as one Mohawk told Europeans at Albany in 1697: "Brethren, you know that we have no forcing rules or laws amongst us."[5] Ceremonies of deliberation, mourning, and requickening, songs, and pledges recalled the past and reminded participants of their commitment to righteousness, peace, and authority.

Non-coercive, decentralized political alliances were not unique to the Northeastern Woodlands. In Mi'kma'ki, the traditional homelands of the Mi'kmaq peoples, evidence suggests that a Grand Council of regional political alliances predated the arrival of Europeans. On the plains, the Blackfoot Confederacy, composed of Piegan, Blood, and Siksika peoples, had "no head chief and no tribal council that adopted a single policy towards Americans, or any other group. Rather, in the early nineteenth century they consisted of well over a dozen autonomous bands, each of which devised its own policies."[6] Whereas one Siksikan band leader, Old Swan, pursued conciliation and trade with Europeans and other tribes, the leader of another band, Big Man, took a more bellicose stance and traded less. Western peoples had their own ceremonies for diplomatic negotiations across different tribes and regions, including the sun dance on the Western Prairies and the potlatch around the Pacific Northwest. Thousands of people gathered every year in the Fraser River canyon to collect wind-dried salmon there, simultaneously forging economic and political alliances. These relationships were much less formal than local village or family ties, but they provided a durable framework for drawing upon a large-scale collective identity when such an identity was needed, as, for example, in years of dearth.

Communities with powerful governing customs do not need a state; coercive laws and states go hand in hand. The most sweeping investigation of states in history is that undertaken by Michael Mann, whose definition of the state may be the best available: "The state is a differentiated set of institutions and personnel embodying centrality, in the sense that political relations radiate outward to cover a territorially demarcated area, over which it claims a monopoly of binding and permanent rule-making, backed up by physical violence."[7] Mann argues that the peoples of North America did not have a state. There was little political differentiation in most Canadian Indigenous societies, excepting political and military leadership, and there was no monopoly of coercive rule-making. Scholars agree that there was greater concentration of power in the more settled societies of the West Coast than the hunter-gatherers of the Eastern Woodlands, but no chiefs wielded powers like those of European monarchs.

Mann usefully distinguishes between stated and stateless societies by suggesting that states operate with social forces to "cage" people, that is, to restrict them to certain roles and powers and to prevent them from overturning political structures and social hierarchies. If we think of the state, backed by the appropriate social and cultural sanctions, as caging people in a way that could not be easily reversed, then it seems obvious that most Aboriginal societies were not caged. They guarded their liberty as, Mann argues, most people did through most of human history: "Movement toward rank and political authority seems endemic but reversible ... the people have possessed freedoms. They have rarely given away powers to elites that they could not recover." There had been no irreversible handover of power.

Scholars argue as to how political leadership emerged in Canada. Some find no sign of organized political leadership before the fur trade, when hunting groups became larger and leadership more necessary. Others insist that the fluidity of social groupings and the need for overall coordination of technology for hunting or fishing lent themselves to political leadership long before contact. Mi'kmaq chiefs did not order people around, but they matched people to resources. Coastal fishing peoples gathered together in larger communities during the spring and summer, when the chiefs were most active, and then moved to smaller encampments in the winter, when authority was perforce decentralized. But the bulk of recent ethnohistorical evidence suggests that specified kinship networks and hunting or fishing territories were commonplace, as were "fishing bosses" and "hunting bosses" to regulate their distribution. Those functions would have been particularly important in years when resources ran short.

The notion of traditional political structures is somewhat chimerical. Early modern Canada saw huge movements of peoples across regions. Around contemporary New Brunswick and Nova Scotia, for example, early French traders identified four linguistic groups: the Almouchiquois and Abenaki (both horticultural groups), and the Etchemin and Souriquois (both hunter-gatherer societies). But warfare and disease decimated and dislocated populations. Whether Mi'kmaq, Maliseet, and Wabanakiak or Abenaki peoples were descended from earlier groups or replaced them has been disputed by scholars, and so too has the specific nature of political representation among both early and late groups. At the beginning of the seventeenth century, Samuel de Champlain mentioned six sagamores, that is, chiefs of local villages or tribal groups. Among them was Bessabez, an Etchemin leader, who enlisted Champlain to broker peace with the Souriquois, led by Membertou, who was both a shaman and sagamore, that is, a person of religious and political authority. Politics and geography tangled lineages as successive wars uprooted and intermingled populations. By the mid-eighteenth century, Abenaki villages around Acadia had large numbers of Maliseet or Canibas peoples who had fled villages on the Kennabec River that the English had burnt down. As peoples were in flux, so too were geographical boundaries. Hunting territories could span hundreds of miles. The fact that some hereditary offices were matrilineal only confused Europeans even more: Madockawando was a Penobscot chief sagamore, his children were Metis, and his grandson described himself as an Abenaki chief by his mother's line.

As the contact zone moved westward, epidemic disease, new trading relationships, and such new technologies as horses and guns all worked to transform and relocate communities that had never been fixed in the first place. Epidemic diseases had decimated European societies many times over the centuries, causing serious political and social disintegration. Indigenous peoples were almost wholly unprepared for their impact, which began with traders and missionaries and spread disastrously in the early seventeenth century and beyond. Thousands upon thousands of people died, in staggering proportions. Not all died from disease: with so many sick, it was impossible to tend the fields or to hunt effectively, and many starved. These waves of devastating disease continued to spread northward and westward through all of Canada over the seventeenth, eighteenth, and nineteenth centuries. The Haudenosaunee, intimate trading partners with the Dutch and the English, were among the first to suffer from the epidemics in the 1630s, and by the 1640s depopulation seriously threatened their ability to conduct trade or defend their territories. Epidemics, thus, caused the Haudenosaunee to launch mourning wars against the Wendat, the Petun, the Neutral or Attiwendaronk and other northern peoples, to replenish their own ranks. Remnants of these conquered peoples dispersed and regrouped in ethnically mixed settlements across North America, forging new cultural forms from the intermingling of traditions.

Such patterns of dislocation persisted more than a century later, as smallpox spread across the Northern Plains in the

1780s, sometimes killing three-quarters of populations and driving some smaller bands, like the Kootenay or Ktunaxa in present southeastern British Columbia, entirely out of some competitive districts. New migrants took up new territorial and economic niches. As the fur trade expanded westward, Cree and Anishinaabe peoples moved west with it, taking up a new role as middlemen and provisioners to the traders. We can only guess at the political changes that these peoples experienced as they reoriented themselves. Such evidence as the 200-year-old remains of an Anishinaabe youth, found at Red Deer River, dressed in chief's regalia although too young to have engaged in chiefly activities, tantalizes scholars with hints of tradition and change.

Many sources refer to the presence of multiple sagamores in maritime and inland communities. Among many peoples, such as the Wendat, the basic political or social unit was the clan segment: matrilineal families inhabiting a single community and claiming their descent from a common female ancestor. Larger villages would have several clan segments, smaller villages only one. Each clan segment had two headmen, according to anthropologist Bruce Trigger: "One was a civil leader, who was concerned with maintaining law and order; coordinating group activities, including feasts, dances, and games; and with all dealings with other groups concerning peace. The other was a war chief, who was concerned exclusively with military affairs."[8] If a chief's son displayed appropriate qualities – intelligence, oratorical ability, generosity, valour – he would probably become a chief in his turn. In some communities, women had an important voice in selecting clan leaders and advising chiefs in village councils. Such councils debated communal projects, such as building palisades or relocating the village, and addressed disputes within or between clans.

Having two chiefs checked the consolidation of power. States often expand their powers during military crises and fail to restore liberties at their cessation. If war leaders cannot exercise civil authority, they cannot use the war to increase their hold over civil society; nor can civil authorities use pretext of war to extend their powers. Often, the older men who exercised sagamore powers and the younger men who served as wartime leaders regarded one another suspiciously and actively subverted the other. Hotheaded young men might foment a war by means of private raiding parties. But to say that one act of violence might trigger a war is not to suggest that war-making powers were decentralized any more than among European countries, where a private act of abuse (such as the severing of Captain Robert Jenkins's ear in 1731) might also provoke a war. Decisions were formulated consensually.

Actions taken by individuals were understood as subject to clan discipline. In the event of a serious offence, such as a murder, the victim's clan demanded recompense or penalty from the perpetrator and his or her clan. Clans bore the burden of disciplining unruly members and did so by, for example, declaring them outside of clan privileges, making them effectively outlaws. Some communities also had secret societies or police societies to help maintain the peace. Chiefs and elders generally tried to prevent a murder from escalating into a bloody feud that might threaten peace by, for example, enjoining an offended clan to accept restitution. The Jesuit Jean de Brébeuf observed in 1636 that such suasion kept public order as well as laws.

If laws are like the governing wheel regulating Communities, – or to be more exact, are the soul of Commonwealths, – it seems to me that, in view of the perfect understanding that reigns among them, I am right in maintaining that they are not without laws. They punish murderers, thieves, traitors, and Sorcerers; and, in regard to murderers, although they do not preserve the severity of their ancestors towards them, nevertheless the little disorder there is among them in this respect makes me conclude that their procedure is scarcely less efficacious than is the punishment of death elsewhere.[9]

More than two centuries later, the same tone of bewildered respect coloured a description by naturalist George Mercer

Dawson, during a visit to the Kwakwaka'wakw at Haida Gwaii, of the local elaborate and time-consuming "ceremonies, apparently meaningless, but which serve to form the bonds and rough working machinery of society among them."[10]

Northwest Pacific coastal clans and communities had their own clearly distinguished leadership, often hereditary, which reflected social standing and influence more than formal political organization. These were socially stratified societies with slaves at the bottom and wealthy elites at the top. Most slaves were captives, but slavery could also be a punishment. Peoples of the interior had designated social ranks, but show less evidence of clearly delineated, self-perpetuating leadership. The mechanisms of early intertribal negotiation in the West and the North remain unclear, but Nisga'a oral tradition records regular councils of chiefs. Further north, Inuit societies were highly egalitarian.

The notion of non-coercive laws may seem paradoxical. There was no coercion if coercion meant armed enforcement, but human laws had divine sanction. They were conceptualized in a spiritual and naturalistic framework that reinforced human authority. Many customs reflected a sense of natural necessity and of scarce resources. Bears, for example, offered themselves to be hunted and eaten by humans in need, but they might withhold themselves if a bear carcass was treated wastefully. The relationship between natural and human lawfulness was reciprocal: as human customs respected nature, so too nature reinforced human customs and punished unnatural deeds. A murder that occurred in northwestern British Columbia in 1935 exemplifies the point. Trespassing onto another tribe's hunting grounds was a serious matter at all times and places and was, according to Witsuwit'en law, sufficient grounds for murder, with the proviso that restitution had to be made to the family of the murdered trespasser. The person who had murdered the trespasser had to mark him- or herself, to signify responsibility for the act, until the act of restitution had been performed; otherwise he or she could be killed with impunity. But in 1935, following such a trespass and murder by a neighbouring group, the killers refused to admit to the murder. The result was long-lived bad feeling between the tribes. The family of the murder victim took no vengeance, but felt that justice was served when the suspected killers all died nasty deaths, none by human hand.

Coercion here existed as a story, a narrative of events that imposed a determinate moral and political meaning to the outcome. That principle infused all relations of authority: leadership was an act of persuasion and of storytelling. Storytelling was the mechanism for socialization and discipline. When adults disciplined children, they told stories with pointed messages rather than by more direct and shaming confrontation – many were horrified to witness corporal punishments inflicted on white and Indigenous children for petty transgressions, and the difference helps to account for the failure of early schools aimed at Aboriginal children. Indigenous emissaries meeting in diplomatic councils told explanatory stories to avoid direct confrontations and to explain their reasoning. Stories were not coercive, but they enjoined a certain way of seeing the world, one that encouraged consensual norms. Stó:lo communities on the lower Fraser River based their definitions of community upon shared histories, rather than geography, and a consequence was fluidity of political identities: overlapping ties of kinship, clanship, and alliance, that confounded early observers and officials seeking to identify discrete polities.

Those consensual norms could, of course, sanction extraordinary violence: war, torture, and slavery were widespread. European-style edicts might not force a prisoner to run the gauntlet, but run it the prisoner must all the same – unless someone managed to persuade the gathered crowd to forego its rites and pleasures. In the 1650s, Pierre-Esprit Radisson narrowly escaped a process of torture and execution already underway in a Mohawk village because his adopted family negotiated for his release. Later, he watched four slaves abruptly killed on orders of an Oneida village council, to rebuke a warrior who had tried to claim them without the council's consent. Consensual rule needed policing no less than authoritarian rule did. On the whole, customs and alliances were remarkably durable, notwithstanding the scholarly insistence on fluidity and fragmentation. Historians have taken Cain's rather than Abel's perspective, privileging settlement and stability over mobility. But freedom of movement was fundamental to such peoples as the Haudenosaunee. Mobility was as important a part of their culture as the assimilation of other nations to enlarge their populations and territories. The ceremonies of the confederacy sustained political consensus amidst such extraordinary mobility, even across such supposed fissures as Christianity. When Christians left their clans to move to a Jesuit mission near Montreal, historian Jon Parmenter observes, "opportunities to reconstitute families, to hunt, to trade, and to establish a functional, persistent, League-sanctioned Iroquois presence in the St. Lawrence valley prevailed over exclusively religious motives."[11]

It is hard to assess the impact of European contact, trade, diplomacy, and missionizing on the First Nations. These were complex societies, well served by their customs, and well adapted to the environmental conditions of northern North America, with sustainable economies, and impressive military prowess. No doubt, contact challenged traditional mechanisms of governance. Epidemics wrought terrible damage, and their effects mingled in complicated ways with the efforts of early traders, missionaries, and royal officials determined to make Indigenous peoples more "European." Contact was a long and complicated process and was always enmeshed in complex cultural webs that cannot be disentangled into a linear narrative. Sometimes contact and the colonialism that followed it prompted Indigenous peoples to join together in common cause, building upon existing political traditions; other times group solidarity frayed and political traditions were ruptured.

While we may suspect that political leadership was never uncontested in any human society, the evidence, mixed and complicated, suggests new challenges to long-standing political checks on the consolidation of power. The epidemics, for example, probably enhanced the influence of military chiefs over civilian leaders. Civilian leaders were generally older than the martial young men and they were, therefore, more irreplaceable. Likewise, the fur trade provoked new grounds for warfare between some old allies. The fur trade did not introduce trade to a pre-trading society: evidence of continent-wide trading patterns dates back thousands of years. But it disrupted traditional trading relationships and may have made long-distance trade more difficult. Indigenous people in proximity to European traders tended to guard that access jealously because they could better acquire European arms and other goods, and they could trade those goods for furs rather than hunting themselves. The emergence of tobacco and liquor as important trading commodities also undermined pre-existing community relations, and missionaries were often appalled at the impact that the liquor trade had on families. Traders also tried to insist that many of the new goods, like jewellery, be consumed or owned privately rather than communally.

Some of the earliest European settlers made it their business to denounce and undermine existing norms as well as the shamans and sagamores who upheld them. Many had honed their skills by denouncing religious heterodoxy in Europe. The early missionaries subscribed to a deeply authoritarian model of divinity, and they laboured to inculcate proper deference and obedience to written law among Indigenous peoples.

The role of Indigenous peoples in seizing upon the new opportunities and trappings of power cannot be downplayed. Membertou insisted that Europeans greet his arrival with military salute, as they did their own commanders. On Vancouver Island, the late-eighteenth-century Nuu-chah-nulth leader Wickaninnish (whose name meant something close to "hereditary leader" and was passed on to his son) consolidated his authority by nurturing trading relations and acquiring an armory. Europeans were keenly aware that access to their goods could influence political relations, and they often tried to prop up a faction or candidate for leadership with such gifts as a captain's coat. Of course, such direct intervention could backfire and create an anti-trade backlash and a reversal of political fortune. But these sorts of negotiations reveal that Europeans and Indigenous people could elaborate mutually comprehensible and even shared political strategies and agendas without a shared understanding of the state. The state was not a necessary element to the psychology and language of power. In many respects, the state impeded Europeans' ability to negotiate with their Indigenous allies and enemies: there were too many hedges, checks, and constraints to let colonial officials negotiate with a free hand.

And yet, once the Europeans came, the state was immediately always implicated in the conversations and strategies. The physical apparatus of the European state was only slowly implanted across the country, but there was also an ideological advance guard. When Europeans came to Canada, they began to join in the conversations that they heard around them. But they were used to political forms wherein conversation had a limited place (exactly how limited was the subject of heated controversy) and could be trumped by something that was taking formal shape as *raison d'état*, or reason of state, during the sixteenth century. Thus, rather than considering deliberation as the best guide to behaviour, they were always following a script, often a hidden one, subordinating that deliberation to the principle of a centralized monopoly on rule making. The point is not that the Europeans thought themselves more correct than Indigenous peoples (an attitude that the latter thoroughly reciprocated vis-à-vis the Europeans), but that the Europeans subscribed to a principle of the state that permitted them, whenever possible or feasible, to override deliberation and discussion, and to impose an already made-up policy that pursued the purported interests of the sovereign. At its most basic and earliest form in Canada, the idea of the state was the principle that the central should trump the local. Much of Europe's statist ideological infrastructure was dedicated to erasing doubt and securing political and intellectual closure. Those principles of closure and of the state as a kind of trump card in effecting closure coloured the European side of the conversations and they ensured that Europeans would systematically cultivate coercive rather than deliberative strategies of diplomacy and governance.

Even as principles of centralized coercion began to work their way westward across Canada, Indigenous principles of resistance to centralized coercion worked their way eastward to Europe. The French were never able to impose their policies and forms on their Indigenous allies. When they came, they landed in the middle of a network of alliances to which they had to adapt. Champlain fell in with the Innu and their Algonquin allies north of the St. Lawrence and so joined them in warfare against their enemies, the Iroquois Confederacy. Initially, the alliance had the advantage, but over the next few decades, as the Haudenosaunee acquired firearms from Dutch and English traders, the French did little as the Haudenosaunee dispersed their allies. Some joined with the Anishinaabeg in present-day Ontario, while others moved further west or took refuge amidst the French settlements. Warfare continued on and off through the century until, in 1701, a Great Peace treaty eased Iroquois attacks on settled French populations. But warfare persisted with the Fox and the Sioux on the western frontier, notwithstanding the French desire for peace. The French could never restrain their allies from quarrelling and warring among themselves. Nor did they entirely fathom familial metaphors for political relations: when Iroquois began referring to them as "fathers" rather than "brothers," the French erroneously understood the change to reflect increased rather than diminished deference. Above all, they could not impose their military priorities. In 1710, the Mi'kmaq were more interested in collecting eels than in rushing to Acadia's defence. War aims were most likely to diverge during sieges: if Europeans negotiated a capitulation, then there would be no loot, no scalps, and no glory. In 1757, when the siege of Fort William Henry, on Lake George, ended in a peaceful capitulation, the thousands of warriors who had come from many parts of the New World seized spoils anyways, deeply embarrassing the French. The Indigenous allies believed themselves betrayed and their military support for the French evaporated, with dramatic consequences at the Battle of the Plains of Abraham two years later. The French persuaded themselves that they genuinely ruled the Indigenous peoples and that Indigenous sovereignty was a fiction. But as the French were increasingly unable to paper over the growing gaps between their interests and those of their allies, French sovereignty proved the greater fiction.

Indigenous resistance to European forms posed challenges for philosophers as well as officials. The discovery of Aboriginal statelessness shocked Europeans into reflection upon their own state. The spectre appalled many, especially at a time when European states seemed to be fragile, threatened by war, famine, and unrest. Surveying English regicide and civil war in the seventeenth century, Thomas Hobbes, the father of modern political liberalism, developed a powerful argument in favour of strong central authority for, he argued, "during the time that men live without a common power to keep them all in awe, they are in that condition which is called war, and such a war is of every man against every man."[12] According to Hobbes, where there was no strong central authority – as he thought was the case among North American "savages" – people lived in such insecurity and fear of death that neither arts nor sciences could flourish, and life was "solitary, poor, nasty, brutish, and short." Only a powerful state could sustain civil liberties and social harmony.

But other writers were more appalled by Hobbes' powerful state than by the prospect of licence, and they saw much to admire and emulate in Amerindian forms of governance. These thinkers had an important influence over European political relations and the construction of the modern state. Even as European states compiled ever more complicated legal codices, they took on some of the attributes of North American lawlessness by easing traditional moral imperatives. Classical and medieval regimes subscribed to the pursuit of a "best regime" whereby the state epitomized (more or less accurately) virtue according to human or divine law. Modern states have, instead, constructed regimes founded upon commerce and liberty. As historian Roy Porter has observed, it was during the early modern period that the great social question changed from "How can I be saved?" to "How can I be happy?"[13] Even Hobbes's authoritarian argument for a powerful state rested upon a repudiation of classical political theories, urging, instead, that human nature was best served by and adapted to a political regime that didn't expect too much morality and virtue from its citizens and left them to pursue their private ends in relative tranquillity.

Direct lines of influence can be drawn from encounters in New France to the new political theories of the Enlightenment. As early as 1649, two "Indians" who visited the French court and commented upon the juxtaposition of wealth and starvation, were branded "two Heathen Levellers."[14] Priests, too, could be important intermediaries for the circulation of new ideas, such as those of the Jesuit Joseph-François Lafitau, who, in 1724, published a study that systematically compared the customs of Huron and Iroquois with those of classical antiquity. Because, he argued, men were "everywhere the same," their politics were similar in structure (oligarchic) and substance (war, diplomacy, and civil and criminal regulation). The most obvious difference was size: European settlements were so numerous they needed a state – "a multitude of inferior magistrates"[15] – whereas the smaller numbers of Iroquois had never called for that division of authority. Lafitau saw parallels in the paganism of both groups of peoples, but other writers reasoned from Aboriginal godlessness and statelessness to denounce the modern alliance between church and state.

Above all, there was the work of Baron de Lahontan, published in 1703, which systematically compared contemporary European and Huron political ideas and structures, displaying obvious preference for the latter. It was widely read, translated, and reprinted. As well as his own sardonic remarks about the unpleasantness of European political institutions in general, especially in a New France all too dominated by priests, Lahontan published an account of a dialogue with Adario (patterned after a wily Wendat chief called Kondiaronk). There can be no doubt that Lahontan put words in Adario's mouth: the fiction of a searching Aboriginal analysis of European institutions served his subversive purposes very well. Lahontan's Adario denounced the corruption, injustice, and ignominy of European customs, arguing that Europeans had sold their liberty and their reason for material comforts that the manly Huron scorned. He rejected the subjugation of peoples "to one who possesses the whole power and is bound by no law but his own will."[16] Lahontan's suggestion was that Europeans could live a more humane and free existence if they were to dismantle their vaunted civilization.

The Baron de Montesquieu's *Persian Letters*, published in 1721, also adopted the literary conceit of a non-European observing and criticizing European laws and *moeurs*; his *Spirit of the Laws*, published in 1748, was a more systematic criticism of traditional European political regimes as dominated by repressive laws and outdated classical virtues. Montesquieu argued that these repressive regimes made men neither wise nor happy; they should be discarded in favour of something more natural – true to man's genuine nature – and more free. He drew upon the emerging model of English commercial society, but also upon Lahontan.

Montesquieu's arguments for greater political liberties and moderation in government were enormously influential; they underpinned the American Revolution. British theorists also drew upon this French discourse to develop their own theories about authority as being in important respects intrinsically consensual. Again, it was Hobbes who first developed the theory of the social contract, but eighteenth-century philosophers such as Adam Smith and David Hume reworked that contract to accord far more agency to ordinary people going about their business, strengthening their state and nation in the process. These theories decisively influenced the kind of state that would govern Canada in the eighteenth century. Cultural influence did not flow only one way; the modern conception of the state still bears the shock of the initial contact.

But the process was not linear. When Lahontan wrote, he wasn't just comparing free Hurons to caged Europeans in the abstract but was writing from his experience of New France, where the dichotomy was particularly stark. Europeans in New France were much less likely to read about natural liberty than they were to observe it around them. Indigenous statelessness was visibly played out before settlers' eyes. At Montreal, French settlers regularly rubbed shoulders with hundreds of Indigenous people – primarily Anishinaabe, Iroquois, and Odawa – who came to fur fairs every summer to trade in their furs and buy European goods. Domiciled villages existed near Quebec and Montreal, developing from missionary settlements. The most important were the Wendat refugees settled at Lorette, near Quebec; the Jesuit mission at Sault-Saint-Louis (Kahnawà:ke) with about a thousand people by the end of the century; and the Sulpician mission relocated from Mount Royal north to Sault-aux-Récollets in the 1690s with about a hundred people (and relocated to Oka in 1721). In the back country, Aboriginal peoples vastly outnumbered Europeans. There, the "middle ground," according to an influential argument by Richard White, was a geographical and a conceptual space where new and hybrid cultural and political forms were established through the process of negotiation: "The middle ground depended on the inability of both sides to gain their ends through force. The middle ground grew according to the need of people to find a means, other than force, to gain the cooperation or consent of foreigners. To succeed, those who operated on the middle ground had, of necessity, to attempt to understand the world and the reasoning of others and to assimilate enough of that reasoning to put it to their own purposes."[17]

A middle ground also characterized Indigenous-settler relations along the St. Lawrence River. Even in Montreal, the French were largely unable to impose their criminal law on domiciled Indigenous peoples who committed violence against European settlers. Chiefs would insist that the culprit had been drunk at the time, thereby absolving him (it usually was a "him") of any responsibility for the crime. Mission councils cooperated with French authorities to deliver criminals, but usually with the assurance that a speedy release rather than prosecution would follow. Officials had some legal leeway because Indigenous peoples were under the governor's sole jurisdiction. Thus, when officials seized smuggled goods, chiefs would persuade the governor to order them released. In short, conflicts were negotiated to more or less consensual conclusions, though much depended on such factors as proximity to French soldiery or the degree of military and economic involvement. Some alliances ran deeper than others, and the costs of causing offence could be higher.

The freedom of Indigenous peoples in and around the St. Lawrence valley posed immediate and practical problems for the governance of the colony. Whether friend or foe, they defied and undermined a European rule of law that was already precarious and that seemed, increasingly, to need serious military and institutional reinforcement.

If, in the long term, the impact of Aboriginal Canada on Europe was to loosen the bonds of government, its impact in the short term was to tighten them. In the face of the serious military threat posed by the alliance of Haudenosaunee and New Englanders, and in the absence of checks upon military rule, by the time that Lahontan came to New France, the French state there was becoming as powerful and oppressive as any in the world.

2

The Ancien-Régime State

Ancien-régime Canada was a frontier: that is, by definition a place of limited state authority. Europeans lacked the diplomacy and the technology to impose themselves effectively on the peoples whom they found there. They made bold claims to New World sovereignty during the sixteenth century but few practical inroads until well into the seventeenth. Frontier violence persisted beyond the end of the eighteenth century, but warlords had, by then, ceded power of place to representative institutions of government through much of the land.

Early modern European monarchs were weak at home and weaker abroad. They provided obvious political centres but controlled few direct mechanisms of power. They governed by delegating powers and privileges to intermediary groups: nobles, trading companies, churches, and local councils. All of these institutions were imported to Canada, and royal authority was largely piggybacked upon them. Even if Europeans could extend their sovereignty more directly over New World colonies, it was not clear that they should. As one adviser told James I, a private company was the best means to occupy Virginia because, if the Spanish objected to the incursion, then James could lay the blame on the Company and "the State suffers no loss, no disreputation," while any success would still redound to the Crown.[1]

Legal theorists agreed that the rule of law among nations did not apply to the colonies. Governments had to justify or punish atrocities committed by their subjects in "civilized" places, but they could close their eyes to such actions overseas. By the end of the century, treaties recognized the difference explicitly. In short, European monarchs initially made only indirect or nominal claims to and impositions of authority upon the territory that is now Canada. They were too weak to do more with any credibility, and keeping an arm's-length distance gave them greater room for manoeuvring.

The state's very weakness provided for its emergent strength. In a world where violence seemed ubiquitous and unpredictable, people looked to the state for protection, hoping for more predictability and constraint. Over time, the limited, mediated state gave way to a more direct imposition of state authority. The change reflected significant investment in royal bureaucracies and state growth in Europe and demands for European-style models of authority on the ground in Canada from both a growing population of settled Europeans and First Nations. Without royal authority backed by royal soldiers to rein in commercial, religious, and political competition, life and profit were profoundly uncertain. The French Crown encouraged settlement that would entrench its territorial claims and develop a market for metropolitan goods. Consequently, pressure mounted upon the French government to mediate between different kinds of inhabitants: settling disputes between seigneurs and farmers, rival trading interests, or quarrelling Indigenous nations. But if state authority began in mediation, it became direct and coercive. French royal authorities parlayed mediation into overt acts of control and enforcement. By the end of the seventeenth century, royal authority was independently imposed, justified by an emergent *raison d'état*, or reason of state. British colonies in Canada were slower to develop settler populations but, as the French state intervened ever more intensely, amidst a developing race to the Pacific, pressure mounted upon British officials to meet and match it.

France and Great Britain were fiscal-military states until the end of the eighteenth century, meaning that most state apparatus and spending was directed towards financing and fighting wars. Britain spent 80 per cent of its revenue on war and war debts in that century, and France spent even more. Both France and Britain used their navy to manage their colonies. Newfoundland had very little state apparatus independent of the British Navy for much of the eighteenth century; in Britain, colonial administration was placed under the Board of Trade, but it relied on pre-existing official structures, including the navy. French colonial officials looked to their naval office to cover their substantial fiscal shortfalls (after 1700 those shortfalls never fell below two-thirds of total expenses); a colonial secretariat was created only in 1749. Naval rule was much attacked by Victorian liberal reformers, who equated it with corruption, arbitrary justice, and the lash, but it was quite effective at securing metropolitan investment and bringing justice to outports. Navies were not the least enlightened wing of the early modern state. Another sign of military predominance was the use of metropolitan taxes to pay most colonial bills. Canada did not pay for its own administration. In France, the navy's budget shrank over the eighteenth century, and the cost of governing Canada put no small pressure upon it. Some local monies were raised by the lease or sale of land or the trade in furs; by customs, excise, and some specialized levies; as well as by fees for such services as justice, but much of the cost of government in Canada during the seventeenth and eighteenth centuries was borne directly by the governments of France and Britain. Their Canadian settlements remained too sparse and too poor to sustain their own government.

Population growth in the Canadian settlements did not match the growth of state apparatus. A population unable to pay for its own state apparatus or defence must be subject to imperial priorities. Neither English nor French inhabitants in early Canada could do much to restrain their states. People had the more or less "natural" freedom of the frontier but not much in the way of civil liberties. Political leadership and commercial orientation remained firmly European, well represented in their respective imperial metropolises. The situation was very different in the New England colonies, where expansive royal charters coupled with population growth created ambitious local elites. As leadership in those colonies passed from British to colonial interests that had little presence or influence in the metropolis, those local elites began to resist metropolitan constraints. Above all, settlers in the Thirteen Colonies wanted to expand freely, and they chafed at the border constraints that hemmed them in: the French, Native peoples, and British officialdom. But if the French state could be ousted, American settlers reasoned, the consequent demilitarization of the borderlands would neutralize all the other constraints; neither French settlers, nor British officials, nor Native peoples would be able to restrain American expansionism. They persuaded Britain to ramp up the war against France in North America.

France sustained defeat in the regions of Canada, ceding Acadia and Hudson Bay in 1713 and Quebec in 1763, and retaining only two small islands off Newfoundland with access to the fishery there. But the military insecurity did not let up as optimists hoped. British soldiers and officials had to pacify France's erstwhile Aboriginal allies, first in Acadia, then around the Great Lakes. And from the mid-1770s Canada was drawn into Britain's war against its American colonies, as well as the French revolutionary wars, culminating, for Canada, in the War of 1812. On the West Coast, where Americans, Russians, and Spanish competed with the British for the sea otter and swapped assertions of sovereignty, the Spanish seized British vessels in the Nootka Crisis of 1790 to enhance their claim. Into the nineteenth century, therefore, populations across Canada continued to look to the imperial state for military protection, and administrators were continually scrambling to maintain alliances and divert money to their defensive projects.

But the same pressures for an expanded state apparatus worked to restrain that apparatus. The state expanded in complexity and size, but civil society expanded still more. The settler population of Canada stood at 18,000 in 1690, and at ten times that number a century later; it had doubled again by 1805. Increasingly, people sought freedom *from* rather than freedom *through* state violence. Civil society developed its own logic, one that state officials had increasingly to respect. This chapter recounts the transformation of a limited fiscal-military state – existing in institutional form primarily to wage war and to garner revenues for those wars, and one that viewed commerce as a strategic adjunct to those projects – into a different kind of state: a state more deeply invested in commerce as providing a new measure of political legitimacy and new scope for political aggrandizement, according to formulae that insisted the state restrict the fearful powers, the systematic violence, that had first justified its extraordinary growth. It interweaves a top-down view of imperial projections with a grounded account of the institutions and everyday life that were gradually incorporated into projects of rule.

Still, Canada remained a frontier: a place where different ways of living and comparative lawlessness persisted on the fringes of everyday life. That lawlessness remained a resource for conversations about the public good, always ready to be translated into arguments for new ways of deploying the power of the state. Slavery, for example, prohibited in both imperial metropolises, was introduced in Canada because it flourished in the borderlands around Canada. Canada could not compete diplomatically or commercially without it. Slavery was tyranny on a domestic scale, and it required of the state coercive interventions that contradicted the emergent language of civil liberty adapted from metropolitan political cultures. The logic of statism versus that of the frontier, civil liberty versus natural freedom, continually collided in Canada. The consequence was not a simple decline in violence but discrete new uses for violence.

Installing European State Institutions

Explorers came first, with royal warrants in their hands, because the new lands were either subject to Christian monarchs or up for grabs. They sought the Northwest Passage: John Cabot, sailing for the English king in 1497; Giovanni da Verrazzano and Jacques Cartier, sailing for the French king in the 1520s and 1530s; and then later, English sailors Martin Frobisher, John Davis, and Henry Hudson. They laid the basis for French and English claims to sovereignty in the northern parts of North America, but their explorations proved that a Northwest Passage would be too far north to be practically useful. They brought home pyrite or fool's gold and reports of a cold climate that effectively quashed interest in the region.

The next wave of Europeans into Canada consisted of fishermen, whom Peter Pope describes as practising "vernacular" industry: industry that was primarily local and traditional in orientation, with fishermen sailing a long way to capture their fish, but preparing them according to market preferences in their local community back home.[2] This was not yet large-scale, directed capitalist exploitation, and attempts to develop that kind of directed industry, in the form of state-granted monopoly charters, failed. But the vernacular fisheries flourished among Iberian fishermen in the early sixteenth century and French and English fishermen into the seventeenth century. Catches in the early eighteenth century approached the magnitude of twentieth-century catches, employing hundreds of ships and tens of thousands of men.

While the fisheries developed freely, some merchants formed trading blocks and petitioned the state for royal charters that would give them trade monopolies. In return, they would generally promise to found a colony, govern it, and represent royal interests in the region. The French Crown issued one charter after another in the late sixteenth and early seventeenth century, but nearly all of these projects quickly collapsed due to intrigues in the French court and difficult conditions on the Atlantic Coast. Between 1534 and 1541, Jacques Cartier and Jean-François de La Rocque, sieur de Roberval, were chartered to trade and to settle Canada; in 1577 the Marquis de la Roche was commissioned as governor, lieutenant general, and viceroy of New France; in 1588 two descendants of Jacques Cartier were awarded a twelve-year monopoly on trade and minerals, but it lasted only a few months. In 1597, La Roche received a new commission and settled two hundred people on Sable Island, southeast of Nova Scotia; a scant eleven months later, Henri IV transferred the fur monopoly to Pierre de Chauvin, sieur de Tonnetuit, who settled a handful of people at Tadoussac, where the Saguenay River joined the St. Lawrence: neither settlement persisted. In 1602, another trade monopoly was granted, this time to traders in Rouen and Saint-Malo, including Samuel de Champlain, who established a settlement on Saint Croix Island, then moved it across the Bay of Fundy to Port-Royal. That site also proved inhospitable, and the initial 100,000 livres investment was exhausted. Champlain established a new and lasting settlement at Quebec in 1608, but the monopoly holder, Pierre Du Gua de Monts, lost control of the fur trade in 1609 and the company as a whole in 1610, when Henri IV's widow, Marie de' Medici, dismissed all Protestants from court. Champlain managed to regroup merchants of Saint-Malo and Rouen into a company backed by the Prince de Condé, and in 1613 this Compagnie des Marchands received an eleven-year monopoly on the fur trade. The terms, requiring annual payments plus settlement, were not fulfilled; in 1621 the viceroy (now the Duke of Montmorency, who had bought the post from his brother-in-law) transferred the colony to a new company, the Compagnie de Montmorency, which held it for six years, once again without fulfilling the obligations. More successful was the quasi-public, quasi-private company chartered in 1627 under the aegis of Cardinal Richelieu, the king's chief minister: the Compagnie de la Nouvelle France, a.k.a. the Compagnie des Cent-Associés (Company of One Hundred Associates), with an initial capital of 300,000 livres. The Company was given full ownership of the St. Lawrence valley as well as the trade monopoly; in return, it promised to settle 160 families per year and introduce priests. Most of the invested money, however, was lost when English privateers led by David Kirke seized and held the colony from 1629 to 1632.

The English Crown had begun issuing trade and settlement charters around the same time as the French, with mixed success. In the 1570s, Elizabeth I tried and failed to plant settlers on Frobisher Bay and granted Sir Humphrey Gilbert a governorship of Newfoundland. Gilbert sailed there in 1583, performed rituals of possession, and then died on the return voyage; his claims petered out. In 1610, the Privy Council bestowed Newfoundland on a company headed by John Guy, a Bristol merchant, who created the first permanent settlement. In 1621, Sir George Calvert, Baron Baltimore, established a small settlement at Ferryland, south of St. John's, but by 1628–9, attacks by French privateers led him to abandon his colony; a few years later, the British Crown named David Kirke, now Sir David, governor of Newfoundland as a reward for his earlier capture of Quebec.

Both French and the English Crowns delegated their powers of governance and warfare to companies and commissioned privateers to prey on enemy ships and settlements. Privateers like Kirke operated on the margins of legality: in times of war, they functioned as an unofficial navy; in times of peace, they were ostensibly reined in. But delegation entrenched violence deeply within emerging commercial networks. Canada attracted too many competing nations, companies, and interests to permit uninterrupted economic development. Traders and settlers pleaded with the state to protect them. The British state responded more slowly, but ultimately more forcefully, to such pleas than did the French state.

Settlement was the crucial factor determining state investment in the colony. The British did not seriously pursue settlement in Canadian territories before the eighteenth century, and they primarily took up arms in Canada to protect their settled colonies to the south. The French state pursued settlement along the St. Lawrence much earlier. French state formation in the area that is now Canada can be seen as following three waves: the stage of chartered companies in Acadia and Canada; the refounding of New France as a royal province in 1663; and finally, the establishment of Louisbourg on Île-Royale (later Cape Breton) in 1717, after the cession of Acadia four years earlier. At each new foundation, the French state gave itself new powers and presence, always for purposes of warfare. New France was continually embattled, and all its activities had to be managed with an eye to strategic interests. The fur trade was a branch of diplomacy: a means of forming alliances with Indigenous peoples. It required substantial investment in forts and soldiers, but that investment made it unremunerative. Only an alliance between merchants and the state could underwrite the fur trade and sustain a settlement colony.

Early rule in New France was corporate rule: governors represented both the king and the Hundred Associates. Samuel de Champlain served as de facto governor in New France until his death in 1635, but his authority was never formally established by the Crown. He made peace and trade treaties, but there were no early land cessions. He also banished or executed lawbreakers and wastrels largely off the cuff, and passed ordinances that have not survived, for lack of a bureaucracy to record them. Local inhabitants could petition Champlain or French authorities for reforms: in 1621, they gathered in a public meeting to negotiate the transfer of goods and powers from one company to another and to request a more formal judicial system, as well as schools, soldiers, money, and a ban on Protestants. After 1635, the king named governors of New France. Charles Huault de Montmagny, a French nobleman, held the position until 1648. He was the first Onontio (Mohawk for "Great Mountain"), a title that was later used by French Indigenous allies to refer to all governors. Montmagny held all administrative, military, and diplomatic powers, aided by a lieutenant, a clerk of court, and an attorney. As new towns were established at Trois-Rivières in 1635 and Montreal in 1642, governors were named for them. The Hundred Associates controlled Trois-Rivières directly, but in 1640 ceded the island of Montreal to a charitable organization based in France, the Société de Notre-Dame de Montréal, which named its own governors, beginning with Paul de Chomedey de Maisonneuve.

The Company of One Hundred Associates was neither fully private nor fully public; such distinctions were still developing in the seventeenth century. Richelieu's involvement made it more state-like than its predecessors, essentially a royal corporation privately funded. Royal involvement prevented intrigues from rival merchants, and royal decrees staved off creditors. The state enforced settlement, fortification, regular supply ships, and missions – financial difficulties notwithstanding – though it let the more profit-minded associates drop out.

But the Company was not doing enough to sustain the colony. Haudenosaunee raiders impeded the flow of furs into the trading posts and trade dried up. In 1644, the queen regent transferred the trade to a group of colonists, the Community of Habitants, which would pay an annual feudal fee of a thousandweight of beaver fur and administer the colony. A public meeting approved the terms of the transfer and elected twelve directors. The queen regent also donated 100,000 livres towards the defence of the vulnerable colony, which was seriously beset at the very gates of the settlements. Settlers hardly dared gather a lettuce or a few sticks of firewood for fear of ambush; one complained that they dared not stand in the doorway to relieve themselves. In 1645, the troops helped French officials to negotiate a treaty with the Mohawks that extended French protection to Christian allies of the French, but left the "Algonquins without shelter" unprotected and paved the way for the destruction of Wendake.

Still, settlers and traders quarreled over control of the trade. The Community tried to restrict the trade in furs to a handful of traders, so as to push up prices, but ordinary inhabitants protested this infringement on their customs through public meetings and intermediaries such as priests. Corporate rule threatened public order. The Crown responded by creating a Central Council in 1647, composed of the royal governor, the governor of Montreal, and the superior of the Jesuits (later replaced by the Bishop of Quebec) to oversee the colony and the fur trade – the freedom of which was restored to settlers. Thus did three distinguished founders – Montmagny, Maisonneuve, and Jesuit Jérôme Lalement – assume direct royal rule in Canada. The council was modelled on French provincial *parlements*, with powers to regulate police, appoint clerks and controllers of the fur trade, borrow money, inspect accounts, and address remonstrances to the king. The three towns of Quebec, Three Rivers, and Montreal had non-voting, later voting, syndics present. In general, the council eased constraints on trade and lowered the Community's profits from 50 per cent to 25 per cent. But with open competition, the fur trade was unprofitable. The income was insufficient for ordinary administration and grossly insufficient to fight a war (exports from New France were as low as 7 per cent of exports from the West Indies to France). By 1658, war had broken out again, with the Haudenosaunee perpetrating deadly raids directly on French settlements. Furs couldn't reach the towns, farmers dared not tend their fields, and many talked of abandoning the colony. Again corporate rule seemed to be failing in Quebec.

Acadia, governed more distantly by the Hundred Associates, was even less secure. The primary threat in Acadia came from rival governors, merchants, and privateers. In 1631, King Louis XIII named Charles de la Tour his lieutenant general and governor for Acadia, in return for a promise to build a fort at the mouth of the St. John River. La Tour, a fur trader, built the fort, but it was overrun by Scots the following year. When the colony was returned to France months later, the Hundred Associates conveyed to Richelieu's cousin, Isaac de Razilly, a large seigneury and the governorship of Acadia. Razilly and La Tour came to terms, but then Razilly died, and his agent, Menou d'Aulnay, also a distant cousin to Richelieu, defended his claim to the colony and persuaded the king to recognize him as governor. D'Aulnay died in 1650, whereupon La Tour had the king restore his title. D'Aulnay's widow petitioned the king's uncle, César de Vendôme, superintendent of navigation, and struck a deal, ceding him the title in exchange for half the land. By marrying the widow, La Tour resolved her claim, but his title was now challenged by Vendôme and by d'Aulnay's main creditor in France. Meanwhile, in 1654, though England and France were at peace, Robert Sedgewick, a Boston merchant with a commission from Oliver Cromwell to make reprisals against French privateers, seized Port-Royal. England returned the colony to France under the Treaty of Breda, signed in 1667, but in order to pay reparations, La Tour signed the colony over to English interests. Privateers, pirates, merchants, seigneurs, and weak governors continued to vie inconclusively for Acadia through the end of the seventeenth century and into the eighteenth. All those bloody rivalries seriously impeded the development of the colony. The state in Acadia was at best nominal, at worst a target. French officials there were, but the lack of French soldiers made them virtually useless. Settlers formed parish assemblies to run their own affairs, and they largely ignored political allegiances as they negotiated taxes, rents, and trade.

Areas of Canada controlled by the English Crown in the seventeenth century also had little direct state control. Newfoundland was largely governed by a system of fishing admirals, whereby the first captain to arrive in a given port served as de facto governor, allotting places in the harbour and judging disputes. This system was enshrined in law in 1699, deemed appropriate for a land with few settlers. The English state came close, in the 1670s, to forcing all settlers to leave the island so as to avert the kind of public resistance to corporate rule seen in New France. When privateers attacked English settlements, fishing admirals were the leading line of defence, as in 1673 when Christopher Martin, a fisherman planter (farmer), fended off a Dutch privateering expedition. As well, the French occupied and fortified Placentia from the early 1660s and used it as a base to attack the British settlements.

The vast inland territory that drained into Hudson Bay attracted even less attention from the British state. A royal charter of 1670 made the Company of Adventurers of England Trading into Hudson's Bay the "true and absolute Lordes and Proprietors" of about 40 per cent of what is now Canada, which it held in "free and common soccage," with power to wage war, build forts, and dispense justice. The Company's claims were challenged by the French all around the bay from the 1680s. Pierre Le Moyne d'Iberville, New France's greatest locally born warrior, took the largely unprotected trading posts by surprise when he marched north from the St. Lawrence colony with sixty voyageurs and half that number of regular soldiers. That raid occurred in the absence of a state of war, but later devastating attacks by d'Iberville on trading posts around Hudson Bay and settlements in northern New York and Newfoundland were acts of war. The HBC governors tried and failed to persuade British diplomats and politicians to send resources to defend Hudson Bay and to represent company interests in their negotiations with France. In defiance of the 1697 Treaty of Ryswick, France held on to HBC posts until 1713.

In short, endemic violence, a weak state, and corporate rule constituted the normal condition of life in early Canada. Coastal and inland settlements alike were extremely vulnerable to attacks and raids. The seventeenth-century practice of licensing private government and private warfare resulted in a system that could generate violence but not quell it, disrupt trade but not sustain it. Given the proximity of competing colonies and Aboriginal nations, it would take enormous resources to change that basic fact of insecurity, well beyond those of a corporation trading in fish or fur. Thomas Hobbes's description of the state of civil war, undermined by continual insecurity, best described the *European* experience of early Canada. This was not a simple dichotomy of order versus chaos. Scholars speak of a "regulatory order" across the Atlantic and other arenas of imperial competition that relied "more on interimperial negotiation than on a connected network of legal forums and naval enforcers."[3] Violence and expropriation were not the absence of order but factors to be negotiated and means of negotiating in a hybrid and legally pluralistic world. Tolerating violence and suspending the "law of nations" in North America were ways of declaring geopolitical boundaries to be part of what was under negotiation.

But tolerance for violence diminished over the early modern period as settled, urban populations increased and sought greater security, private expectations here dovetailing with new state ambitions. The French state began the seventeenth century neither centralized nor integrated; by the end of the century, it was both. Louis XIV built upon a process already initiated under Louis XIII, expanding the use of the Intendant de justice, police et finances, appointed directly by the Crown to represent it in the provinces and colonies. Greater standardization and extension of royal justice, substantial increases in taxation and the army, expanded the French state. Overall, French state spending increased in the seventeenth century by a multiple of between five and eight. Still, the core purpose of the state under Louis XIV remained unchanged: to finance and wage war. Much of this expansion was directed at enhancing the king's authority rather than that of the state per se, but "the state, not the king, was the great winner from increasing absolutism: the state, a permanent and autonomous entity, could do without the monarchy."[4]

The new apparatus of government was exported to New France, which Louis XIV decided to rule directly. The Hundred Associates was dissolved, and the colony returned to the Crown in 1663. Louis XIV secured the province militarily by sending out a regiment of professional, uniformed soldiers, deployed in two attacks upon Iroquoia, and resulting in a momentarily successful treaty between French and Iroquois. He vested the administration of New France into three branches: commercial, civil, and military. A new company, the Compagnie des Indes Occidentales, had feudal or "seigneurial" title to the land as well as the fur monopoly. This was one of two new companies created by the new minister of the marine and colonies, Jean-Baptiste Colbert, to manage French imperial trade. Colbert subscribed 30,000 livres, while Louis XIV subscribed three million. The new company had a seat on the Central Council, now renamed the Sovereign Council, but civil administration was under direct Crown control. The Company went bankrupt within a decade, as did subsequent companies, including one chartered to wrest the fur trade from the Hudson's Bay Company.

Civil concerns as well as military ones prompted the royal takeover. The Community of Habitants resisted its seigneurial burdens (paid to the Hundred Associates) while settlers protested the Community's monopoly on trade and all pressed their claims on the French court. The reorganization took two years, 1663–5, as a weakened governor fought a losing battle against church and oligarchy, seigneurial and royal courts of justice alike were paralyzed by conflicting decrees, and the civil administration stuttered to a halt because the first intendant named by the Crown remained in

Europe. It may well be that the Crown's intentions changed during the process, so that a modest redistribution of powers became a deeper realignment.

The most important change was the new post of intendant, a civil administrator who exercised new administrative powers, such that "his integration into the administrative structure more or less shattered it."[5] The governor would henceforth focus on military concerns, though this left him considerable scope because diplomacy and trade remained closely aligned. Mandated to work with and oversee the Sovereign Council, powerful intendants took control of it: there, the "Great Intendant" Jean Talon routed such rivals as Bishop François de Laval, defeating the churchman's attempts to increase the tithe or restrict the liquor trade. Intendants also worked to rein in seigneurs, forcing them to fulfil settlement obligations, for example, while a series of new courts purveyed royal justice, though some seigneurs continued to dispense some forms of justice on their personal domains. Above all, the intendant managed state spending in the colony, and Colbert's mercantilist policy of promoting economic development in the colony (albeit a development subordinated to metropolitan economic interests) sent more than a million livres through his hands between 1665 and 1672.

The most important aspect of the change was centralization. We might borrow Peter Pope's distinction between vernacular and directed trade and apply it to the state in the same period. Government in Canada before 1663 was vernacular government: it reflected and responded to local contingencies rather than to central direction. Indeed, much like Aboriginal forms of government, successful leadership depended largely upon the personal strength and charisma of the leader in question. In Newfoundland, Sir David Kirke represented civil power on the south Avalon, "de jure among the planters and de facto among West Country migratory crews within his sphere of operations. Kirke held courts and was capable of enforcing his decisions, executive or judicial, by force majeure."[6] He was finally undone by rivals in England and died in prison in 1654. No later merchant in the region enjoyed his prestige, and the result was an absence of civil government in that region.

French absolutism aimed at overcoming vernacular government in France and colonial holdings. It marked a change in the way power was delegated. When the early modern state delegated powers, it did so in its own image. A chartered corporation or a seigneur exercised powers of governance similar to those that the king enjoyed. Offices were usually sold, often irrevocably, and they tended to become autonomous and hereditary rather than responsible to the king. Bourbon absolutism took a different form. New offices, like the intendancies, were not sold and derived their authority directly from the king. Louis XIV relied on increased taxes for his income, and he obtained the nobles' collusion by exempting them from those taxes. Seigneurs still collaborated in the constitution of royal authority, but their powers became more circumscribed, while those exercised by royal officials – much more precisely defined – expanded. There remained very considerable overlap: most intendants also purchased venal offices, for example. And office holders still quarreled among themselves – so intensely in 1682 as to provoke the recall of both governor and intendant of New France. But the quarrels could not be translated into the armed territorial disputes that devastated Acadia. Appointed directly by the king and subject to recall, these officials were less likely to lose sight of the king's interest than were nobles or corporations. The reforms reduced complexity and overlap, and they united central policy and local governance within a mercantilist framework.

France and Britain seemed to go in very different directions at the end of the seventeenth century, with royal powers enhanced in France and weakened in Britain. The British Revolution of 1688 resulted in an assertion of parliamentary sovereignty and the restriction of monarchical powers. But in the colonies, the effect was the same: centralization of power in the metropolis. Whereas royal charters had conveyed expansive powers of government, those issued by Parliament after 1688 were far more limited. At the turn of the eighteenth century, French government in Canada looked more enlightened and responsive than British rule in Hudson Bay and Newfoundland, where independent state authority remained close to nil. The intendant existed to check military and corporate rule, both of which held sway in those territories (unlike in the British colonies to the south, where a more lively civil society resulted from higher levels of immigration). Indeed, Louis XIV patronized apologists for royal prerogative who described his projects of state-centred modernization as more progressive than the looser, commercially driven modernization of the Dutch or the British.

Whether or not the intendant actually checked corporate or military rule is another question and a controversial one. Scholarly debates have long raged about the extent to which local and imperial policies genuinely cohered. Accusations of corruption, of substituting private gain for public benefit, were levelled against governors and intendants from the beginning. Jean Talon was told to encourage local industries that might serve the empire, such as ship-building, mining, agriculture. Investing his own money in a brewery and even fur trading was one thing, but Talon went further, shipping consumer goods from France to New France duty-free and selling them in competition with merchants. When the merchants complained of being undercut, Talon explained to Colbert in 1670 that new settlers could not afford the merchants' high prices, so his goods were indispensable aids to the new settlements and industries. Colbert took Talon's side. Intendants could, apparently, engage in commerce that served the interests of consumers. Strategic interests could also outweigh private concerns: soon after his appointment as governor, Count de Frontenac established a fur-trading post on Lake Ontario, at what is now Kingston, to forestall traders based downriver. When the fur-trading governor of Montreal protested, Frontenac threw him in jail. For these misdeeds and for committing military resources to his trading ventures, Frontenac was reprimanded and recalled in 1682. His successor promised to renounce private profits, but did not; nor did Frontenac himself, restored to office to confront a renewed Iroquois threat in 1689. By contrast, Intendant Michel Bégon was, in 1715, reprimanded by the Council of Marine (the body vested with colonial affairs) on the grounds of "having engaged in commerce," an activity that was "not permitted and was in no way suitable in the position you occupied."[7] Among other misdeeds, Bégon had responded to reports of dearth by requiring farmers to bring one-fifth of their harvest to royal warehouses in Quebec and Montreal, only to resell the produce, profitably, in the West Indies.

At delicate moments, the state was prepared to make delicate decisions as to what sort of commercial activity was appropriate to state officials. But in a world where officials operated as "profit-making entrepreneurs in government finance,"[8] the boundary between public and private could not be other than vague and shifting. Where strategic interests or public tranquillity were too scandalously sacrificed to personal profit, the central government could intervene. But that capacity for responsiveness should not be confused with genuine sympathy for public opinion in New France. Unlicensed popular assemblies were illegal in New France (as in France) on the grounds that they encouraged "all sorts of monopolies, secret associations, and plots."[9] Popular opinion in New France had legitimate avenues: from time to time officials convened public assemblies to take advice on such matters as the fur trade or defence. Individuals could also petition royal officials, as Montreal women did in 1714 to complain of the bad quality of available bread. But officials controlled the agendas for such public meetings. Independent initiative, as in 1675 when Montrealers gathered to demand a syndic be restored to the superior council, was met with gubernatorial reprimand. The state constituted itself as the protector of the people, but there was no intention to generate individual or public liberties – rather the reverse. The state's concern was to ensure public order and tranquillity and to prevent agitation for such necessities as food and security that might become agitation for rights. Enlightenment philosophers might insist on the distinction between state and civil society, but these were polemical concepts, idealizing the notion of a bounded state and individual liberties. They did not describe conditions in the early modern colony.

Scholars have tended to exaggerate the binary of state and society in New France because the geographical and political distance between Versailles and the *pays d'en haut*, the back country, was so vast. The imperial court and the colonial frontier became archetypes of extreme statism and statelessness, autocracy and freedom, so that analyses of their practical interface tend to drift towards one pole or the other. Some see a largely autonomous frontier society very like the American frontier that historian Frederick Jackson Turner identified as the foundation for America's greatness in 1893. They point to flurries of edicts and regulations restricting the fur trade, regularly reiterated because regularly ignored. Wayward officials who ignored instructions from Versailles and pursued their own interests could seriously undermine French imperial policies; such was the case with French diplomats mandated to seek peace with Western tribes who instead enslaved tribe members, thereby inspiring military reprisals. Others see in New France an effective imperial state: "In the final analysis, Louis XIII and his ministers would prove capable, when they wished and when their attention could be brought to bear upon the issues, of exercising a commanding influence on the way in which colonial ventures developed."[10] They argue that colonial officials were members of a cosmopolitan network, one often rooted in familial connections. Such officials served in many different arenas and imported a genuinely imperial vision to the administration of the colonies, a vision that does not always show up in documentary archives. Indeed, these complex networks of private sociability and political influence greatly complicate questions around the state's responsiveness: nobles or merchants or farmers who might not gather publicly to demand a reform could, nonetheless, exercise considerable influence through such networks. Other recent work breaks down the dichotomy between metropolis and colony, noting, for example, that legal disputes about New France reflected and reshaped metropolitan legal cultures. There was not one metropolitan authority but, rather, overlapping jurisdictions that mined colonial experiences to enhance rival claims.

Historians of the imperial state in New France play an elaborate game of Whac-a-Mole: no sooner is any hint of statist intervention spotted than it is blamed for the colony's eventual failure. They argue that the colony was designed and administered to serve metropolitan rather than local interests. Were it not for the military expenses and the interference with market forces, New France might not have been conquered. In his classic study *The Fur Trade in Canada*, Harold Innis explained that the French state responded to growing British competition by expanding its military outposts and troop manoeuvres, fatally undermining French traders and stunting other industries, with the final result that "French power in New France collapsed of its own weight." Other scholars point to exactions on fishermen around Placentia or an edict of 1704 that prohibited all industries capable of competing with French interests. They condemn a short-sighted focus on fiscal gains at the expense of colonial economic needs and opportunities and argue that the colonists made their own world, largely in defiance of mercantilist prohibitions; small wonder that they outlasted the French state in Canada.[11] But still other scholars play down the dichotomies of empire and colony, state and non-state, finding local advantage in certain kinds of statism. French traders probably exaggerated the effects of foreign competition for political purposes, and the few

French soldiers stationed in the trading regions probably did help to keep English traders away and sustain French profits. Only after the Conquest did the fur trade open up to all comers, leading to a collapse in prices, extensive cutthroat competition, and eventual consolidation. One recent study tallies all the different state economic ventures: the aid given by royal officials to entrepreneurs in pitch extraction, soap making, beer brewing, potash production, slate quarrying, hemp cultivation, fishing, and ironworking, and finds that "without the crown's intervention, New France would have been a more primitive and fragile colony, dependent upon the mother country for its basic needs."[12] Historians who denounced these failed state projects were guilty of focusing too much on export statistics and ignoring the developing domestic economy.

But if recent scholarship blurs distinctions between public and private and gives more credence to local economic agency, there is nonetheless substantial evidence for a state trajectory of coercion and despotism. Traditional archival documents may exaggerate central policy over local practice, but they also conceal the state's coercive reach within those local practices. For example, French Canadians were purportedly freer because they were less taxed than French peasants, but such arguments underestimate statute labour. "The peasant at the start of the eighteenth century who provided fifteen days of corvée on the walls of Quebec, a dozen more to build or maintain the roads in his parish, which is to say almost a month of a growing season that counted only six months, might also consider that he contributed largely to the public works."[13] New France also lacked some important checks on state authority. Food illustrates the point well. Royal officials made sure that urban populations would not lack for food, lest they rise up in protest if bread, a key dietary staple, was too expensive or unavailable. Consumers could buy at markets before innkeepers or peddlers could buy their stock. But other regulations to protect French consumers were not introduced. Officials could freely engage in the wheat trade, and they regulated themselves less than they regulated farmers and small-scale sellers. They could buy and sell where they liked, secretly hoard grains, supply bakers, or form secret price-fixing associations – all things forbidden them in France. Bakers could be merchants, something that became a serious conflict of interest in the early eighteenth century, as both cities and the export trade grew, during a period of modest harvests, renewed warfare, and inflated prices. Because New France's cereal production was closer to subsistence levels than in France, and supplies often ran short towards the end of the long winter, the state was more likely to intervene aggressively to requisition wheat.

When New France was under military threat, the colonial authorities tended to expand their powers of intervention and control, in food as in everything else. The intendants did not check military rule but drew greater strength from it. However moderate the system of state exaction might have been during time of peace, in time of crisis – ill defined and frequently invoked – it permitted extraordinary state intervention. Commerce could be brought to a standstill, all manner of property seized in country and town, and people summarily conscripted. Incidents of resistance did occur, including a pillory thrown into the river or a demonstration at Montreal to demand lower prices on food and salt, but they were rare in the seventeenth century and not much more frequent in the eighteenth.

War justified much of the permanent institutionalization of the state, in New France as in France. Into the eighteenth century, as the British threat to French presence in America grew, so did the heavy hand of the military state. If the French state was at its weakest in Acadia, the loss of the region led to new heights of statism there. Louisbourg, founded in 1717, was a fortress town where the state was a powerful and fully militarized presence. The earliest officials and nearly half the founding settlers were soldiers, and even in peacetime, as in the 1730s, a quarter of the inhabitants were soldiers. Soldiers outnumbered civilians on the colony's Superior Council. This was visibly a very well ordered community – although officials could be heard complaining that Acadians in the vicinity defied their authority. Nonetheless, Louisbourg also fell to the British in due course, as did New France as a whole in 1763.

Conquest hovers in the background as the standard for determining success or failure of "the state" but it provides only a partial measure. Metropolitan officials wanted the colony to be as profitable and peaceable as strategy permitted; colonists wanted the same thing in reverse, with profit and tranquillity trumping geopolitics. Given that the imperial connection failed but the colony itself continued to grow under new rulers, it might be argued that the state in New France served the local population better than it served the imperial court. Indeed, most local institutions of government persisted, largely unchanged, into the post-Conquest era. The Catholic Church, the courts of law, local administrative units such as the militia, even feudal land tenure were all perpetuated by the British Parliament. Eighteenth-century British rule in British North America was an ancien-régime form of government, with some mechanisms for sounding opinion but scant formal integration. Newfoundland and Hudson Bay looked more like New France than New England; Nova Scotia alone received a legislature before the 1770s. Thus, ordinary life could persist largely unchanged across the Conquest, as an overview of the churches, the courts, and the institutions of land ownership reveals.

State Institutions in Everyday Life

Political apparatus in ancien-régime Canada reflected an essential tension between metropolitan need for and distrust of local elites. French and British authorities sought to create local landed gentry, but they also tried to prevent them from becoming powerful enough to challenge

metropolitan interests. In this matter, there was surprising
continuity. Britain's southern colonies enjoyed greater powers of self-government because they held royal charters that
predated 1688. Parliament guarded its sovereign powers
more jealously than had the king, exercising them more directly over colonial populations and with fewer delegated
powers. Colonial rule in Canada was exercised primarily by
appointed officers operating under a centrally appointed
governor. Acadia, and later Quebec, full of Catholic subjects
traditionally loyal to the French Crown, were long denied
local powers of representation, incorporation, and taxation.
British local government was by magistrates and county
courts, under the supervision of the provincial governor.
Magistrates – unpaid amateur justices of the peace – put
up public buildings, regulated markets, issued licences to
tradesmen, and supervised taxation and such local work as
road surveying. There was almost no incorporation of towns
in Canada before 1830. Thus, in comparison to Britain and
New England, Canada lacked institutions of self-government, particularly at the local level. Long before the Revolution, New Englanders considered Nova Scotia's government
too military and centralized to suit them: "The power of the
crown, in conjunction with the musketos [mosquitoes], has
prevented men from settling there."[14] Because the British
state was more centralized and more authoritarian in its Canadian holdings, radical ideologies that spread like wildfire
through the American colonies failed to catch in the north.

But if neither Versailles nor Whitehall sought to empower
Canadian elites politically, they also did not adopt levelling
principles. They incorporated the interests of local elites and
governed through them. Metropolitan officials might balk
at providing political powers to the colonial elite, but they
encouraged social distinction and deference. A state could
not be run without such things. When the Crown granted
commercial or seigneurial or ecclesiastical privileges, it had
a vested interest in seeing them observed, for royal authority
was, through such intermediaries, personified to ordinary

people. In proclaiming himself a father to his people, a king drew upon and reinforced the paternal authority that a father exercised over all the people in a household, including women, children, servants, and slaves. Louis XIV infused the most mundane daily activities with elements of the ritual authority and symbolism of his coronation ceremony, believing that "the people over whom we rule, unable to see the bottom of things, usually judge by what they see from outside, and most often it is by precedence and rank that they measure their respect and obedience."[15] Claims to paternal authority reinforced one another and they knit together old-regime society from top to bottom, with a cultural resonance that exceeded their immediate coercive powers. The precise terms of dissemination differed in New France and British North America – the one characterized by seigneurs, the other by householders with more restricted powers – but seigneurs and heads of households both served as the most important intermediaries between inhabitants and the state, and both exercised near-feudal powers over their extended households – powers that the post-Conquest authorities worked to reinforce. Historian Nancy Christie sees in a (Lower Canadian) Master and Servant Act of 1802 an attempt to extend paternal rule both within and beyond the family: "In a society without the regulatory apparatus of a poor law, few charitable societies to reinforce values of deference, a paucity of churches to morally regulate the population, and minimal governmental institutions outside the courts, the master-servant laws served as a form of omnibus legislation with wide cultural implications for the governance of all types of subordinates and potential delinquents, including masterless youths, vagrants, and the poor."[16]

All monarchical states encouraged deference and social distinction, but imperial states had reason to carry things rather further. Imperial rule was exercised over very different subjugated and Indigenous populations. Sometimes a small handful of metropolitan officials or merchants ruled vast and populous territories. The greater the disparity of numbers and of cultures, the more coercive the process of subjugation was likely to be. Empires built up technologies of differentiation that justified "enlightened" imperial rule – what came to be known as the "white man's burden." An extraordinary amount of social and political capital was spent distinguishing between "Indians" and "Europeans," and much of the state apparatus and many of the laws introduced into Canada were designed to create, perpetuate, and administer the so-called racial differences. The process was begun in the eighteenth century but became much more developed as ideology during the nineteenth.

In Canada, the local state was founded upon distinctions of religion, class, race, and gender, based upon theories of property, colour, and sex. Property formed the basis of legal citizenship and could be used to manage all the others. In British North America, as in New France, "Indians" and women faced legal obstacles to holding property, while working people faced practical ones. By British tradition, people without property were considered incompetent to govern themselves, and they were, therefore, enormously disadvantaged in their dealings with the emerging imperial state, which claimed the authority to dictate policy and interests to them. Property was a kind of ballast: the gentry with large estates, observed Edmund Burke, a conservative philosopher and legislator, tended to support conservative policies that prevented social or economic upheaval. In both Britain and France, ownership of land was connected to political privileges, though that relationship was becoming complicated by the eighteenth century with the emergence of new and powerful interests, particularly mercantile and financial capital. Things were even more complicated in North America because land was so much more freely available than in either France or Britain. That meant it was both cheaper and far less lucrative, especially in the early years before there was much in the way of settlement.

There was a conflict of interest between the imperial state's desire for large landed estates and its need for intensive settlement to make areas economically viable and ethnically French or British. Large conveyances of land slowed down the rate of clearing and settlement. That tension was very visible in land policies in New France. The French principle of feudal tenure, *nulle terre sans seigneur* (no land without a lord), was imported to New France, and the land was given, initially by the Hundred Associates and later by the Crown, to seigneurs who would be responsible for peopling it with tenants or *censitaires* (so named for the *cens*, a small annual fee, distinct from rent, owed by all peasant holders) and providing such services as mills and courts. Under the Hundred Associates, seigneuries went to men holding colonial office, and the process worked to consolidate power within a handful of families. But elite consolidation impeded actual settlement. Thus, from the late seventeenth century, a series of edicts threatened to confiscate lands if seigneurs did not properly settle them. Louis XIV instructed Jean Talon to reclaim and redistribute unsettled or overly large seigneuries, and he repeated those instructions in 1711. But intendants balked at alienating large landowners, and seigneurs found ways to evade such rulings by claiming they had ceded the land or were farming it themselves.

The French state intervened on tenants' behalf so as to get them onto the land, but largely ignored their complaints once they were on it. It prohibited seigneurs from writing a seigneurial corvée into the terms of tenure, but tenants who had already signed such documents were told they must fulfil their contract. In a dispute that occurred in Rivière-du-Sud, near Quebec City, during the 1730s and 1740s, a seigneur let his mills decline, the better to pry them from his co-heirs. When his *censitaires* resorted to other mills, he sued them. The case went all the way to the minister of the marine in France, the Comte de Maurepas, who ruled against the "unruly" *censitaires*. Officials found it more useful to punish insolence and confirm seigneurial exactions than to discipline a neglectful seigneur. When *censitaires* sought to rebuke seigneurs in petitions or the courts, the cases were apt to be dismissed, often with accusations of popular insolence. The French state in New France lent its authority to sustaining seigneurial standing and privilege.

The slow pace of settlement delayed but did not prevent land ownership from generating an elite, and the tensions persisted under British rule. In 1787, an early governor of Quebec, Guy Carleton, Lord Dorchester recommended reserving five thousand acres in every thirty-thousand-acre township for the King to "create and strengthen an Aristocracy, of which the best use may be made on this Continent, where all Governments are feeble and the general conditions of things tends to a wild Democracy."[17] One way to build up a loyal elite was to grant land to military veterans, who were offered fifty acres if they were private soldiers and up to five thousand acres if they were of field rank. After the American Revolution, the grants were reduced and in 1791 capped at 1,200 acres by the imperial Parliament. But in Upper Canada in the late 1790s, a local acting governor, Peter Russell, took a Dorchesterian view and made larger grants of up to six thousand acres for councillors like himself. Such grants paved the way for enormous speculation and the creation of powerful landed dynasties, like the Baby family, which owned 13,400 acres by 1805, or Robert Hamilton, who dominated trade and politics in the Niagara Peninsula and owned over forty thousand acres. On Lake Erie, Thomas Talbot parlayed a five-thousand-acre grant into sixty-five thousand acres under his control. The larger landowners proved some of the most conservative members of Upper Canadian society. In the early nineteenth century, their languid pace of developing land became a major political complaint among local populations. Similar tensions infused politics in Prince Edward Island, where distant British landlords virtually monopolized land ownership.

In Quebec, the new British overlords needed different strategies because good farming land was largely settled.

British merchants soon took over the transatlantic trade and began to constitute themselves as a powerful and landed bourgeoisie in the colony, but a dense society of farmers, traders, and professionals remained stolidly in place on the land. The early governors soon decided not to tear up existing property relations but, instead, to govern through them and other institutions already in place. New grants of seigneuries ended, and freehold tenure was introduced into unsettled lands, but existing seigneurial titles were confirmed. To a considerable degree, the British perpetuated French laws, offices, and elites, quickly grasping that these provided the best means of managing the eighty thousand or so French-Canadian inhabitants. Well might Benjamin Franklin predict that the conquest of New France would be followed by a flood of northward-bound immigrants or the Archbishop of Canterbury predict that missionaries would secure mass conversions from Catholicism to Protestantism in Quebec. These fantasies were soon unmasked, and it became clear that Catholic and French-speaking inhabitants would outnumber Britons in the new province. Therefore, existing elites would have to be co-opted, with offers of military and civil commissions. Many left, but many others remained to enjoy British patronage. Seigneurs like Joseph-Dominique-Emmanuel Le Moyne de Longueuil and René-Amable Boucher de Boucherville fought for France at the Plains of Abraham and for Britain during the Revolutionary War, and were rewarded with seats in the Legislative Council (the nominated upper house). French Canadians made up the majority of justices of the peace in Quebec during the late eighteenth century.

Existing local institutions of self-government were perpetuated in both Acadia and New France after their respective conquests: elected delegates in Acadia and parish officers in New France. These men gradually assumed growing responsibilities, from settling local disputes, to negotiating with local Amerindian groups, to organizing defences. Local elections persisted in Acadia through the

French regime and into the British. The British council established at Annapolis Royal tolerated the elections, formalizing them as annual events after 1721, and relied on them to advise on and resolve petty complaints. It was these elected deputies who tried and failed to negotiate watered-down oaths of loyalty that the inhabitants were willing to swear, thereby providing imperial-minded opportunists with an excuse for mass deportation in 1755. A legislature was finally established in Nova Scotia in 1758, after the deportation prompted Protestant immigration. In New France, appointed captains of the militia rather than elected delegates tended to oversee local administration. Rather than establishing new, potentially troublesome local institutions, the government let the existing ones bear the brunt of such local organization as road-building and policing. The one effort that was made – to replace captains of the militia with elected constables (*baillis*) – was abandoned in 1774. Protestant parishes were not given the same powers. Local officers remained under the British as they had been under the French: centrally appointed and representing the central state's interests rather than local public opinion. The flow of services to local communities did not much exceed infrastructure for roads and justice.

The British state rested heavily on French-Canadian officials and intermediaries. Indeed, as tensions mounted in the American colonies, the British legislators passed the Quebec Act in 1774, confirming tolerant gubernatorial policies with explicit legislative protection for French-Canadian religion and civil law. The result was stability within Quebec, albeit a stability purchased with outrage in other British realms. Dorchester was disappointed by the tepid attachment that French Canadians showed towards their government during the American Revolution, but on the whole the northern colonies remained unmoved by the revolutionary fervour. The transition from a French to a British state was achieved with remarkably little unrest. Still, British and American immigrants were dismayed to find

Quebec Frenchified, centralized, and unrepresentative, while those remaining in the Thirteen Colonies saw British imperialism in much the same light. Their political affairs, previously negotiated discreetly through such mechanisms as instructions to governors, were now subject to direct parliamentary legislation. Distance had fostered an autonomy, unthinkable in the home colonies, that seemed threatened by technological and bureaucratic innovations in a shrinking Atlantic world.

In Quebec, British imperial agents sought legitimacy by balancing old and new instruments of rule. Thus, the Catholic Church persisted, but in a new form. The men and women of the Catholic Church were almost a state within the state, with its own institutions, personnel, and rules. It enjoyed formidable political influence in Canada as in France, and state officials relied on its impressive local organization to provide such things as education and care of the sick or poor. Nominally under the Bishop of Quebec, the Church was not singular but organized into more or less powerful institutions, including seminaries and parishes. Ecclesiastical seigneurs, including the seminaries of Quebec and Montreal, held a quarter of all Crown-granted land, which they settled and administered as other seigneurs did. Religious orders did much for public welfare, running hospitals and hospices, often in return for state payments. In the eighteenth century, state subsidies made up as much as 40 per cent of the Catholic Church's income. State and church officials did quarrel from time to time but, on the whole, they collaborated to uphold public order, patriotism, and piety. Sermons denounced theft, drunkenness, and raucous assemblies, as in 1704 when riots against the high price of salt were denounced by priests. French military victories were marked by the churches with bell-ringing, enthusiastic sermons, and banners hung from cathedral rafters; defeats by public penance. For its part, the state enforced the tithe and punished sacrilege, profanation, and even witchcraft. The clergy complained continually of impiety, especially in

Montreal; nonetheless, if the Enlightenment of the early eighteenth century, with its critique of the oppressions of church and state, largely bypassed New France, this was in no small part because church and state collaborated closely.

Conquest left the fate of the Catholic Church in question, because papal hierarchies were prohibited in British territories, and Catholics had few political rights. In Acadia, where priests were scant even before the transfer, the British authorities perpetuated parish authorities. And in June of 1765 the British government determined that a Catholic establishment, headed by a bishop, would be tolerated in British North America. But this would be a national church, its appointments made by British authorities. Priests and bishops swore and upheld loyalty to the British Crown. The rituals of thanksgiving and penance to mark important public events continued and, after an initial dip, they increased considerably from the 1790s, when priests fleeing the French Revolution reinvigorated the church in Quebec. The British also installed their own established church. An Anglican bishopric was created in Nova Scotia in 1787 and another in Quebec in 1793; Toronto waited until 1839. The British Crown was intimately partnered with the Anglican Church and placed resources at its service. But Anglicans never constituted more than a fraction of the colonial population and their legal privileges enraged rival denominations that denounced any formal ties between church and state. Savvy Scottish Catholic veterans persuaded the War Office to subsidize their church establishment, doing an end run around jealous Anglicans. Denominational battles intensified in the nineteenth century, as immigration created a more religiously eclectic influx. Religion was one of the great ideological projects of the state, but by the nineteenth century it was a problematic one that provoked as much resistance as compliance.

The other great ideological state project, justice, went from strength to strength. Both French and British justice rested on the premise of fearful and spectacular display. In the courts, royal officers of justice articulated the state's position on all manner of behaviour; at the scaffold, the whipping post, or other public places of punishment, words and deeds together exemplified the state's purpose and power. Prisons were used primarily for storing prisoners before trial or punishment, and they were ill-equipped for long-term confinement, especially in wintertime. The judiciary was a substantial part of the state, employing eighty salaried officers in the early eighteenth century. French justice was prescribed by a code promulgated in 1670, though local officers regularly modified procedures and penalties to meet local circumstances. In one study of 569 trials, thirty-eight convicts were sentenced to capital punishment (most of them men of low birth), thirty-nine to flogging, forty-five to banishment, thirty to branding (usually for theft), and twenty-seven to the galleys. Only 10 per cent of those accused were convicted, but the prospect of trial with torture during legal interrogation and without legal counsel must have been terrifying.[18]

The substitution of British for French criminal justice had the result of abolishing some of the most severe aspects, including judicial torture. Defence lawyers were an eighteenth-century innovation in Britain, and they were brought to Canada. Nonetheless, the British "bloody code" was, no less than French justice, designed to strike terror into the hearts of evildoers, whether petty pilferers or radical levellers. The emergence of Atlantic economies based upon slavery and a widening gyre of oppression and rage against oppression, prompted new extremes of torture and repression by authorities at all levels: from slave owners and ships' captains to statesmen. The unpropertied proletariat continually threatened to become a violent enemy of the state – and quashing its enemies was a particular forte of the early modern state.

British justice came to Quebec in terrifying, spectacular form in the spring of 1763, in the unprecedented gibbeting or public display of the body of Marie-Josephte Corriveau, sentenced by a military tribunal to execution and "hanging in chains" for the murder of her husband. The gruesome spectacle became the stuff of local legend. It also fuelled a larger argument that French Canadians experienced the Conquest as radically alienating, leaving them at the mercy of an alien justice system peopled by their conquerors and conducted in a foreign language. But new work by Donald Fyson overturns this account. Many of the new laws passed soon after the Conquest re-enacted old ones, such as those aimed at preventing fires. Others reflected changing circumstances experienced across the Atlantic world, including a rise in felonies. Above all, French Canadians showed no hesitation in initiating criminal or civil procedures against one another under the British regime. For most people, justice consisted of negotiations between neighbours, with the state serving as an arbiter. French and English subjects in Quebec underwent a process of mutual adaptation in the years after the Conquest. Indigenous people generally did not seek imperial justice, preferring their own customs, but they were increasingly subjected to European-style prosecution for crime as legal pluralism declined over the next century.

Similar trajectories marked Newfoundland and Nova Scotia. First, the executive authority – the governor – was empowered to dispense justice; then, a judicial wing of government was established, complete with a chief justice and a supreme court distinct from the executive council. Under the British criminal code, which operated in Nova Scotia after 1749, the number of capital crimes increased, but the royal pardon was used to keep the execution rate stable. In Britain, convicts who had a good reputation were often pardoned for non-violent crimes, and fewer than half of criminals condemned to death were actually executed. In Nova Scotia, local discretion operated slightly differently: the governor used the pardon primarily to let off soldiers, in a colony that was overwhelmingly military in character and population. The execution rate remained unusually high, perhaps for lack of such alternatives as banishment.

Local preferences and mores shaped the colonial state in eighteenth-century Canada. Empire was made on the ground as well as at the centre. Imperial identities and norms were translated and negotiated, and made to serve local realities and interests. Indeed, problems that British legislators encountered in Canada led to a rethinking of imperialism at home. British legislators, realizing that they must woo French Canadians if Canada was to be militarily secure, granted some unusual liberties. Even as they restricted local instruments of government, ensuring that control remained firmly under the king in Parliament, they confirmed the local customs and expanded the civil liberties of subjects of British North America. Legislators and pundits began a new and prolonged debate about British rights: Were they historically and culturally specific, or abstract and transferable to peoples with an alternative history? Could they be partial? Could they apply to groups? Local inhabitants had rights and interests that legislators ignored at their peril. Often, it proved more convenient to cede power to the periphery than to wrestle dissent into submission and squeeze local peculiarity into ill-fitting imperial categories.

The law was not a crude instrument of either imperial or social control. Ordinary people who used the legal system to mediate their disputes appropriated a legal regime long understood to serve their political and economic masters, but they believed that it served them as well. Women, who had little legal identity of their own once they were married, regularly turned to the courts – entirely staffed by men – to complain when men beat, raped, or abandoned them. Their success rates varied, but they were higher than the success rates for male complainants. The courts treated women as credible defendants and witnesses, and it took their part. Unpropertied men complained against propertied men, peasants complained against seigneurs, servants complained against masters. According to the oath of office drawn up by Sir Guy Carleton, justices of the peace swore that they would "do equal right to the poor and to the rich" and enough apparently did so that the poor thought they had a chance before the courts. The distorted view of the ancien-régime state concocted by nineteenth-century liberals is being rewritten by recent historians: "An older view of 18th century politics as an increasingly restrictive system dominated by an increasingly unrepresentative oligarchy has been toppled by studies finding reciprocity, mutual recognition, openness and high degrees of contestation in elections and local government."[19]

The State as Social Mediator in an Age of Enlightenment

Though it was not a crude instrument of social control, the law did reinforce social differentiation. It was riddled with biases that privileged property and connection, both local and imperial. Patrician values served as an essential solder for the early modern state and empire by knitting together networks of office holders across British and French territories. Shared culture lent coherence and solidarity to their dealings with other groups and interests. Gentlemanly ideals provided "a shared code, based on honour and obligation, which acted as a blueprint for conduct in occupations whose primary function was to manage men rather than machines."[20] Patricians in legislative, executive, and judicial offices often engaged in internecine rivalries, but they also protected one another by upholding class values. Sometimes they openly flouted the rule of law in ways that reveal much about the workings of early modern society.

Duels illustrate a double standard that permitted elites to simultaneously uphold and flout both the law and the Crown. They were fought by gentlemen reluctant to relinquish the defence of their honour to state apparatus; only gentlemen had honourable reputations to defend. European monarchs passed proclamations against duels on the grounds that they breached the king's peace. But British legislators – honourable gentlemen determined to defend their privileges – rejected all bills against dueling until 1819. Duelists in Canada usually wound up before the courts only when someone died or nearly so. Juries had to decide whether to enforce the law or to let duelists off lightly. In January 1800, John Small, clerk of the Executive Council of Upper Canada, killed the attorney general, John White, af- ter White credited Small's wife with a long and varied sexual history. Small was acquitted of all charges. Acquittals of well- bred, public men persisted until the last fatal duel in British North America in 1833. Murder was treated lightly in such cases, because it greased the wheels of oligarchic rule. In a culture of political patronage, duels served to reinforce trust or "social capital": the value derived from connections with other people. Patricians were deeply invested in so- cial capital: their power lay in their connections, in their inclusion in a network of office holders, landholders, and business elites. The duel helped to cement the connections between such people and ensure that all members shared genteel status. Such mechanisms of trust reminded both patrons and the patronized that their true loyalties lay as much with one another as with the state.

Canada never quite conformed to metropolitan stan- dards of gentility. Governors were supposed to choose of- ficials from among the respected citizens of the colonies, meaning that they should not be criminals or of known im- morality, and they should be of better-than-middling social or economic status. Respectability was both material (a cou- ple of servants and £200–300 a year) and cultural. Not all officials met this standard. In the 1760s, Guy Carleton de- scribed the Quebec magistracy as "bankrupt butchers and publicans." Later governors in Upper and Lower Canada worried that the creation of legislatures would put govern- ment in lowly hands. John Graves Simcoe described Upper Canadian legislators in the 1790s as "men of the lower or- der, who kept but one table, that is who dined in common with their servants"; and in 1810 Sir James Craig moaned that Lower Canadian legislators were either shopkeepers' sons or illiterate farmers who worked their own fields: "They are a people with whom it is impossible I can have any connection not even the common intercourse of a dinner."[21] Without shared cultural capital, there could be no political consensus.

Rival groups resented one another's power. In post-Conquest Quebec, distrust between civil and military networks was rampant. One civil magistrate, Thomas Walker, mandated to administer the billeting of soldiers, tried to make them as uncomfortable as possible. In December 1764, he was assaulted by a group of disguised men, obviously military officers, who beat him and cut off most of his ear. Could justice be done in such a case? A reward was offered for information, but no soldier ever came forward and the assault went unpunished. Walker blamed a conspiracy among state officials, above all Governor James Murray, who preferred to surround himself with Frenchmen and soldiers rather than Britons and merchants, to the detriment, Walker complained to British authorities, of the colony's proper development. Murray was recalled though ultimately exonerated.

The violence of a Walker affair or a duel was exceptional and notorious because it amounted to public admission that some people could flout the law and that the state had no monopoly on violence. The justice system rested, ultimately, on public opinion, and if public opinion deferred to privilege, then so did justice. Privilege was both content and form for social elites. In any dispute with inferiors, social elites were quick to identify insubordination as the root problem; the very fact of dispute – coming before the courts, for example – exemplified insubordination. Arguments that did not exemplify the principle of vertical hierarchy were suspect when viewed from above. Governors might urge identical treatment of rich and poor individuals alike when they appeared before the court, but the system tended to work to prevent their appearing on such equal terms. Slaves, in particular, had almost no legal recourse against abusive masters, though prosecutors were quick to punish slaves who took matters into their own hands. In 1734, after Marie-Joseph Angélique, a Portuguese-born slave, supposedly burned her owner's house – and much of old Montreal along with it – in protest against being separated from her lover, she was tortured and executed.

The courts, like the governors, had at least to *seem* responsive to popular mores and the rule of law, and they largely accomplished that. But there was also much opportunity for abuse that might spark powerful public outcry. By the turn of the nineteenth century, debates about slavery began to reflect gaps between popular and elite values, as ordinary people turned against an institution that wealthy elites tried to perpetuate. Other kinds of property divided the population in similar ways, with the powerful landed gentry working to protect their large holdings, while ordinary inhabitants agitated to break them up. In the eighteenth century, juries were probably the most important vehicle for expressing public resentment, followed by the nascent press. By the nineteenth century, a vibrant popular press and lively debate in the legislatures considerably amplified public protest against such abuses.

For all the continuities that marked French and British governance in eighteenth-century Canada, here was one big difference: the role accorded to public opinion. Parliamentary sovereignty in Britain meant that government rested ultimately on public opinion. French kings had mechanisms for taking advice, but they were less responsive to opinion and slower to provide for its systematic representation. The French state discouraged people *sans caractère* (without standing) from reflecting on national politics, but, from the mid-eighteenth century, it failed to contain their critiques. The tone of public debate in France became openly confrontational in the aftermath of the military and economic failures in New France. Discourse enjoyed a more positive political status in Britain, where the Crown had to call Parliament together annually in order to levy taxes. Parliament fulfilled its mandate by debating and passing legislation, and its members were elected by propertied people who had the right and duty to discuss public matters. Even in Britain, however, the government resisted public printing of parliamentary debates until the 1770s; that gallery seats were provided for reporters from 1803 reveals how quickly things changed after that. British countenance of public discourse made for one post-Conquest discontinuity in Canada: French constraints on public meetings, petitions, and publication were relaxed, and printing presses entered Quebec for the first time. Immediately, they were put to use airing debates about the rights of British subjects to criticize their governors.

The point was moot before the mid-eighteenth century because no Canadian colony paid for its own administration. But once the French threat was removed, inhabitants began to demand British economic and political liberties. Slowly and cautiously, Whitehall introduced legislatures to its Canadian colonies, so that colonists could levy taxes and debate policies. Nova Scotia was conceded to Britain in 1713 and given a legislature only in 1758, after the deportation of the Acadians. Prince Edward Island, initially run from Nova Scotia, was given its own governor in 1769 and its own legislature in 1773. Loyalist New Brunswick had a legislature from its creation in 1784, but Quebec, with its large population of Catholics (grounds for disenfranchisement in Britain) did not until 1791, when Upper and Lower Canada each received one. Newfoundland, which had a large Irish Catholic population, had to wait until 1832. But Parliament retained some important checks, including power of veto and control of appointments. By controlling patronage, governors rewarded men who supported imperial projects. Large tracts of lands reserved for the Crown were expected to provide an independent source of gubernatorial funds.

New theories of public opinion by Enlightenment philosophers shaped the state that the British constructed in Canada. The Scottish essayist David Hume observed in 1742 that, because rulers were always outnumbered by the ruled, state power was always negotiated, never simply imposed. The most brutal dictator might drive his subjects like animals, but he must lead his army, "like men, by their opinion."[22] This discovery of public opinion was an important factor in the decision to confirm Catholic French-Canadians in their customs, rights, and rites. British legislators were confident that the people of New France could be won over to their political regime, a regime that many thinkers, some of them French, believed to be the most rational, progressive, and free in the world. The first Lieutenant Governor of Upper Canada, John Graves Simcoe, believed that Americans could similarly be won back over to British rule, and he offered free land to American settlers. But most colonial legislators remained deeply distrustful of oppositional discourse. They equated it with American and French republicanism, which seemed especially dangerous after those republics went to war against Britain. The notion of a loyal opposition evolved slowly, and criticism of the government was apt to be interpreted as treasonous or libellous by the officials concerned. During the 1770s, when the *Gazette littéraire de Montréal*, published by political radicals, complained that Quebec suffered from partiality among judges, unlawful convictions, the lack of representative institutions, and other aspects of civil despotism, incarceration swiftly followed. In the 1790s, Loyalists, trembling for the security of their Canadian haven, passed a law that condemned as sedition any uttered or printed words or false news that tended "in any manner to disturb the peace and happiness enjoyed under his Majesty's government."[23] People could be rounded up and interned on the say-so of a magistrate, without reference to the common law and without a trial. Canada had a garrison mentality that made it fearful and repressive.

Whereas Hume privileged the political use of popular reason, Adam Smith privileged its economic use in *The Wealth of Nations*, published in 1776 as the culmination of economic arguments that had been evolving for a century. According to Smith, the free use of individual self-interest and judgment in the marketplace transmogrified into a rational, self-governing economic sphere; and most state intervention to manage the economy – such as bounties for home producers of linens or restrictions on sales of wheat during dearth – impaired national wealth and people's ability to provide for themselves. Bad seasons might cause dearth, but only government meddling could turn dearth into famine. No legislator, Smith insisted, could better judge anyone's interest than that person, and people should exercise their "natural liberty" to buy and sell in nearly all circumstances. This was a politically explosive argument, a direct attack on the principles of centralization and paternalism that underpinned the early modern state. Without some visible mechanism to diffuse purpose and policy from centre to periphery, state sovereignty over the periphery is illusory. In the short term, Smith's debunking of the knowing, purposive state was not much more immediately effective than his friend Hume's debunking of the knowing, purposive self (in arcane philosophical texts that were much less popular than Hume's state-centred histories and essays). The model of public opinion remained, in the eighteenth century, wedded to a trickle-down model of emulation, interlaced with coercion.

But in the long run, the effect of such Enlightenment theories was considerable. The ancien-régime state foundered upon them. Scholars have written extensively on the ways in which liberal reasoning, grounded in the individual's liberty to make free contracts, collided with and overturned customary laws and privileges. Commercial freedom gradually became a kind of trump card that could overturn other kinds of interests and concerns. The Conquest accelerated this movement towards commercial freedom, but the process was already underway under French rule; once again, continuities should not be overlooked.

On paper, the Custom of Paris restrained free disposal of property: noble property was subject to primogeniture; seigneurial property was preferentially given to the eldest son, but with other siblings inheriting substantial proportions; and peasant property holdings were divided equally among all children. Neither seigneurs nor tenants really "owned" land as in a freehold tenure system; both, rather, had certain claims upon it, not easily dislodged. The Custom of Paris also constrained property relations between wives and husbands, making it harder for husbands to dispose of property that wives brought to the marriage. But people found ways to circumvent constraints, for example, by giving the whole estate to their son during their lifetime in return for promises of upkeep. Such arrangements became more frequent in the eighteenth century.

British law more openly favoured contractualism over traditional constraints; the "cash nexus" over the "human tie." Feudal tenure was formally abolished in the seventeenth century, though primogeniture persisted. Dower protected widows' interest in family property, but if their husbands were still alive, women could be stripped of assets more easily in British North America for lack of the equity courts found in Britain. Relations between landlord and tenant were primarily financial, without the various verbal and symbolic expressions of homage, such as the annual capon or chicken that many *censitaires* had to produce. Deference was sacrificed to contractualism, privilege to competition. The process, even as it gathered momentum, was widely protested as a violation of popular "moral economy": an expectation that bread would be made available and affordable when and where it was needed. Defying those traditions, politicians began to let bread find its own price. But this was a slow evolution. Metropolitan legislators overturned laws against grain merchants (likened by Smith to witchcraft laws), but local officials such as colonial governors, more exposed to popular resentment over high prices, perpetuated old prohibitions on forestalling (preempting or monopolizing sales at the public market) well into the nineteenth century.

Negotiating the Ancien-Régime Frontier

State paternalism and illiberal property relations also persisted in the unsettled parts of Canada, where Indigenous
property relations posed different problems. The French
Crown long tried to restrict its civil population to the St.
Lawrence River valley, to control the price and flow of
beaver pelts and to minimize conflict on the borderlands.
Desperate to maintain military alliances across the length
and breadth of New France, it deferred everywhere to
Indigenous commercial and political priorities. This was always a losing battle, as the example of slavery suggests. Slavery was widespread throughout Native societies of North
America, but that slavery was very different from Atlantic
chattel slavery. Aboriginal slaves had a symbolic political
importance that outweighed their commercial value: they
served as a reminder of political relations – of warfare or
alliance – and could be restored to their people at any
moment, to cement an alliance. French officials made a serious mistake when they sent away a group of captured Iroquois to work as galley slaves, and peace talks foundered on
the failure to return them. The French legalized slavery in
New France in 1709, the better to be able to negotiate this
complex but necessary brand of diplomacy, but the consequent expansion and commercialization of the slave trade
made it all the harder for French officials to appropriate
and return captives without undermining private property.
The problem went well beyond incommensurable property
regimes. Indigenous consensus ensured that slaves, though
they belonged to a particular family, remained a diplomatic
resource. The French state had nothing like that consensus or flexibility and could not appropriate a commercial
good without undermining the commerce. Its powers were
more restrained than those of the supposedly stateless Indigenous peoples; it was less able to articulate and sustain
a definite common good. France's Indigenous allies used

the slave trade to cement their alliances, but they also used it to obstruct French ambitions of western expansion. With large numbers of Fox and Sioux slaves in French hands, the French could not form peaceful relations with those nations and extend their westward reach. But commercialization of the slave trade led to comparable problems among such French allies as the Illinois; they, too, began to deplete their diplomatic capital, as well as their population, by trading away slaves as commodities. The ancien-régime state in New France promoted commerce as a necessary foundation for a colony, but commerce often pitted private against public interest, as propertied people, like slave owners and slave traders, some of them state officials, defined and managed their property and their interests in ways that suited themselves and defied state purposes.

Conquest by the British exacerbated the tensions between public policy and private interest. In pursuit of an empire founded on trade, British imperial agents determined to put their North American holdings on an economically sound basis: they would pass the costs of imperial defence onto the American colonists (who were, after all, the instigators and objects of all that expenditure), and they would reduce the distribution of presents to Indigenous allies. Both policies proved immediately disastrous, provoking resistance among settlers and Indigenous allies alike. Pontiac instigated a general uprising around the Great Lakes and beyond in 1763, in response to General Jeffrey Amherst's refusal to provide presents as well as more general fears of encroachment on Indigenous lands. Land speculators and settlers had long been encroaching on Aboriginal lands, provoking violent encounters and necessitating expensive troop manoeuvres. Colonial legislators seemed rather to encourage than repress the land rush as they sought to expand their borders at the expense of other states. So in October 1763 the British Crown issued a Royal Proclamation that reserved all unsettled and unceded land in North America as Indian hunting grounds and that prohibited any survey or patent, purchase, or settlement of that land without "our especial leave and Licence." Both the Treaty of Paris and the proclamation seemed to regard Indigenous peoples as free and unconquered, and this was, of course, how they saw themselves. Nonetheless, the proclamation clearly expressed British sovereignty over the back country. Its provisions were regularly confirmed, beginning in 1764 with the Treaty of Niagara – negotiated by Sir William Johnson, the capable superintendent of Indian affairs among the northern tribes – which contained pledges of mutual support and a promise of annual presents. Thomas Gage, a conciliatory British general, similarly built alliances with the Toronto chief Wabbicommicot, and with the Kahnawà:ke Mohawks, recognizing them, rather than the Jesuits, as owners of that land.

Thus, in the back country as in Quebec, the British upheld pre-existing relations of property. Only a few British officials like Johnson grasped Aboriginal tenure of property; for most, that tenure was opaque and, according to the preeminent seventeenth-century liberal philosopher of land, John Locke, probably illegitimate. Nonetheless, to hold their own colonies securely, British legislators upheld that strange opacity. The result was to create new relations between Crown and subject, with the special status of Aboriginal land confirmed in perpetuity. Many American colonists were as aghast at the proclamation as at the new tax policies. Their resistance led Whitehall to impose further constraints on trade in Indian territory. It signed treaties with southern nations and placed the northern Indian territories under Quebec civil jurisdiction in the Quebec Act of 1774, so as to ensure centralized control and prevent individual American states from issuing their own trade licences.

The Quebec Act and Royal Proclamation provided a framework for negotiations, but the protective provisions were breached more often than they were observed. True, alienation or transfer of title over land had to be negotiated through state officials, but officials could apply pressure to force sales for a pittance and without proper community consultations. Pressure to transfer land to freehold tenure began to mount in the 1780s, as the British government had to find land to settle Loyalists, including Haudenosaunee Loyalists who had lost traditional homelands. The land once inhabited by Wendat was now peopled by Mississaugas who had probably migrated from the Ohio valley, and further west and north were the Potowatomi, the Odawa, and the Anishinaabeg. The Mississauga sold the land that became the Six Nations Reserve at Grand River in 1783 (though reserve land constituted only one-fifth of the three million acres sold for a little over £1000). Joseph Brant, the leader of the Grand River Iroquois, was furious to learn that the provisions of the Royal Proclamation, rather than freehold tenure, would apply to the reserve. A township-sized plot was allotted on the Bay of Quinte for the Tyendinaga reserve at the same time, and a few years later the north shore of Lake Ontario was ceded according to terms that were never written down and later disputed. Resettled Iroquois Loyalists, meanwhile, helped negotiate access to hunting lands from the Haudenosaunee further east along the St. Lawrence. Some important concessions were made during the 1780s and 1790s, but relations deteriorated at the end of the century. The Mississauga began to refuse further sales as the impact of settlement upon hunting became increasingly apparent, leading to some violent confrontations, while sexual trespass precipitated the murder of a Mississauga chief, Wabakinine. However, they could not hold out indefinitely as, into the nineteenth century, growing pressure on the land and the decline of game, fish, and timber in areas adjacent to white settlement, prompted further surrenders, often on fraudulent or coercive terms. The Royal Proclamation, by creating a monopoly buyer, worked to lower prices, while political divisions among and within Indigenous communities weakened the bargaining position of the sellers. State centralization on the one side and political multiplicity on the other facilitated the transfer of land into colonial hands. Time and again, state officials intervened in disputes to protect the interests of settlers, squatters, and speculators, all well represented in colonial officialdom. Indigenous farmers, of whom there were many in early nineteenth-century Upper Canada, were more likely to be resettled than protected.

Much of British North America was not explicitly covered by the Royal Proclamation. Quebec was largely exempted on the grounds that the inhabitants there were later migrants and had no more claim to proprietorship than European immigrants, and also because it had been claimed by conquest from the French, as had Nova Scotia. British agents negotiated a diplomatic treaty with the Mi'kmaq in 1726 to transfer their allegiance from the French to the British Crown, but they did not realize just how much French-Amerindian relations in British North America differed from those in New England. Thus, the British state presumed a transfer of sovereignty and fealty that the Mi'kmaq had never yielded to the French. Because settlers and traders were not yet pushing into Mi'kmaq land, British officials undertaking the negotiations did not have to spell out distinctly the new way that Europeans would use those lands. The Mi'kmaq were dismayed by the new settlements that sprouted around Nova Scotia at mid-century, at Halifax and Lunenburg, Fort Lawrence and Fort Edward. They had promised to respect "lawful" British settlements, but the British consulted neither Mi'kmaq custom nor opinion. A subsequent attempt to delineate lawful Mi'kmaq land on the Restigouche foundered on settler opposition, and the Mi'kmaq were gradually pushed onto small reserves. Narrow understandings of *property* were used repeatedly, from one coast of Canada to the other, to justify reducing Indian reserves to pathetic sizes. By the end of the century, petitions complained of dire effects following the loss of hunting grounds to settlement. For all the rhetoric of a free frontier, the primary function of the nascent colonial state in Canada was to orchestrate the orderly transfer of land from Indigenous to European hands.

Direct ownership by the Hudson's Bay Company exempted Rupert's Land from the Royal Proclamation; treaties were signed only after Canada purchased it in 1869. The Company faced more challenges to its tenure from European rivals than from Indigenous inhabitants. Early instructions to local Company officials, dated 1680, recommended concessions to local sensibilities: "contrive to make compact with The Captns. or chiefs of the respective Rivers & places, whereby it might be understood by them that you had purchased both the lands & rivers of them, and that they had transferred the absolute propriety to you, or at least the only freedome of trade, And that you should cause them to do some act whch. by the Religion or Custome of their Country should be thought most sacred & obliging to them for the confirmation of such Agreements."[24] But any agreements remained unrecorded and untested. Generally, the HBC did not try to impose British law outside trading posts, and until the fall of New France it concentrated trading posts on the Bay; its one inland post on the Albany River was withdrawn after violent confrontation. Chief officers or factors ran their posts much as captains ran their ships, imposing summary corporal punishment on their employees, but the proximity of the frontier tended to stoke disobedience, illicit trade, and abandonment.

After the Conquest, Montreal-based traders extensively infiltrated Rupert's Land. By the end of the 1760s, they were already predominant around Lake Winnipeg and the Saskatchewan River. The Company's monopoly powers were hard to uphold, as there were no courts anywhere in its territory, and courts outside the territory had scant sympathy for what the British solicitor general described (a century after the Company's charter had been granted) as its "many extravagant and illegal clauses."[25] The competition frequently became violent, as exemplified by Peter Pond, a Montreal-based trader reputedly responsible for a series of murders during the 1780s. But the British state apparatus was so feeble in Western Canada that it needed the HBC to represent its sovereign interests; certainly that Company made a better stand-in than the defunct South Sea Company, which supposedly held title to the Pacific Coast in the eighteenth century. Into the early nineteenth century, thus, the leading HBC trader on the West Coast, James Douglas, was, like Onontio in New France, simultaneously chief factor and royal governor. British imperial agents exercised scant powers inland but more powers along the coast, where they could exercise gunboat diplomacy.

The Western regions, like early New France, lacked European settlers. In their absence, there could be no strong distinction between public and private, state and society. That situation had seemed normal in the seventeenth century but came to seem anomalous by the end of the eighteenth, after a century's worth of Enlightenment philosophizing about the differences between them. The HBC, with real sovereign powers over Rupert's Land, conflated commercial and political authority, and because it owned the land and controlled justice, there was no independent civil society. In theory, serious court cases could be transferred to Britain, but it was never practicable to send accused, witnesses, and evidence across the ocean. In the early nineteenth century, a more practical solution was found by placing the territory under the jurisdiction of Canadian courts. But only the most important trials, such as that of Simon Fraser and others accused of the murder of twenty settlers at Seven Oaks in 1816, actually came to Canadian courts. Most of the time the HBC informally upheld "club law" in its territories, and the British state tolerated the situation.

Changing frontier diplomacy reflected new state trajectories. When seventeenth-century officials negotiated with Indigenous peoples, their primary concern was political advantage and military alliance. Profit was subordinated to security, according to principles expressed in a French memo of 1717: "There is no middle course; one must have the Native as either friend or foe; and whoever wants to have him as a friend must furnish him with his necessities at conditions which allow him to procure them." For strategic purposes, therefore, the French sold goods below market value.[26] But over the course of the eighteenth century, those priorities began to reverse, as officials pursued liberal economic relationships, a process that accelerated in the nineteenth century. The change reflected lessened need for Indigenous military support, but it also reflected a broader change in the conception of what a state was and what it should do. In pursuing its fiscal-military goals, the state became more intimately committed to protecting commerce, and the result was to make the constitution of market relations and private property more central to the very conception of a state. The Duke of Newcastle, secretary of state for the three decades preceding the Seven Years' War, declared, "By trade we do, and must, if at all subsist; without which we have no wealth; and without wealth we have no power, as without power we can have no liberty."[27] According to that logic, security must serve trade, rather than the other way around. In the seventeenth century, the British government neglected the HBC's requests for military and diplomatic support; in the eighteenth century, it met them. Governments reclaimed powers of governance that they had delegated to corporations, and they involved themselves more prominently in commercial diplomacy. Rather than keeping violence at arm's length from the Crown, corporations had tended to drag their governments into military engagements. When Pierre Le Moyne D'Iberville lay waste to settlements along Newfoundland's eastern coast in the 1690s, there wasn't much resistance beyond what local merchants could muster, but the land was quickly reclaimed for Britain by a Royal Navy squadron and 2,000 land troops. During the eighteenth century, companies transferred more expensive protection costs to the state, with an enlargement of state powers as the consequence. British overseas trade expanded enormously because the state invested in its navy and in colonial political institutions. This was still the fiscal-military state, judged in terms of expenditure and public intervention, but as the rationale for warfare became increasingly wrapped up in commercial projects, the stage was set for a far more extensive intervention into private enterprise and public life.

From that perspective, the most important factor in the history of the Canadian state in the eighteenth century was not the Conquest of New France or the American Revolution but rather the habit that ordinary British subjects developed, over that century, of taking a cup of tea regularly, along with a spoonful or two of sugar – a habit that emigrated everywhere with them. By the end of the eighteenth century, the British consumed nearly half of all the sugar and most of the tea shipped to Europe. Tea and sugar were just the vanguard of the modern consumer revolution characterized by the trans-shipment of colonial produce and the industrialization of Britain. Because taxing commerce was far more lucrative than taxing peasant farmers, the British were better able to fund and win their wars and to pluck New France from France.

As the British Empire grew more intertwined with commerce, the political function of commerce became more salient. For philosophers like Smith and Hume, popular agency, exercised as consumption or public opinion, was a positive foundation for modern society. Their arguments owed much to earlier French theorists of liberty, especially Montesquieu, for whom the French spirit of monarchy, privilege, and honour compared unfavourably with the British spirit of commerce, freedom, and equality. But Montesquieu tempered his admiration for commerce, fearing that in Bourbon France consumption must emulate the corrupting luxuries of a Versailles. Hume and Smith, by contrast, looked to popular consumption as providing a solid foundation for modern liberty. Wealth or revenue could emerge only from economic surplus, Hume argued, over and above subsistence. You could force people to work, but it was usually violent and impracticable "to oblige the labourer to toil in order to raise from the land more than what subsists himself and his family [i.e., as seigneurial levy or taxation].

Furnish him with manufactures and commodities and he will do it himself."[28] In other words, a commercial society in which people worked to buy themselves such luxuries as tea and sugar, could be wealthier and freer than a more traditional economy. In such a society, state exactions could be virtually painless.

Hume was describing a century's economic expansion in Britain, fuelled by a huge increase in market-oriented labour by ordinary people keen to buy new goods. A parallel increase occurred among the Indigenous peoples of North America. They, too, were at the vanguard of the early modern consumer revolution, a process – accomplished without state coordination – that successfully translated Indigenous consumer preferences into metropolitan profits. Hume and Smith may have observed that process of translation in their native Scotland, where HBC artefacts were manufactured, only to be returned if they failed to meet satisfaction. The HBC, for all its supposedly despotic powers, relied primarily on popular consumer agency to extract surplus value from the inhabitants of Rupert's Land. And therein lay the larger lesson that British philosophers and pundits drew from Canada. Early defeats in the Seven Years' War prompted a panic that Britons had been too softened by commerce, unlike their more spartan French and Indigenous enemies. But eventual success reaffirmed their confidence in their trading vocation: not state coercion but economic exchange must carry the continent.

So extraordinarily positive seemed this new equation between commodities and national well-being, protected and directed by the state, that the logic was obvious to many: the modern state, epitomized by the British Parliament, could flourish only where commerce flourished. Where commerce did not flourish, the modern state would be weak; therefore, commerce should be encouraged – and perhaps even imposed at gunpoint. The state became more profoundly invested in economic relations as a project of rule; trade became the tail that wagged the dog.

But metropolitan theories were not easily adapted to Canada. Philosophers talked of freedom of exchange as both a natural and a civil liberty, that is, as one both prior to and guaranteed by the state. That kind of conflation was problematic in a frontier society like Canada, where Indigenous people continued to resist the state and its supposed liberties. Hobbes's social contract required that natural freedom not be on offer any longer – and yet there these people were: consumers par excellence, but flouting the deference and the disciplines of modern civilization. Traits that study-bound philosophers celebrated as freedom looked to officials on the ground like recalcitrance, savagery, and an unbearable restraint upon the profits to be made from the conversion of hunting grounds into farmlands. Colonial legislators began to insist that the Indigenous peoples of Canada must exchange freedom for liberty, if necessary under coercive laws designed to teach them their proper economic interests: not hunting over vast territories but engaging in disciplined labour exercised on small holdings. Such arguments gained force as first the beaver and later the bison were hunted towards exhaustion, but they also reflected the rising value of Western lands.

Therein lay the other great problem of commercial society: a deep vein of violence. The philosophers advocated commercial society because it empowered civil society in ways that seemed to restrain state violence. Rulers vying for commercial empire might obtain temporary advantage through privateering and expropriation, but in the long run, commerce required security of property. Such was the promise of British rule. However, opportunistic profiteers and politicians found it relatively easy to justify extraordinary violence against people they defined as outside of civil society and resistant to the marketplace. Such was the effect of British rule upon the Acadians, or the Beothuk of Newfoundland, who refused to trade with settlers and perished in the early nineteenth century, victims of murderous raids, starvation, and tuberculosis. Indeed, history was against the philosophers. Hume and Smith reflected back upon a century of economic growth and of relative abundance. But from the middle of the eighteenth century, the prices of basic foodstuffs and fuel began to rise, at first gradually, then, from the 1780s, dramatically and calamitously. Poverty, dearth, and social unrest gripped communities across the Atlantic and beyond. Some districts saw riots, others the emergence of serious political confrontations. New accommodations would have to be worked out, and the state would be transformed in the process, playing an ever-increasing role in maintaining order. Liberal philosophy presided over a transition from the fiscal-military state in Canada to the modern administrative state, but governance remained a bloody and coercive business.

3

The Liberal State in the Nineteenth Century

At the turn of the nineteenth century, the state in much of what now passes for Canada was in a parlous way. The British North American colonies were precarious, dwarfed by a hostile nation to the south that looked likely to over-run them by either peaceful or warlike means. British and American state institutions thumbed their noses defiantly at one another across the long border but, in the face of American demographic and economic expansion, Canada looked like a ninety-seven-pound weakling bullied at the beach. While Canadians could expect British forces to come to their defence, they were painfully conscious of their own feebleness. Some blamed the harsh northern climate, others the state. Compared to the expansive, egalitarian political institutions to the south, Canadian monarchical rule looked conservative and repressive, unequal to the great task of holding, settling, and developing the vast continent, as visitors continually observed in travelogues and political treatises.

The governing institutions that the British installed in British North America reflected an imperial project perched ambivalently between progress and tradition. British North America was a bastion of British liberties, but those liberties were understood to be conservative and even counter-revolutionary, resting on arcane historical negotiations and treaties dating back to the Magna Carta rather than on abstract appeals to individual autonomy and freedom. Especially after the American and French revolutions of 1776 and 1789, British political discourse was a tangled, contradictory mix of appeals to liberty and authority, reason and tradition, rights and duties – appeals that did not transfer easily to newly conquered territories and peoples. Apologists for this discourse called themselves liberals and their political philosophy liberalism. They privileged political and commercial liberties as the foundation of the modern British state and empire, including liberty of the press, liberty of the body (habeus corpus, i.e., no detention without due process of law), liberty of contract, and a host of other rights that were more or less shared by British subjects, depending on their age, gender, class, and sometimes their "race." These liberties reflected a view of the state as able to exercise extraordinary powers over its subjects, but restrained by law from doing so. This was a state with limited administrative powers, but capable of fearsome violence. Liberal theorists were those who explained how the state could be held to such moderation in a world where political ambition and other kinds of "sinister interest" (the phrase occurs in James Mill's 1820 *Essay on Government*) continually conspired against public liberty. Most such theorists traced their lineage back through Adam Smith's arguments for laissez-faire economics to Thomas Hobbes's theory of social contract.

Early British North Americans had most of the civil protections of British subjects but few political rights. Frontier violence accounted for the fragility of liberalism. The War of 1812 was the last paroxysm: the inhabitants, with British help, fought off the invaders convincingly enough to prevent a recurrence. But the sense of threat was slow to fade and left a political legacy of illiberalism. The British government still sent military men to govern Canada, still invested in defensive infrastructure (including the Rideau Canal, fortifications in Kingston, Quebec, and Halifax, and a new naval station in Victoria), and still maintained paternal control of Canadian politics. But over the half-century after 1815, measures against invasion came to seem pointless, not to say foolish. The French state no longer mattered in North America; the western frontier was secured with treaties rather than by military force; and the Americans seemed more interested in western than northern expansion. Should they change their minds and seriously renew the invasion of Canada, well, the colony was probably indefensible, the British concluded, and they withdrew their troops. The last British soldiers left in 1871; there remained only two coaling stations, both serving British rather than Canadian purposes.

Gradually, external threats ceded to internal ones, questions of defence to ones of liberty, and the double standard of British and colonial rights was challenged. The British Parliament was responsible to its electors in Britain, but colonial populations did not participate in those elections, nor could they control local affairs in colonial legislatures; these were regularly overruled by Parliament and its Canadian appointees. If British rule was legitimated by consent, in Canada that consent was show rather than substance. Colonial reformers began to argue that the real threat to British rule in Canada was illiberal, un-British rule by authority, and to demand local self-government or "responsible government," in the parlance of the times.

Traditional theories of authority, grounded in classical and medieval notions, posited that some people were specially endowed with the ability and power to govern other people, and kings divinely so. But according to liberal theorists like Smith or Mill, people could govern themselves better than others could govern them, and they had a natural liberty or right to do so. Representation there could be, but it must have the consent of the governed. For some, that consent was primordial to society itself; for others, it was ongoing, and revocable – the sort of qualified consent that one might give to an elected representative. Conservative electoral candidates deferred to British Parliament; reforming ones demanded greater local autonomy and the transfer of power to the people. All pointed to the United States to prove their point, whether to condemn it as corrupt demagoguery or to praise it as a flourishing republic. Liberalism was capacious enough to frame most of the debate in British North America and contain it within British constitutional forms, but there were also excruciating deadlocks and violent uprisings.

Liberalism won out, but in a particularly conservative form, as backwards-looking collective "British" rights that owed much to patrician rule. Economic, political, and legal privileges riddled the various legal codes of Canada before and after Confederation, as did arbitrary boundaries of political citizenship. More than half the population – including racialized groups, the poor, women, and children – was declared to lack crucial constituents of liberal identity and was governed paternally. Before they could exercise liberties, they had to be educated up to them, coercively if necessary.

Coercion was hard-wired in nineteenth-century Canada as both frontier violence and internal repression. The frontier remained, conceptually and practically, a place of limited state authority and limited rule of law. Eastern Canada had frontiers, but was no longer a frontier; there, the state could claim rough control of both territory and population. Legitimate liberal governments did not govern over populations but through them, as state and society mutually infiltrated one another. The violence of the frontier was intolerable in civil society. The model of state violence that liberal theorists sought to banish from civil society (if not from the frontier) – the armed soldier – would be dispelled by shifting the burden of police into institutions of civil society. If breaches of order required violent arrest, civilian employees would make the arrest: sheriffs, constables, or private contractors operating as something like bounty hunters. By mid-century, most authorities were organizing special police forces, usually unarmed, to reduce disorderly behaviour and protect property. If soldiers exemplified a potential for violently transgressive states of exception, police exemplified peaceful, civilian principles of rule that upheld security of property and contractual exchange. Likewise, the spectacular punishment and execution of criminals moved out of the public square, behind closed doors, and prison sentences replaced capital and corporal punishment or the stocks for petty crimes. But such changes could succeed only in a population that accepted the basic premise of liberal rule: the need to restrain violence in both the state and civil society.

Indigenous peoples in British North America and Canada were governed illiberally: the state exercised quasi-despotic powers. Initially, Whitehall controlled relations with Indigenous peoples; defence was too important to leave to colonial legislatures. But as the spectre of war receded, "Indian Affairs" was transferred from military to civilian and colonial administration. In eastern and central Canada, immigration ensured that settler society had little to fear from the Indigenous people living among them, on or off reserve. Western Canada was very different: there, Indigenous people outnumbered settlers for most of the century. When Canada purchased Rupert's Land in 1869, it acquired a vast new territory of illiberal subjects. Until the West, too, could be settled by farmers governed by consent, it would remain a frontier, a place of limited state authority and limited rule of law. Even as representative institutions began to appear – in Assiniboia (later Manitoba) during the 1830s, in British Columbia during the 1850s, and across the Prairies from the 1880s – policing remained quasi-military under the North West Mounted Police from the 1870s.

The nineteenth century oversaw the growth and extension of a liberal state, one newly accountable to civil society, but a civil society that it arduously reconstructed according to new standards of citizenship. Ancien-régime household government was a kind of binary opposite to state government: people were either free and governed by the state, or dependent and governed by the head of their household. But the patriarchs seemed to be failing the people as much in private as in public life. Patriarchal rule of the household and patrician rule of the country stood and fell together. Too many husbands failed to provide for their dependants: wives, children, the elderly and incapacitated, and defunct servants or slaves. Customary solutions, such as private charity or the billeting of the poor, were expensive and inadequate in the face of the growing numbers of people in need of such provision. When emigrants failed, they could not fall back on familial networks. So legislators created specialized institutions: orphanages, insane asylums, poor houses, hospitals, prisons, and schools. The result was growing state responsibility for public welfare. Expense was one reason, and gatekeeping was another: only the state could provide for forcible confinement in such institutions. The decline of patriarchy created a new kind of state with more extensive powers for civil administration. Ordinary people gained more control over the state, but the state also gained more control over the management of their lives. As state and society mutually infiltrated one another, the bars of the state's "cage" grew stronger.

This account follows the chronology of Ian McKay, the historian of the "liberal order framework" in Canada, whose argument for liberal hegemony between about 1840 and 1890 has attracted a host of reflective analyses in its wake.[1] The new history of liberalism differs from an older, Whiggish version that celebrated the triumph of popular agency and freedom. The liberal order repressed and trampled people as much as it liberated them. Liberty and equality were elaborate legal constructs, tendentiously defined to safeguard property, which was usually the liberal state's primary concern. For all their incoherence, liberal principles expanded remarkably among a society deeply fissured by region, class, ethnicity, religion, and gender. Initially the great challenge to liberalism was how to modernize the pre-liberal elements of society; by the end of the century, it was how to repress the growing postliberal elements that, having experienced liberal rule, rejected it.

Liberalizing the State

The state in British North America in the early nineteenth century suffered from a serious credibility gap. Its constitution was modelled on that of Britain, but it was far from being the "image and transcript" that Governor Simcoe of Upper Canada claimed to see. British North American colonies remained more liminal and more violent than the metropolitan culture that they emulated. The War of 1812, which was provoked by American war hawks and left much of the Canadian borderlands pillaged and burning, reflected the tail end of that frontier violence and its consequences for ordinary rule of law in the colony. The war provoked extremes of loyalty and disaffection in occupied areas like Niagara, where many people had only recently emigrated from the United States. After peace was signed, the ostentatiously loyal governing clique passed legislation to disenfranchise American-born inhabitants throughout Upper Canada. The mixed population experienced the law as an unprecedented attack on well-established, constitutional rights and, over the ten years it took to reverse the legislation, political culture settled into highly polarized camps, each claiming that British liberties were under extraordinary threat from the other. But only one of those camps could force the point and control the political process.

Legislative assemblies were largely in place, based upon a fairly broad franchise, but the imperial Parliament retained control of Canadian affairs. Local elections, newspapers, and legislative debates created a colonial public opinion that grew ever more frustrated by executive veto. Governors reflected imperial interests but they had to rule through local elites, whom they appointed to legislative and executive councils (i.e., upper houses and ministries). The local elites, often self-made land speculators or lawyers who used their powers to enrich themselves and abuse their critics, were impervious to either imperial or local checks. Overlap between different branches of government (judges executed laws as well as enforcing them) meant that there was little local recourse against abusive laws or abusive application of the laws. Reformers fumed indignantly but risked a beating or imprisonment when they spoke out.

On the one hand, government officers winked at violence that served their purposes. At York (Toronto), in 1826, when journalist William Lyon Mackenzie described the attorney general's female forebears as loose and syphilitic, a group of young law clerks, some articled with the attorney general and others with the solicitor general, broke up his press. About the same time, in Hamilton, George Rolph, the brother of a prominent reformer, was tarred and feathered by government supporters, including two magistrates and a sheriff. In both cases, the only recourse proved to be a civil suit, decided by sympathetic jurors. On the other hand, government officers ruthlessly suppressed dubious infractions committed by their critics. When Francis Collins, editor of a reform newspaper, censured those involved in the types riot, insults escalated, and Collins was soon on trial for slandering the attorney general for his "native malignancy." The presiding judge, father to one of the rioters, sentenced Collins to jail for a year and imposed exorbitant fines and securities. Collins had served all but seven weeks of his sentence before he was freed by imperial clemency. A few years earlier, when juries persisted in overturning charges of criminal libel against Robert Gourlay (who blamed corrupt and self-interested officials for failing to develop the province), Gourlay was arrested on a trumped-up charge of sedition and deported after a stint in jail. This was not a wholesale attack on civil liberties, but it did undermine confidence in the rule of law.

Comparable grievances in the Atlantic colonies ranged from Joseph Howe's complaint of excessive exactions by the magistracy and police in Halifax (prompting a charge of criminal libel against him that he persuaded a jury to dismiss), to violent floggings for debt in Newfoundland, to imperial protections extended to absentee landlords of Prince Edward Island against legislative projects of expropriation or "escheat." Abusive acts by robber-baron officials were not the only cause of widespread discontent during the 1830s, but they were an important one. Economic and financial crises were also blamed upon corruption and neglect in local and imperial legislatures. Corruption was a serious indictment of patrician rule. Honourable gentlemen of good birth and education supposedly made good public stewards because they conformed to higher standards of behaviour than the state could articulate or enforce. But time and again, they gamed the system to rob the public purse. Reformers equated privilege with corruption, and the patricians could not return the accusation against adversaries who had never held power. Upper Canadian Tory scion Samuel Peters Jarvis, Indian superintendent, exemplified the problem: acquitted after a fatal duel in 1817, he went on to a career in the Indian Department from which he was dismissed for financial mismanagement in 1845. Some whispered that he had dishonourably killed his opponent (aiming point blank at an unarmed man) to escape his debts. Such infamous, money-grubbing behaviour discredited the patrician class as stewards. If they could not be governed by honour, they must be governed by the law like everybody else.

In Atlantic Canada, the political debates were less radical and republican; in Lower Canada they were more so. Political tensions had begun to emerge in Lower Canada after the French Revolution, when the French population suddenly seemed more menacing to English-speaking elites who passed anti-sedition legislation stronger than anything in Britain. If the laws were bad, their abuse was worse – as in 1832 when two editors, Ludgar Duvernay and Daniel Tracey, were imprisoned by order of the Legislative Council (the upper house) after describing that body as an "oppressive incubus." The Court of King's Bench, full of legislative councillors, confirmed the council's powers and sentence; the men were released only after the legislative session ended. Duvernay returned to jail in 1836 after he criticized the treatment of a prisoner who had died of privation and exposure in there. Even more menacing was the Montreal election "riot" of 1832 when troops fired, unprovoked, into a fleeing crowd and killed three of Tracey's supporters. Politics were more polarized in Lower Canada because, unlike their counterparts elsewhere, reformers won decisive victories in election after election, only to see reform legislation vetoed by the upper house. Their demands for self-government were continually rejected on the grounds that the population was too ignorant to be trusted with such powers. But because ignorance justified illiberal rule, illiberal rulers in the colony perpetuated it: they blocked the assembly's attempts to create local schools on the grounds that an illiterate population could not be trusted to oversee schooling. The Lower Canadian experience of the British constitution was replete with the rhetoric but none of the reality of self-government, and finally the reformers rebelled against British control. The result was crushing military defeat and harsh repression both there and in Upper Canada, where a much smaller uprising occurred. So harsh was the repression in Lower Canada that it left no legitimate form of local government or justice in its wake, not even enough to administer martial law. An imperial plenipotentiary with unlimited powers but a liberal reputation was sent to restore order: Lord Durham

Durham largely capitulated to conservative anglophone opinion that condemned reform opinion as irrational and uninformed because it was French, and he concluded that French Canadians rendered themselves unfit for political liberalism by their failure to read British newspapers. Only assimilation, Durham argued, could bring French Canadians into the polity. This was nonsense: French-Canadian politicians and editors debated English Canadians point for point, and they collaborated with English-speaking reformers. Durham had a narrow conception of liberalism, one unsympathetic to the republican strain that was, by the 1830s, giving new life to platforms of reformers frustrated by British intransigence.

Durham was spooked by the remarkable degree of saturation between state and society that he found in Canada. His famous description of "two nations warring within the bosom of a single state" could have been reversed to read "two states warring within the bosom of a single nation." The English and the French had monopolized distinct branches of the colonial state. The former, controlling the executive, threatened to subvert liberal government from above, by reversion to despotic oligarchy. The latter posed a comparable threat from below. Unusually close relationships between voters and the liberal professionals who populated the legislative assembly, coupled with the lack of intermediary state institutions, such as municipalities that elsewhere undermined such alliances (by pitting propertied ratepayers against the unpropertied), combined to create an extraordinary degree of statism among the French-Canadian inhabitants. Deprived of innervating self-government, they had, Durham lamented, become "accustomed to rely entirely on the government." An unlimited, popular statism of that sort could result in something like the French Revolutionary Terror.

The two nations and the two states had to be reintegrated to create a balanced liberal polity. Durham tried to accomplish this by infusing both state and society with new principles of self-government and monarchism. His viceregal tour of the Canadas, replete with elaborate performances of imperial grandeur and mixed receptions for English and French participants, aimed at turning an ancien-régime politics of display performed *before* quasi-literate crowds into a liberal and discursive politics performed *by* an educated public. The Canadian public was, Durham lamented, less educated than the "middle and lower orders" in Britain – for whose enfranchisement he had long advocated precisely by reason of their "improved intelligence" – but it was ultimately no less worthy of political self-determination. His formal recommendations were twofold: self-government (in municipal institutions as well as the colonial legislatures) and union of the Canadas. The British government enacted the second and not the first, but (as Durham almost certainly anticipated) the end result was the same because, once united, reformers were able to deadlock public affairs and force Westminster to concede local self-government.

According to the history long taught to Canadian schoolchildren, political rights and civil liberties could not be forever withheld from a political system purportedly modelled on Westminster. By refusing to cooperate with governors, elected reformers forced Parliament to subject the colonial executive to colonial assemblies, achieving responsible government by the end of the 1840s. And, over the next two decades, those empowered colonial legislators transferred sovereignty from Britain to Canada, largely placing the state in the hands of Canadians. They created a political structure that was, if not democratic, at least broadly representative and accountable. Moreover, they achieved this process on a transcontinental scale, creating a federal government to unite and oversee local provincial entities, excepting only Newfoundland, which joined Confederation in the mid-twentieth century. Britain relinquished control of Canadian politics at the same time as it relinquished protective imperial tariffs, moving to adopt freer (though never quite free) trade.

Revisionist historians tell things differently. The crises of the 1830s, when the legislature was suspended in Lower Canada and a Special Council governed, permitted dramatic alterations that made political and economic elites more powerful and secure in their power. As historian Brian Young has argued,

The Special Council's work subjected a whole envelope of social relations – the family, childhood, marriage, community, work, and region – to a regime of "positive" [i.e., innovative and interventionist] law and an expanding role for the state. Granted that its legislation was only temporary, was often hastily conceived, and was unlikely to receive popular support; the Special Council's crucial contribution was the structuring of an institutional framework that would be legitimized later by Lower Canada's indigenous political class under the rubric of responsible government.[2]

The new laws would persist within a legislature reconstructed and combined with that of Upper Canada for that purpose. The union of the Canadas was a forced modernizing project.

Corruption and cronyism probably intensified. The fight over responsible government was largely a fight for the control of state spending. The group that controlled spending could use it to promise money – investments, contracts, offices – to supporters and could thus create a political block or party cohesive enough to pass whatever legislation it liked. Conservatives, once they overcame their reluctance to see themselves as a party rather than as the natural governing class, took to the new patronage politics with alacrity. They spent wildly and governed Canada for most of the period between 1854 and 1896. Spending on projects such as railways outpaced spending on bureaucratic oversight, with corruption scandals an inevitable consequence.

The new executive looked even more authoritarian than the old one. There were no longer any political checks upon the leading minister: by leading the majority political party, he controlled the legislature, appointed all officials, and dispersed all patronage. Canadians briefly experimented with an elected upper house, but an appointed upper house was reintroduced at Confederation. Indeed, the plan for Confederation was never submitted to the Canadian public for approval but was pushed through by John A. Macdonald, heir to the old Upper Canadian Tory party. He masterminded a constitution that strengthened his powers as prime minister and kept him in office almost continually until his death in 1891. The success of this anti-democratic Anglophile, who left office in a corruption scandal in 1873, but *still* returned to govern Canada for another thirteen years, was the most compelling proof of the persistence of patrician ways. So was the succession of Wilfrid Laurier, onetime liberal firebrand who remade himself in Macdonald's image in order to inherit his mantle. Still, Macdonald's death did permit a handful of long-awaited reforms, including the codification of criminal law and gun control.

Political liberalism in Canada looked a lot like conservatism, and Macdonald called his party Liberal Conservative. The colonies had been designed as a counter-revolutionary project and were recommitted to that outcome by warfare in 1810s and rebellion in 1830s; conservatism adhered to them for decades longer. To the end of the century, democratic reasoning was castigated as American-style demagogy. And yet an important change did occur around mid-century. People felt genuinely empowered and freed by the new responsible state. The "cage" of the liberal state was legitimized by an insistence on freedom. Power was no longer seen only to descend from the state but also to ascend from the population towards the centre. Rather than pleading with imperial statesmen to remove officials who were corrupt and abusive, only to be jailed or beaten for their pains, electors could vote the bastards out. Opinion was newly empowered as the key liberal interface between state and society.

Appeals to public opinion had become central to British political life during the eighteenth century, and they assumed that same centrality in Canada during the nineteenth. When they rejected their king in 1688, British parliamentarians made public debate, as epitomized in Parliament, the highest standard of legitimacy and authority. Something like an alchemical transformation occurred through the process of public debate, turning private into public interest and national purpose. The process was riddled with contradictions and blind spots, but nonetheless, appeal to the public use of reason became authoritative. Liberal advocates of reform took up ideological arguments in favour of public opinion and liberty and disseminated them in popular newspapers. Conservatives had their own newspapers but hadn't previously used them to make popular political appeals to electors. As the reformist arguments spread, and the accusations of corruption and misrule mounted, conservatives had to respond. If they tried to defend traditional political relationships grounded in authority, they had to appeal to the reader's understanding of those traditional forms. They could and did draw upon irrational appeals to patriotism and the spectacle of monarchical grandeur (as when the governor of Upper Canada mobilized the ostentatiously patriotic and Protestant Orange Order during the election of 1836), but no politician could tell his electors, no journalist his readers, "This point will elude your understanding." Once the appeal was made to ordinary reason, interest, and agency, there was no way to justify a political regime that bypassed the decision-making powers of the electorate.

Together, elections and newspapers silenced diehard Tories who refused to "stoop to conquer," as John A. Macdonald advised they must in 1856. Barring some sort of demographic reversal ("Immigration & Copulation"), British Canadians in Montreal must abandon dreams of political ascendency and "make friends with the French ... Treat them as a nation and they will act as a free people usually do – generously. Call them a faction and they become factious." Flattery of the electorate's sense of agency and freedom was necessary for winning elections but, Macdonald explained to his correspondent, the editor of the Montreal *Gazette*, it could also conceal the quiet workings of cronyism: "It would surprise you to go over the names of Officials in a Lower Canada Almanac & reckon the *ascendency* you yet hold of official positions. Take care that the French don't find it out & make a Counter Cry."[3] Here was Macdonald's formula for political success and liberal conservatism in a nutshell: insistence on freedom, liberty, and agency, counterbalanced by careful control of patronage that long perpetuated a political cronyism directly descended from the old patrician networks of Upper and Lower Canada. It cohered with the broadly liberal principles underwriting the nineteenth-century public sphere (Macdonald and Conservative British Prime Minister Benjamin Disraeli met as what Anne of Green Gables would call kindred spirits), but it was a far cry from the dreams of transparency and equality that had inspired the great reformers of the previous generation.

The public sphere in nineteenth-century Canada did advance reform agendas and did subject governments to greater scrutiny and accountability. But it was channelled and moderated by some important elements that grew exponentially with responsible government: partyism, public education, commodification, and moral regulation.

Most early newspapers served political parties and followed a party line. Political parties policed unorthodox opinions and allocated resources to loyal party members. They tethered political opinion to institutions and resources and blurred the distinction between the categories of "state" and "nation." Party loyalty ensured that, when Macdonald took up a policy like Confederation, a whole series of newspapers and other organizations would follow his lead. André Siegfried, who brought French sociological methods to the study of Canada in 1906, observed that, "in the absence of ideas and doctrines dividing electors into opposite camps, there remain only questions of collective or individual interests for the candidates to exploit to their own advantage," which was to say that Canadian politics consisted of fierce fights for the spoils of patronage. Sage politicians, knowing that Canadians could agree on little, sought to keep substantive questions off the agenda and to make their parties "entirely harmless."[4] Unorthodox or radical opinions commanded much fewer resources. Political parties overlapped with and shaded into other more or less partisan organizations, ranging from voluntary fire brigades to mechanics' institutes to the Orange Order. Persuaded by Alexis de Tocqueville's arguments that a vibrant association life reined in the state, men and women reformers formed high-minded voluntary associations aimed at regenerating civil society, and they fumed to see them undermined, time and again, by the infusion of party spirit and booty politics, effectively extending the state's reach into civil society. Reformers in government also used political patronage to prop up party discipline, but they usually expressed some regret at having to do so. And because Macdonald kept them in opposition so much of the time, his critics preferred other forms of party discipline. It was reformers, rather than Macdonald's Liberal Conservatives, who began to publicize political platforms at the end of the 1850s. Reformers inclined to voluntary reforms, but their frustration at the failure of such voluntarist projects as temperance propelled them towards coercive statist reforms, such as prohibition.

Conservatives largely trusted newspapers to manage public opinion; reformers dreamed of improving it by means of state schooling. Public education promised to ground opinion in knowledge and self-discipline, thereby creating a stable basis for moderate political consensus. For reformers like Durham, education was a key constituent of liberalism. In the first half of the century, it was voluntary: parents could send children to school or simply set them to work. Subscription schools were too expensive for ordinary inhabitants: only state support permitted mass education. In the second half of the century, most provinces established compulsory state schools. Wherever publicly funded schools were established, they sapped their private rivals and attracted most of the local children. Quebec alone resisted the trend: there, the Catholic Church held the provincial state to a more strictly liberal, non-interventionist, standard. School attendance in Quebec lagged behind that of other provinces, and Catholic journalism lagged as well, emerging only after mid-century. The Catholic Church had financial resources far beyond those of other denominations (especially after clergy reserve lands were finally put towards public schooling). Catholics managed to secure state funding for their schools, especially in areas with substantial Acadian, French-Canadian, or Metis presence, but these special accommodations were fiercely attacked by Protestants and fuelled some of the most heated political controversies in the half-century after Confederation.

Education illustrates the coercion inherent in the new liberalism. Egerton Ryerson, superintendent of education for Upper Canada from 1844 to 1876, insisted that education was a child's right that "the State" must uphold. The parent might choose the school, but "he has no right to the choice as to whether his child shall, or shall not, be educated at all, any more than he has the right of choice as to whether his child shall steal, or starve, as long as he is a member of a civil community, whose sole interests are binding upon each member."[5] Such a breach of parental authority would have seemed tyrannous in earlier days but, by mid-century, most voters outside Quebec apparently agreed with him. And because they felt a vested interest in such public policies, those policies could reasonably impinge upon the life of the household. The urgent need to reconstruct working-class or other kinds of "undisciplined" households – Indian residential schools promised the greatest transformation of illiberal subjects – to fit them for raising new liberal subjects, justified the intrusion. Legislation to prohibit child labour in factories followed logically and chronologically, from the mid-1880s.

There was a good deal of resistance along the way to what was, essentially, a middle-class project of discipline. In 1840s Quebec, the *guerre des éteignoirs* (candle-snuffers' war) reflected organized hostility to public schooling and school taxes, but many families quietly resisted elsewhere. Public education was supposed to eradicate unruly, radical potential by instilling both intellectual and physical disciplines, teaching people to display the decorum of the schoolhouse even when school was out. School children were taught to sit still and learn, acquiring mental and physical discipline; they even learned to defecate in toilets rather than indiscriminately around the school yard. Vagrants and criminals were put to hard labour, so that they could learn to work; even lunatics in asylums were encouraged to act out plays, on the theory that role playing would teach them to "act" appropriately in civil society. In innumerable ways, thus, institutions constructed a new kind of disciplined, rational citizen. Standards of civility continually shifted according to new fashions or discoveries, such as germ theory, which killed off beards, long dresses, and public spitting.

The battle was never fully won. Popular culture remained stubbornly unruly, infused with casual violence, drunkenness, uproariousness, and unwillingness to suspend disbelief in the state's claims to authority. Many acts criminalized by the state continued to appeal to popular opinion and to flourish more or less overtly, ranging from trivial defiances, such as nude bathing in the local river, to more organized expressions of popular defiance, such as the charivari – the crowds and cacophony that greeted breaches of popular norms, as when, for example, a rich old man married a young woman, or an official behaved too officiously. Alternatively, the official might be hanged in effigy. Ribaldry and political caricature constantly accompanied such outbursts. This sort of behaviour was not a minor historical footnote but was, rather, a vibrant public presence that looked backwards to peasant traditions and forwards to emerging traditions of working-class radicalism. When political tensions polarized, as in the 1830s, popular unruliness aligned with them, and their conjuncture could threaten to break the bars of the state's cage. Corrupt patricians made marvellous targets, but so did reformers. One radical ditty penned in 1837 urged,

Take this piece of advice from an ignorant elf

Let each ipso facto reform one himself

And then my dear Roger, you'll see in conclusion,

A glorious, a grand, a great, Revolution.[6]

Public education did not aim simply at imposing mental and bodily disciplines on the unruly classes. It was also a middle-class project to pool the costs of education that middling people could not otherwise afford. Paying for the school was not an incidental problem but rather reflected another kind of popular discipline, one that transformed the local state. As Michael Mann observes, "Through most of history subordinate classes had been largely indifferent to or had sought to evade states. They were now caged into national organization, into politics, by two principal zookeepers: tax gatherers and recruiting officers."[7] In Canada, the latter were negligible: John A. Macdonald largely eschewed military forays. Tax officers were more important intermediaries between state and society. Customs and excise (indirect taxes that people didn't feel directly) largely paid for the costs of central governments, but the new local institutions of governance, such as schools, were largely paid for by taxes collected from people directly, often in face-to-face negotiations. State schooling was an expansive disciplinary program, as much material and economic as it was physical and intellectual.

Gathering taxes to pay for the schools was everywhere, year after year, an enormous effort, always accompanied by lawsuits, forced sales of properties for unpaid taxes, and endless correspondence. Taxes were the most common, banal constituents of public debate and local politics. Newspapers filled columns with ratepayers' complaints, and their editors catered to that public sentiment by demanding greater accountability and retrenchment. Many people strenuously resisted such state encroachments, and the new police forces regularly had to enforce the new taxes. But liberal states could not impose their exactions willy-nilly; many new taxes failed and lapsed. Liberal state modernization was always a dialogue, never a monologue. But the dialogue is the story, reflecting a new kind of political and civil relationship. People negotiated their value and their interests directly and indirectly with state officials.

Everywhere that these debates occurred, ratepayers were reminded that governments taxed property because they protected property, and that property owners were natural allies of the liberal state. But taxes could prove devastating to people with modest holdings, so devastating, indeed, as to threaten the public order that the taxes supposedly upheld in the first place. In 1877, a year of great hardship, county councillor George Longard, JP, advised the people of Upper Prospect, Nova Scotia, not to pay their county rates and refused to execute a warrant against them; in 1870 he refused to assess poor widows according to the strict letter of the law. That year, a collector in Hants County, Michael Burgess, exclaimed, "You never heard such a cry about a county tax as there is about this one here the people are exasperated some swares and some prayes and I dont know wither I shall get out of the scrape with a sound head or not." In 1881, a constable in British Columbia, trying to extract a province-wide school tax of $3 from Chinese railway labourers on the Canadian Pacific Railway line, had to run in fear for his life. It took five months and nearly a dozen men "in battle array, all well armed with first-class revolvers" to overcome that tax revolt. This was liberalism gone far astray: the newly arrived workers could not benefit from the provincial schools, and the overt use of military-style violence belied the basic premise of a civil society engaged in peaceful self-policing. As one outraged newspaper correspondent remarked of the incident, "Taxation is tyranny when the tax is collected with pistols."[8] In fact, state violence was (and remains) latent in even the most trivial transactions, all too apt to explode into beatings, and even killings, of people who seemed, individually or collectively (like the Chinese at the time), deaf or immune to the disciplines of liberal civil society.

The obverse of public education through schools was public education through the courts. "What liberalism could not rule by freedom, it ruled by other means."9 All levels of government had their own courts, from the municipal recorder's court, through the provincial and territorial courts that did most of the heavy lifting, to a federal system that culminated in the Supreme Court of Canada, established by statute in 1875. Courthouses and jails proliferated, and the apparatus of justice gradually stretched more effectively into rural society. Jury trials declined, ceding to summary justice before a magistrate or judge in the vast majority of cases, and the scale of punishments inflicted underwent a decline in severity as well. New kinds of crimes emerged, even new kinds of police, around the emergence of the automobile, for example.

Punishment, public education, and partyism collaborated with commodification in constructing the broad outlines of the public sphere in Canada. Public debate in Canada matured as a consumer product, sold by and through newspapers. If the public sphere was ruled by market relations, philosophers and pundits reasoned, it would nurture progress, choice, and freedom, rather than subserving a tyrannical state. Egerton Ryerson, an editor as well as an educator, always insisted on the importance of a practical, commercial education. The pace and tenor of commercial appeals intensified through the century as, from the 1860s and 1870s, advertising came of age, newspapers grew rich on it, and popular consumption spread. More powerfully than the other constituents of the public sphere, commodification enhanced popular choice and agency and undermined traditional restraints upon it. The insistence on individual choice was universal, but it was particularly novel with respect to women: the same paper might juxtapose editorial homilies that celebrated women's self-sacrificing mission as wives and mothers with advertisements encouraging women to spend on themselves. The discourse of empowered female consumers gradually popularized a discourse of empowered female political agents. Women, too, asked themselves the great modern question, "How can I be happy?" and began to challenge moral, material, and legal obstacles to their happiness and to organize themselves to that end.

Commercial and political discourse shared methods and values, including a slick boosterism that appealed to individual and national vanities. One symbol of this new discourse was Sam Slick, a fictional American salesman (created in the 1830s by Thomas Haliburton, a Nova Scotian judge), who continually remarked upon the slower pace of life north of the border and used flattery to sell fancy clocks to foolish farmers. Slick advised Nova Scotia legislators to emulate American prosperity by building railroads, but this time Haliburton, himself a proponent of railways, was in earnest. The farmers' clocks and state-sponsored railways had more in common than Haliburton understood. Britain and the United States experienced railroad booms in the 1830s and 1840s, a time when British North American colonies were too poor and too politically polarized to follow suit. At mid-century, with full control of the public purse, colonial legislators began to pursue railroad dreams, each trying to out-aggrandize the other. In Canada, almost the first act of the first responsible government, led by Robert Baldwin and Louis-Hippolyte Lafontaine, was a law to guarantee interest payments for railway debts, and subsequent legislation hugely expanded both central and municipal indebtedness for these ends. In 1854 the Conservative Party (including John A. Macdonald as attorney general) won and held power on a policy of railroads. But the early railways could not pay their way, and within a few years, many towns and railways were near or in default. The colonial government was scarcely better off, with nearly half its revenue directed towards servicing debts generated by railway projects. The colony was in a full-scale fiscal crisis that had far-reaching effects. One was the introduction of new regulations and bureaucracies to better manage the railways and finances: Canada acquired an auditor general. Another was an increased tariff on imports, which whetted the appetite of businessmen for protection. Still another was a growing pressure in business circles to combine colonial governments so as to consolidate their debts under an imperial guarantee. Similar scenarios played out everywhere. In Nova Scotia, Liberal leader Joseph Howe predicted in 1851 that a railway would make Halifax the great continental entrepôt on the east coast and open up undeveloped resources, simultaneously connecting all of British North America as "a great and prosperous nation."[10] Future Conservative leader Charles Tupper agreed that the railway would establish the colony's prosperity and that the government must build it. In 1854 the legislature approved the project, just as it would later approve Tupper's grandiose solution to the fiscal obstacles – Confederation.

Railroad projects enmeshed colonial governments in intricate webs of financial speculation and regulation. Power could not be understood apart from such things. Canadian railways were statist projects because the local bourgeoisie lacked the necessary capital (and the initiative, some said) to take up the kinds of expensive infrastructure projects that generated power and wealth. But the reverse was also true: politicians built railroads for the same reason robbers rob banks – that's where the money was. At mid-century, British prosperity was spectacularly on display at venues like the Crystal Palace Exhibition in London, which included state-sponsored collections from British North America. Canadian governments aimed their sparse bureaucratic resources at grabbing all such available investment capital and, for all their many limitations, here they excelled. Counter-intuitively, despite all manner of financial failings that should have provided a compelling argument against investment, British capital continued to flow into Canadian railways, above all the troubled Grand Trunk Railway. "By 1872, its ratio of debts to equity was an almost unbelievable 25–1. The ideal ratio was 1–1 with each dollar of debt paired with a dollar of equity securing the debt. The British continued to invest because they thought the Canadian government would bail them out."[11] Private enrichment (often very brief) and public debt (much less brief) could not but follow from this irrational exuberance. Speculative catastrophes of this sort discredited state building projects elsewhere – especially in American states where, for example, only New York got any return from building canals – but in Canada, the result seems to have been a permanent expectation that this was how governments should behave. Voters didn't much want to hear the dour message of one-term Liberal Prime Minister Alexander Mackenzie that a transcontinental railway was unaffordable; they responded much more enthusiastically to the promise that the transcontinental railways would lay the foundation for a wealthy Dominion. Canadians continued to build massive, unprofitable railways for many more decades. In the process, they reconstructed the state as profoundly interventionist, even as they veiled it in the rhetoric of liberalism.

It was hard to sustain the language of rational, economic self-interest under such conditions. Adam Smith warned that economic meddling tended away from transparency, self-government, and generalized prosperity, and towards oligarchic enrichment of the few at the expense of the many. Canadian politicians took his lesson to heart – and began the work of oligopoly building. Newspapers proved poor watchdogs of these state-building projects. Slim broadsheets, dominated by text and text-heavy advertisements, became bulky packages, dozens or even a hundred pages long, filled with colourful advertisements and frothy plaudits to consumption. As advertising became big business, it was transformed by professional advertisers who projected a view of the consuming public as irrational, feminine, governed by opinion rather than reason, and easily manipulated. The language of rational self-interest gave way to the language of desire – desire for a happiness that would ultimately be material rather than moral or political.

Reconciling the material and the moral was largely left to private organizations like churches and the many associations that they sustained. Quite a few of those organizations received some state support, such as tax relief or annual subventions. But there was considerable perplexity about the relationship between religious institutions and the state. In English and French Canada, many Protestants and Catholics insisted that the state had no business meddling with religion. Catholics in Quebec freed themselves from secular oversight when, in 1836, they persuaded the Pope to create a bishopric in Montreal without first obtaining British permission. The Bishop of Montreal between 1840 and 1876, Ignace Bourget, made the Catholic Church again a powerful social and political organization unaccountable to the state, according to the view, expressed in a pastoral letter in 1875, that "it is not the Church that is comprised in the State; it is the State that is comprised in the Church."[12] Outsiders like André Siegfried were shocked to find scant conception of a civil state in Quebec; the Pope himself rebuked the Quebec bishops for flagrant political meddling. By contrast, Protestant dissenting sects subscribed to voluntarist principles that would rupture state-church relations entirely, and they fought heated battles with established churches over such questions as denominational public schooling and universities, battles that reverberated through the various legislatures at mid-century and that were, finally, won by the voluntarists. One consequence was that Anglican colleges and universities – such as McGill University in Lower Canada and King's College in New Brunswick – founded as instruments of consolidation by governing cliques, began to liberalize their admissions and cater to a more broadly professionalizing middle class. Denominational battles were particularly fierce in Nova Scotia, where the Anglican King's College, founded by Loyalists in 1789 and defended by the upper house, battled a Presbyterian academy supported by the assembly, while Lord Dalhousie's non-denominational college began to admit serious numbers of students only after mid-century. In Upper Canada, amidst torrents of vituperation, Robert Baldwin's newly responsible government nationalized the Anglican university that Bishop John Strachan had founded in 1828.

No less perplexing than formal questions of funding and appointment were informal questions of public morality: was it the state's business or not? There was no clear answer to that question, only a gradually shifting consensus, away from a patrician double standard between public and private morality and towards a middle-class morality that tried to reconcile the two. Thomas Turton personified the perplexities of early Victorian morality: in 1838 Lord Durham named as councillor a man who had left his wife for her sister. Durham's critics insisted this was a breach of morality, church law, and by extension state law; his supporters defended the relationship as private and not illegal because not *really* incestuous. On his return to England, Durham instantly silenced his critics by insisting that his honour was pledged to the defence of Turton, and so was their own; if they persisted in such a line of attack, he would "go into an inquiry into the case of every public man who may have received official employment after having committed adultery."[13] Red-faced lords resumed their seats and moved on to other business. Partisan sniping sought any chink in the armour but was rebuffed when it threatened upper-class male sociability and patrician values. This distinction between private and public decorum kept Macdonald's drunken sprees and George-Étienne Cartier's adultery out of the press. But the schooling that Durham advocated worked to erode the double standard. As the middle classes – nurtured on public education and the project to improve public opinion through it – gained political ascendency, they rallied to organizations that promoted public *and* private morality. The primary locale for constructing private morality devolved, over the nineteenth century, from churches to the family, and this led middle-class reformers to aim at reconstructing working-class families – to make them less violent, less ignorant, less idle, and less drunk – by organizing libraries and reading rooms, or sports and other improving recreations. Temperance organizations first appeared in 1827; by the turn of the century, prohibitionists numbered tens of thousands and were winning legislative victories, beginning in Prince Edward Island in 1900. Moral regulation, crossing private and public spheres, became an important constituent of public opinion.

This, then, was the basic organization of liberal consent to the modern state. The state, a concatenation of officials both elected and appointed, centralized and decentralized, was organized into partisan blocks and infused with a commercialized, moralized public opinion to which it was now accountable, but which it took good care to manage. The federal state that these men erected was much like the one that preceded it: liberal in principle, conservative in much of its practice, and profoundly implicated in the construction of a capitalist economy.

Constructing a Federal State

Between 1867 and 1873, five colonies joined together in a centralized state, to resolve a number of political and economic problems. The primary pressure for Confederation came from the united province of Canada, where English and French Canadian nationalisms clashed. George Brown, a leading journalist in Canada West, lamented that "unenterprising" French-Canadians held back the colony as a whole, as did their Catholic Church. Frustrated by the conservative alliance between Macdonald and George-Étienne Cartier, the Canada-West reformers began to denounce the union of the Canadas. Well aware that his political career could not survive the loss of French Canada, Macdonald supported a different solution: union of all the British North American colonies in a federal system, with a national government to administer shared national interests – primarily trade – and local governments to administer the identity politics that threatened to weaken national interests. Newfoundland refused adamantly, but by 1873, Canada, New Brunswick, Nova Scotia, British Columbia, and Prince Edward Island had all joined the new Dominion of Canada, while Rupert's Land was added by purchase in 1869.

Confederation did not make Canada stronger or more autonomous: local government had already devolved, leaving Britain in control of diplomacy, constitutional reform, and judicial appeal – all powers it kept after 1867. What Confederation did do was strengthen the federal government's ability to promote local prosperity: it could borrow more money, under British imperial guarantee, and it could focus on economic development with infrastructural spending and, from 1879, a protective tariff that stoked big business in central Canada. Critics at the time and historians in retrospect agree that the federal state fulsomely pursued the interests of the business elite. Turn-of-the-century journalist Gustavus Myers remarked, "Politics was, in fact, a business; the Canadian Parliament was crowded with men who were there to initiate, extend, or conserve class or personal interests." Macdonald's party took huge donations from businessmen seeking favours: the Canadian Pacific Railway alone donated more than a million dollars during the last decade or so of his tenure. One historian observes that "the Conservative Party must have been so flush with CPR and manufacturers' money in the 1880s that general elections were close to meaningless."[14]

Macdonald predicted that provincial governments would decline to the insignificance of municipalities, if they did not wither away entirely. Municipal governments – widespread thanks to enabling legislation passed in the 1840s – managed roads, police, water, and other utilities but, funded by direct taxes, they were much more accountable to ratepayers, who invariably punished tax hikes electorally. Direct taxation, along with the paralyzing effects of religious quarrels, promised to hobble provincial governments. Not all the "fathers" of Confederation shared Macdonald's political goals: Cartier, for example, espoused a more decentralized union. Ultimately, the decentralizers won that battle, foiling Macdonald's plans for a quasi-imperial federal state. Provincial governments grew to resemble mini-states more than municipalities. They gained a powerful counterweight in a last-minute change to the constitution by the Colonial Office in 1866, removing final jurisdiction over "property and civil rights" from Ottawa. When trade and property, federal and provincial governments clashed, appeals went to the Judicial Committee of the Privy Council in London (the final court of appeal until 1949). Macdonald had no powers to control that court, and, time and again, it upheld provincial rights over federal ones. Nor did Macdonald succeed in banishing religious controversies from federal politics: a constitutional guarantee in favour of minority religious rights that was written into the constitution failed to restrain provincial governments from abolishing funds for Catholic schools. Every time that happened, the federal government was subjected to intense lobbying both for and against intervention. The provinces grew stronger by yoking religion to provincial rights campaigns and wealthier by imposing new corporate taxes and natural resource sell-offs.

Cities, meanwhile, stumbled along under the rapidly growing burdens of urban infrastructure and social welfare. Such things were closely connected: when unemployment hit Montreal's casual labour force, the city would expand its road-building operations to create work for the men. In Winnipeg, the city woodyard was the staple recourse of the relief office. Unemployment and poverty were seen as short-term problems to be met with short-term arrangements. Still, an entrenched infrastructure of long-term institutionalized poverty gradually emerged over the course of the century: something had to be done for the aged poor, the disabled, and the orphans. Even where it made no provision for the poor, the local state remained their last resort, as one municipality discovered at the turn of the century. Burdened with an indigent old man lacking property, relatives, or income, it sought expert advice: must it pay for his keep or could it send him somewhere? The answer came back: no, council need not maintain him at its expense, but there was "no place to which he can be sent."[15] Charitable organizations provided much of the essential infrastructure for the chronically poor, though they often relied heavily on state subscriptions. Ontario in 1900 spent $800,000 on public institutions (prisons, reformatories, asylums for lunatics and for the deaf, dumb, and blind) and subscribed another $200,000 to charities. Quebec, where the Church even ran asylums, spent half as much and only $40,000 went to charities. But officials still eyed the vast, tax-exempt wealth of the Catholic Church covetously, especially in Montreal, where one-quarter of all real estate paid no taxes.

After Confederation the nation state remained a ninety-seven-pound-weakling. The federal government had its own technologies, such as the postal service, but the BNA Act handed most administrative responsibilities over to lower levels of government. Even as he dispersed patronage freely, Macdonald kept his bureaucracy small, cheap, and inexpert. Occasionally, one of those patronage appointments turned out to have real administrative powers. Joseph-Charles Taché was a washed-up legislator before he became deputy minister of agriculture and created the first modern census of Canada in 1871. But Taché's census was strategically partisan, designed to exaggerate French-Canadian demographic strength. It zigged where aspirant bureaucracies in other nations zagged in constructing objective knowledge of populations. Likewise, into the early twentieth century, the Department of Indian Affairs found it more useful to be ignorant rather than knowledgeable of Indigenous demographies, and deputy minister Duncan Campbell Scott actively suppressed early tallies of atrocious death rates in the residential schools.

The first responsibilities of a modern state were defining and defending boundaries. While unambiguously federal, these were very restrained powers in Canada. The imperial government used its diplomatic powers (which it kept until the Statute of Westminster in 1931) largely to benefit itself rather than Canada. American trade and goodwill were more valuable than Canadian trade and goodwill, so British negotiators regularly conceded to American demands, including access to fish in Canadian waters and a generous boundary for Alaska. Canada lacked the military and political resources to defy either Britain or the United States. The British North American colonies had always relied upon Britain to guarantee their borders; the departure of British troops in 1871 left Canada largely reliant on the peaceful intentions of the United States. American expansionists still sought to annex Canada but, after the trauma of the American Civil War, they chose to rely on peaceful mechanisms, such as high tariffs, rather than invasion, to that end.

Vast borders and permeable jurisdictions continued to challenge and confound Canadian politics. Local, national, and international problems fuelled one another and continually undermined the authority of the Canadian state. If Canada was not a frontier – a place of limited state authority – then its limits must reflect political choices. Violence provided a good measure of that distinction: either the state had a monopoly on violence and exercised that violence in ways that people recognized as legitimate (such as the incarceration of lunatics and criminals), or violence occurred without the state's sanction, and revealed the state's weaknesses (such as the charivari). The authors of the British North America Act crafted it to write state violence largely out of federal politics: policing, justice, and punishment were largely, though not exclusively, provincial responsibilities. But it remained a huge problem for Canada that American violence continually spilled over into Canada. Americans made themselves an independent, vast, and powerful people over the century after 1776 by deploying extraordinary violence against internal and external threats. State and individual violence there continually reinforced one another. Andrew Jackson insisted that his guns were his passports;[16] when he became president, the US Army became his passport. The objects of such violence streamed into Canada seeking asylum, led by such iconic figures as Joseph Brant, Sitting Bull, and Harriet Tubman. Time and again, the refugees provoked political crises, as the case of slavery shows.

Canada had always owed its slavery to its borderlands. The French legalized slavery in New France because they could not sustain military alliances without it. The British legalized slavery in Canada at the behest of Loyalists who wished to keep their slaves. These were strategic military decisions that reflected the distance between metropolitan and colonial regimes. But if British North America genuinely emulated British liberties, it must abolish slavery. When Chloe Cooley was violently carried across the border in 1793, resisting to her utmost, Upper Canadian legislators were appalled at the violent public spectacle and responded with laws to prohibit further enslavement. Propertied elites, slave owners themselves, used their executive powers to overturn abolitionist legislation, unsuccessfully in Upper Canada and more successfully elsewhere. But judges often refused to put the state's powers to work to force runaway slaves back to their owners. In Montreal, slaves freed themselves by walking away in 1898. The value of slaves plummeted and investment in such an uncertain property dried up. Slavery was moribund in British North America by the time it was formally abolished by imperial law in 1834. But, under American pressure for extradition, Canadians still had to negotiate what to do with slaves who had escaped to Canada: were they to be extradited as criminals or protected as free human beings? What if they stole or murdered in order to escape? There was no simple answer to that question; some were freed, others returned, though an aroused public sometimes violently sprang from jail a slave destined for extradition. Every case provoked heated debate and creative readings of "natural freedom" and "international law." There could never be a uniquely Canadian version of authority or rule of law impervious to all the challenges that modernity could yield up.

The western borderlands of British North America posed even greater challenges of sovereignty and control. Inhabitants there moved north and south, east and west, in defiance of political boundaries. Louis Riel, who was of mixed, Metis descent, was born in Rupert's Land (at Red River, near present day Winnipeg) in 1844, educated in Montreal, and worked his way home on the American side of the border, returning as a refugee there in 1870, after the Red River Uprising. The Canadian government badly underestimated the Metis when it purchased Rupert's Land in 1869 and failed to consult local opinion; armed uprising was the result. The government sent troops, but it also belatedly recognized the need to secure consent and meet grievances, and resolved the dispute by negotiation. The rebels' demand for provincial status was accorded with the creation of Manitoba. There were also special land grants for Metis settlers and some other concessions, but the Metis did not flourish on scrip land in Manitoba. Their holdings passed into the hands of English settlers, while the Metis migrated westward to new lands in Saskatchewan and, increasingly, laid claim to the Northwest as a whole, held in common with Indigenous people. When surveyors came to draw survey lines on those lands, Metis settlers believed their tenure to be at threat. Casual violence exploded into uprising in 1885.

Would the Aboriginal peoples of the Plains join the uprising? The Canadian state could easily put down a Metis rebellion; not so a wider uprising of First Nations. These had good reason for disaffection. On the Prairies, where there were no provincial authorities until 1905, federal negotiators signed treaties with Indigenous bands to settle them on reserves and free up the bulk of the land for immigrant settlement. That, at least, was how the government saw things; Indigenous signatories less so. Oral histories of Treaty Seven, signed in 1877 by the Kainai or Blood Nation, the Piikani or Piegan Nation, the Siksika or Blackfoot Nation, the Tsuu T'ina or Sarcee Nation, the Stoney Nation, and the Assiniboine Nation, insist that it was not a land deal but a peace treaty to end violence, share the land, and provide protection from starvation, disease, and the whisky trade (Indian Commissioner David Laird assured them that the government was successfully protecting the buffalo and suppressing the whisky trade). The chiefs believed that powerful and principled governance would come to the region, according to something like their own standards of decision making. The Canadian government, on the other hand, saw such treaties as the means to unleashing market relationships in the region, and its own role as a helpmate to those market forces. Its signatories probably recognized the gap between the different understandings but expected to close that gap by education that would reorient First Nations' expectations from state to market; just such a reorientation was, to their mind, the promised form of protection from starvation.

It was a bad moment for rule by market. The treaty process coincided with the near extinction of the buffalo and the loss of traditional ways of living. Famine forced reluctant leaders to sign treaties providing reserves that the Canadian government considered sufficiently far from one another to avert serious trouble. State responsibility for the health and welfare of its citizens was far from self-evident in the late nineteenth century, but beginning in 1876, negotiating the surrender of much of central Saskatchewan, the Cree and Assiniboine demanded provision and medicine for the poor, unfortunate, blind, and lame. The Canadian negotiator, Lieutenant Governor Alexander Morris, explained that the Canadian state intervened only in the event of a national famine, but, reluctantly, he did agree that the state would relieve "famine and pestilence" and provide "a medicine chest" for every band that signed what became Treaty Six. Morris argued that such a commitment was new, though there was some precedent in earlier treaties. As a new departure in federal welfare, the promises made to the peoples of the Prairies were distinctly unpropitious. The Plains people experienced a calamitous collapse of their way of life, but unimaginative federal officers responsible for overseeing relief understood the situation as part of a normal transition to modern political economy, requiring no more than normal spending. The half-million dollars being spent to feed Indigenous peoples on the Prairies in the early 1880's was becoming a scandal in the House of Commons, and severe cutbacks were imposed. Starvation rations were reduced or denied outright, and the consequence was violence but not, ultimately, widespread uprising. The rebellion of 1885 was essentially undertaken by the Metis, who tried but largely failed to bring Aboriginal communities into the rebellion. It was put down by troops hastily sent west and was followed by trials for the purported ringleaders, including Big Bear and Poundmaker, both of whom were sent to jail on faulty evidence. Nine men, including Louis Riel, were executed in November 1885. Macdonald remarked that the executions "ought to convince the Red man that the White man governs."[17] The events of 1885 weakened terribly the Plains peoples' ability to resist state projects of assimilation. The Upper Canadian conservative tradition, which had long resisted Jacksonian-style frontier violence, now embraced it.

In British Columbia, Indigenous peoples were managed differently because authority was divided. In the early part of the century, the imperial state largely delegated inland governance to Hudson's Bay Company officials. James Douglas, an HBC agent and colonial governor, signed only a few small treaties and resolved confrontations between Indigenous peoples and incomers with rough justice. Consequently, most settlement and treatying occurred after Confederation. Federal and provincial authorities could not agree on such matters as how much land a reserve should contain, so no new treaties were signed and nations were unilaterally pushed on to small reserves that shrank still smaller over time. Nor could authorities agree on responsibility for policing: after an outbreak of violence at Metlakatla, in northwest British Columbia, during the mid-1880s, the provincial government blamed the lack of Indian agents, and the federal government blamed the lack of provincial police.

Indigenous peoples across Canada still did not partake of liberal rule: the state ruled over them in ancien-régime fashion, rather than through them. The Department of Indian Affairs took scant interest in generating or responding to public opinion among Native peoples because it believed them ignorant of economic and political rationality. The Canadian state sought to implant that rationality through Indian agents, schools, agricultural societies, and instructors. But it lacked an objective measure of its success or of Indigenous knowledge and rationality more generally. Elsewhere in Canada, property served as that measure, but the Royal Proclamation and the Indian Act of 1876 insisted that status Indians could not buy, sell, or own property as individuals. In late Victorian Canada, by definition, federal electors must be propertied; by definition, Indians must not. Given that the federal government constituted itself as the government of prosperity, eschewing identity politics, it was particularly ill-equipped to understand or govern anything that could not be translated into liberal individualism and economic self-interest. The consequences for Indigenous peoples, as wards of the federal state, were truly terrible: the government tried for many decades to force them to conform to an economist's caricature of human behaviour.

Liberal rule in Canada was usually rule of, by, and for property. Property was covalent with opinion as a political agency; the two measured and shaped one another. Most political jurisdictions had property restrictions on the franchise for most of the century, though there were some noteworthy exceptions. British Columbia entered Confederation with racialized voting criteria but no property requirement, as provincial politicians struggled to create white rather than class rule. On Prince Edward Island, where politics were largely polarized around absentee landlords and landless tenant farmers, not property but four days of statute labour earned men the vote. Nova Scotia abolished property qualifications at mid-century only to restore them soon afterwards. In most places, property qualifications persisted until the final years of the century.

Property taught people how to be good citizens; if you owned property, that was a sign that you knew how to make good choices; if you had no property, then your reason as well as your stake in a stable, self-reproducing social order were both in question. A state responsible to the propertied classes would be smaller, cheaper, and limited in its grasp. Violence and property seemed incompatible; even the smallest property owner could be trusted to prefer state protection to mob violence. But for property to serve its vital civil function, it had to be upheld, regularized, and protected. Only the state could protect property to the necessary standard, and that was one of the liberal state's most important functions. If property guaranteed reason, the state should guarantee property.

Property was an important measure of reason, but it was a measure of just about everything else as well. Social questions often began as problems of property. Slavery was a problem of property. Religious disputes were often disputes about the disposition of state funds, whether in the form of clergy reserve lands to support churches, separate taxes for separate schools, or the disposition of the vast estates confiscated from the Jesuits a century earlier. Public schooling was really just advanced property protection, argued the school promoters – only uneducated people ran to thievery or revolution. Macdonald's version of liberal rights turned on property relations: "We must protect the rights of minorities, and the rich are always fewer in number than the poor."[18] What turned out to be the definitive delineation of provincial versus federal rights (the rivers and streams dispute that wended through the courts in the 1880s), was fought over the question of whether individual or community property rights prevailed over running waters. The federal spokesman, D'Alton McCarthy, went so far as to suggest that not "inappropriate exercise of legislative power," but "vested rights" of property alone justified federal veto over local politics.[19] McCarthy's was a weak argument for federal control of a provincial right, and the Judicial Committee of the Privy Council rejected it.

The family, the state's most important ally in civil governance, was endlessly mired in legal disputes over property that pitted its claims against those of creditors and debtors. Abandonment, debt, and drunkenness all caused severe distress in nineteenth-century families, strained local welfare, and prompted legislation that strengthened the property rights of wives and children at the expense of paternal authority. Interracial sexual relationships that produced offspring posed problems of inheritance for Canadian lawmakers, especially when the husband abandoned his Indigenous companion for a European wife, as many fur traders did. Drunkenness provoked temperance legislation in many Protestant jurisdictions, but that could rebound, as in New Brunswick in 1865 when the prohibitionist Leonard Tilley went down to defeat by the anti-Confederate and "wet" vote. Prohibition was one of the new coercions of the liberal state, and it provoked new, ideological attacks on statism. Quebec instead passed legislation permitting families to declare drunkards legally incompetent, while British Columbia passed a Habitual Drunkards Act that had much the same effect. But married women with feckless husbands remained vulnerable; they needed an independent income or property that their husbands could not seize. Widows were better protected with dower rights that entitled them to a life interest in lands owned by their husband (one-third of shared property in English common law, one-half in Quebec's code), but dower, too, was under attack in mid-Victorian Canada as an invisible encumbrance on land that could tie up property transfers and sales in courts. The reform of dower and protection from feckless husbands was accomplished from mid-century by giving women greater power to control their own property, i.e., that which they had brought into marriage and that which they earned independently after a separation. After married women's property laws passed, daughters began to inherit more often. Still, judges and legislators refused to recognize that wives had any interest in family property, such as a farm, until the 1970s.

Women's property issues reflected the contradictions between a traditional paternal property regime and the liberal fantasy of transparent contracts by fully empowered agents. Only quasi-propertied, women were also only quasi-rational, according to such influential theorists of patriarchy as Jean-Jacques Rousseau. They could, therefore, be classified as friends or as enemies of rational, propertied rule, depending on a host of complicated factors. Early nineteenth-century reformers disenfranchised them; late nineteenth-century reformers worked to enfranchise them, seeing propertied women as allies against an unreconstructed, unruly public. The mid-century transition to responsible government was seen to reflect masculine political virtues, and it prompted some provinces to contemplate and even experiment with male suffrage. But validation of male agency flagrantly conflicted with rule by property and prompted soul-searching about the hidden threat of violence under illiberal rule. If husbands could legally beat their wives, what was to prevent them from forcing their wives to alienate their property? After 1841, Quebec women who allowed their husbands to sell their property had to swear before a judge that their consent was voluntary. Efforts of this sort to prop up women's contractual property rights and insulate them from violence exemplified the liberal political project, but they affronted popular domestic norms, especially a more casually violent working-class masculinity. More than a few episodes of domestic assault and murder in late-Victorian Canada began, accused husbands testified, by wives claiming that they owned some part of the household property – wives who, for instance, planned to run off with the hired man. Jurors were slower than were judges to lose sympathy for male heads of household who had been "driven" to violence in such cases, but the long-term trend was to enhance the state's claim to a monopoly on violence and to make households more subject to public reconstruction. From the 1850s, custody of children, traditionally awarded to men, began to be granted to women in cases of desertion. Lighter penalties for rape led to more frequent convictions. The trend remained limited in the nineteenth century – divorce was still very difficult to obtain, rape was still seen primarily as an injury to fathers rather than to women – but this was the beginning of change. Some legislators, not yet a majority, were coming to see that the definition of women as illiberal subjects, outside the realm of the fully human, was anomalous, and that liberal property relations required greater legal equality. A new alliance between the state and a group of citizens emerged.

Property provided a useful logic for and mechanism of liberal rule, but it never fully encompassed that rule. There were always other forces at work, including a logic of power itself. The philosopher and historian Michel Foucault helps to explain this. Fascinated by the government of the physical body, he insisted that the analysis of political relations must go beyond discourse to examine how those relations were embodied – inscribed upon the deviant body of the lunatic or the criminal – in ways that rebounded upon the discourse. For example, the techniques used to contain madness "generated a certain economic profit, a certain political utility, and they were therefore colonized and supported by global mechanisms and, finally, by the entire system of the State ... They consolidated the system and helped it to function as a whole."[20] Institutions such as asylums, prisons, and schools subjected bodies to perpetual surveillance that would be internalized by individuals, creating a new self-awareness and new moderation in their behaviour. Canadian historians mostly agree that madhouses, prisons, and schools were part of the complex web of institutions that exemplified and upheld modern systems of state power, for example in the work disciplines imposed at Kingston Penitentiary or the Provincial Lunatic Asylum on Queen Street West in Toronto.

Foucault pushed the logic still further in subsequent work on the history of sexuality. Sexuality defied liberal projects of rule; it was a space, par excellence, of individual choice, but following a logic that was irreducible to reason or property. Disciplined control of sexuality promised to bring order to much of what was most unruly about civil society as a whole, so sexuality was regulated in obviously repressive ways. But, Foucault argued, despite itself, the regulatory apparatus had a liberating effect. Discourse about sexuality exploded – in asylums, prisons, schools, universities, novels, manuals, treatises, and just about every other imaginable institution or genre – and the long-term effect was to redefine people as profoundly sexual beings, their sexual desires and choices providing a better model for human behaviour than the limited, austere models of classical liberalism. Foucault brilliantly identified the limits of certain kinds of statist projects, and his model of power as productive rather than simply repressive, widely diffused rather than state centred, illuminates much. We better understand the ways in which all laws connect in a complex matrix of physical and intellectual constraint and resistance. But even here liberalism fell back on its usual proxy: sexuality, where it was not openly proscribed as deviant, was largely governed as a relationship of property. Not contraception as a practice but the sale or advertisement of contraceptive devices was prohibited by federal law in 1892. Traditionally, prostitution fell under vagrancy laws, but after Confederation, new legislation targeted the commercial transactions connected to prostitution, including habitual purchase and "living on the avails," i.e., pimping, procuring, and profiteering. Precisely because the old laws could not be enforced and officials refused to try, reformers changed tactics and redefined prostitution as a species of slavery, calling forth the new laws. The spectre of uncontrolled sexuality, with its threat to the family or to labour discipline, might underlie liberal legislation, but property was often the preferred regulatory focus.

Property was the iron of which the modern cage was forged. The influential twentieth-century Canadian political philosopher, C.B. Macpherson, argued that liberalism became hegemonic by recasting social relationships as relationships of property. Rights were valued and protected because they were property. The liberal order transplanted the patrician order by reconstructing political privileges as legal privileges, largely through the use of incorporation, which became the usual mechanism for bestowing powers and rights, whether as joint stock companies or civic corporations. No surprise, then, that many of Canada's most prominent and successful Victorian-era statesmen were lawyers – virtuosos at reasoning with property – including Robert Baldwin and Louis-Hippolyte Lafontaine, Conservative premiers John A. Macdonald and George-Étienne Cartier, Liberal challengers Edward Blake and Wilfrid Laurier, as well as such provincial champions as Ontario's Oliver Mowat, Quebec's Honoré Mercier, and British Columbia's Richard McBride. They promised constituents both order and opportunity: not just the "possessive individualism" that C.B. Macpherson identified as the motor of modernity, but, rather, a grasping, *acquisitive* individualism, always seeking new profits just beyond the frontiers of settlement to the west or the north. Lawyers, politicians, and businessmen formed unusually close relationships in nineteenth-century Canada for lack of the professional distinctions seen in Britain between barristers (who oriented their careers entirely around the courts) and solicitors (who negotiated with other professions and interests). Benefitting from a unified profession, lawyers in British North America and, later, Canada, could dabble in business and politics simultaneously without any loss of professional dignity. Consequently, lawyers in British North America did not merely provide technical advice to their business partners; instead, they behaved more like entrepreneurial partners, and the legal relationships they wove blurred distinctions between business, the law, and the state.

People aspired to property for their own comfort and for the political and civil rights that property provided. They experienced as beneficial a state that protected their property as well as their persons. In theory, they could have the best of all possible worlds: maximum individual autonomy through freedom of contract, upheld by a powerful state that respected their private agency. But people had vastly different expectations of that protection and their infinitely complex arguments about their properties embroiled the state in extremely fine distinctions and negotiations. Where women's interests coincided with the establishment of a more liberal property regime, women experienced the transition to a modern capitalist economy as beneficial. The opinions of the propertied – as individuals and as families – were translated by elections into public policy and their interests were carefully negotiated. But where people held property in different forms, they were much more likely to be unrepresented, ignored, and dismissed. Thus, middle-class women had a better transition than Indigenous women or working-class women. As the liberal state became more securely established, it became increasingly intolerant of alternative forms of property.

The State as an Agent of Liberalization

Courts, legislatures, and bureaucrats struggled to make property transparently governable. They were constantly called upon to translate ethnicity or sexuality into property and vice versa, provoking quasi-theological projects of delineation and definition. Women's property rights reflect one example of the transition to liberal market conditions; another was the reform of feudal institutions already implanted in Canada: Quebec's legal code and the English commons transplanted to the Maritime provinces in the eighteenth century. More difficult and less successful were attempts to force race and class into a liberal, property-oriented mould.

Across North America, economic relations were generally governed by negotiated contracts or by English common law, which deferred to contracts (where a valid contract existed, the common law did not pertain). By contrast, Lower Canadian legal traditions limited the scope for contracts and individual free choices. For example, obligatory title deeds required farmers to grind their grains at the seigneurial mill. It wasn't that the grain didn't come to market, but that it did not come under fully competitive conditions. British settlers objected, from their arrival on, that maintaining French customary laws regarding property made it hard for British settlers to do business. But the British government refused so drastic a measure as abolishing existing property relations. Britons could move to areas such as the Eastern Townships, where freehold tenure prevailed, or they could adapt to existing laws. But gradually, property owners, politicians, and *censitaires* liberalized property relations. They converted seigneurial obligations into limited contracts, for example, or they circumvented the Custom of Paris's inheritance provisions by making lifetime gifts to keep farms intact. Negotiations and complaints gathered momentum until they amounted to significant pressure in favour of a more legalistic, contractual civil code and the general conversion of feudal into freehold tenure. Voluntary commutation of seigneurial tenure was passed in 1854, and a new civil code came into effect in 1866. But it is to be remarked that the reforms were gradual and were negotiated carefully with existing property owners.

In Nova Scotia, a different preliberal economic "problem" was the persistence of the commons. British settlers in late-eighteenth-century Nova Scotia carried with them the idea of a common ground that whole communities could draw upon for subsistence and that could not be privately owned or legally monopolized. It was the work of a liberalizing, modernizing state to overturn that commons and impose freehold ownership and specific contracts for specific resources. Like seigneurs and *censitaires*, private agents and tenants quietly negotiated these relations, but sometimes legal challenges brought them before the courts. In Minudie, Nova Scotia, all sorts of people cut grindstones on tidewater lands held by Joseph Des Barres from the late eighteenth century. After Des Barres died in 1824, the land was sold and a monopoly on the stones awarded to one man. Locals were initially successful in persuading local magistrates to uphold their right to harvest grindstones, but eventually the monopoly holder made a successful appeal to imperial authorities. In this case, local authorities, who would have to provide for poor families without resources, upheld the local traditions, but distant, high-ranking officials found it more logical and more lucrative to privilege individual, contractual ownership.

Other kinds of commons were also under attack, above all Indigenous traditions of the shared use of land. The attacks took many forms, because different nations had different ways of owning and using their lands, but across the country the result was to undermine their traditions – practically, legally, and politically. Although the Royal Proclamation existed to protect Indigenous peoples from encroachment on their lands, that protection was illusory. Across British North America, officials treated squatters on reserve lands with the same "forbearance" shown towards squatters on Crown lands. Military officers such as H.C. Darling, reporting in 1828 to Governor General Dalhousie (a veteran of Wellington's Peninsular War), advocated a beefed-up Indian Department, including provision for schooling, on the grounds that the Crown must interpose itself between still-useful Indigenous allies and land-hungry colonials. But as the Colonial Office gradually disengaged from Canada, it abandoned Indigenous nations to colonial legislatures, first creating a local bureaucracy and devolving treaty powers, then transferring all responsibility in 1860. Colonial governments openly sided with the squatters or used them as leverage. In 1841, when the Six Nations on the Grand River protested encroachment by thousands of squatters, officials replied, "Very great difficulty will be found in any medium course between the expulsion of all the intruders or non-interference ... The Lieutenant-governor therefore, considers that it would be very much for the benefit of the interest of the Indians if they surrendered into the hands of the Government the whole tract, with the exception of such part of it which they may choose to occupy as a concentrated body."[21] Colonial protection for Indigenous people was very like patriarchal protection for women: there existed avenues of redress for scandalous abuses – flagrant instances of murder and rape – but on the whole, the system worked by muffling their voices and their political and legal agency.

Canadian lawmakers rejected the legal foundation for collective ownership. John Beverley Robinson, Attorney General for Upper Canada, argued in 1824 that "Indians" had no more collective identity or treaty-making powers than, say, Huguenots or "the Jews in Duke Street," and his views were confirmed in a series of late-nineteenth-century judicial decisions in provincial and federal courts as well as at the Judicial Committee of the Privy Council, in what amounted to a revision of long-standing relationships. Early observers had recognized that Indigenous peoples formed nations with discrete political territories and unwritten but functional mechanisms for recognizing lands as reserved for particular families; statelessness was no bar to governance and possession. But states were supremely useful for confirming title and, in nineteenth-century British North America, the apparatus of the colonial state was put to work to delegitimize competing forms of property. Native peoples remained stateless; barred from representation within the colonial state (on the grounds of either race or property), they still relied heavily on chiefly persuasion to formulate political consensus, but, as the Mississauga chief and Methodist minister Peter Jones told a government inquiry at mid-century, "The power of the chiefs is very different from what it was in former times, when their advice was listened to, and their commands implicitly obeyed." Officialdom and alcohol abuse had undone them.[22] Jones recommended that the colonial authorities recognize chiefs as government agents. Instead, an increasingly white bureaucracy strove to undermine Indigenous traditions of leadership and replace them with liberal forms of government, legislating its right to do so in 1880 and subsequently imposing triennial elections. The gap between governance and state institutions became a growing liability to Indigenous people, who were unable to overcome internal divisions that Indian agents and fraud artists exacerbated.

But an insidious double standard was at work. The great problem besetting Indian officials at mid-century was how to stop settler encroachment – above all, squatting and logging – on Indian lands, a practice that amounted to asset stripping. That is to say, the state's inability to control its population justified the imposition of treaties that restricted Indigenous access to traditional resources of land, trees, fish, and game. But those treaties presupposed that chiefs and elders could impose on their peoples a degree of economic and political discipline that colonial legislators could not impose on theirs. When Canadian governments imposed illiberal and coercive rule over Indigenous peoples on the grounds that they could not govern themselves, they did so according to a logic that presumed effective Indigenous governance and ineffectual colonial governance. That the Canadian frontier was less violent than the American frontier was attributable, in no small part, to articulate, influential elders across the country who persuaded their people to adapt to the new regimes.

For all that, the Indian Department was a shambles at mid-century – inefficient, corrupt, and unaccountable – yet it went from strength to strength, persuading legislators to vest it with growing powers over Indigenous interests and rights. It did so by developing a body of evidence to show that Indigenous identity and property were radically incommensurable with liberal claims and projects. Interlocking, illiberal traditions of tenure were normal in ancien-régime Canada; if property rights were like a bundle of sticks, few people held the full bundle. In New France, settlers and Native peoples hunted over the same land without serious quarrels. Indigenous communities often welcomed settlers, who offered new economic resources. But in the nineteenth century, as the flood of immigrants with livestock depleted fish and game and drove up the value of land, settler society sought to grasp the whole bundle of sticks. And whereas Darling had toured reserves for his report of 1828, the influential Bagot Commission of the mid-1840s instead heard dozens of expert witnesses – Peter Jones was a lonely Indigenous voice – and concluded that the Canadian government owned Indigenous land, could unilaterally resettle Indians, and should "civilize" them by imposing freehold private tenure wherever possible.

Reconstruction of Indigenous land use met with terrific resistance across the country, and sometimes it failed. In Kahnawà:ke, a Mohawk reserve near Montreal, anyone could fell any trees for domestic firewood, excepting only sugar bushes, which were generally understood to belong to certain families. But such understandings were vulnerable to legal challenges, as individual speculators (such as settlers who married local women), claimed a "right" to market their own trees and stop others from felling them. As it became clear to everyone that the courts and the Indian agents would not protect traditional arrangements, the commons in Kahnawà:ke began to give way to an open-access competition for resources, and even sugar bushes were cut down and sold commercially as firewood. The Department of Indian Affairs then used the resulting crisis – a crisis largely of its own making – to try to obliterate existing property relations. The Kahnawakehró:non of Kahnawà:ke successfully fought off that reform, primarily because the project would have required more compensation for landowners than the Department was willing to expend.

Kahnawà:ke had a viable economy and long-established relations of property; even the Department of Indian Affairs could not pretend otherwise. In Western Canada, it pretended otherwise. There, the stakes were considerably higher, with more land and more people on that land, sustaining dense (illegible to officials) social relations that seemed to defy state modernizing projects. Here as everywhere, property and agency mutually expressed one another and had to be repressed together, in ways exemplified by the war on the potlatch. Traditional inhabitants of the Northwest Coast practised potlatch to display wealth and disseminate goods through society, as a means of establishing status and leadership. To bureaucrats this seemed perverse; authority figures should gather, not disperse, wealth and should encourage individual accumulation. Canadian lawmakers were shocked enough at this ritual of giving wealth away that they outlawed it, imprisoned its practitioners, and confiscated their goods. They were determined to yoke community organization to explicitly capitalist projects. But Indigenous people could not speak for themselves. They lacked the interface that property and opinion provided with the state, and so they could not translate their point of view into political influence. No legislators represented their point of view, so they were stripped of property rights in ways that voters were not.

Similar contestations between traditional and imposed forms of authority characterized relations in eastern Canada. Indian agents struggled to replace traditional chieftainships with council elections among the Mi'kmaq peoples, with a variety of illiberal strategems. They insisted on chairing nomination meetings, for example, and they debarred or even deposed supposed "troublemakers." But an understaffed, ill-informed bureaucracy was unable to supplant the old ways with the new ones; the informality of traditional political choices made them particularly irrepressible. If a chief was essentially someone who gave wise council, how to suppress such a thing? Some agents confirmed and sustained them. Many Indigenous communities across Canada discovered that hybrid systems, combining elements of election and tradition, could prove a useful barrier to protect traditional ways of life.

The Canadian construction of racial difference followed imperial templates, both formal and informal. State racialization projects were deeply invested in appropriating Indigenous land, but they were never simply about that land. They always reflected the larger social project of defining and constructing the modern liberal subject. The Indian residential schools built across Canada during the late nineteenth and early twentieth centuries, were operated in partnership by churches and the state according to the same logic as prisons or asylums. By creating optimal conditions of surveillance over pupils, they facilitated control and reform over all aspects of the children's life and culture, far from the supposedly baneful influences of their parents. No such total control could be exercised over Indigenous adults, but an approximation was created by the establishment of Indian reserves, separated from the "corrupting" influence of cities and towns, and managed by Indian agents who enjoyed extraordinary inquisitive and dictatorial powers. For lack of political voice, Native peoples were continually subjected to exploitation, robbery, and petty tyrannies at the hands of the men empowered to govern them.

Indigenous people were, like the insane or criminals, outside of liberal society, and they experienced the imposition of liberal rule as violent conquest. Where they were seen to pose a threat to public order, the state devoted serious resources to pacification and rehabilitation. For example, to teach farming on the new prairie reserves, it sent equipment and instructors. But supplies always ran short, and they were ringed with all sorts of restrictions and impediments to genuine commercial production. Indigenous people needed special permission to leave the reserve or to spend band money, whether on buildings, implements, or coffins. Bureaucracy stifled human agency, and if failure ensued, then failure justified still more bureaucratic restrictions on those categorized as "Indians." The more elaborate the state bureaucracy grew, the more this terrible logic of state racialization and impoverishment played itself out in the century after Confederation.

John Lutz's account of Indigenous-white relations in British Columbia blames the state more than the market for the terrible poverty that took hold of Indigenous peoples over the nineteenth and twentieth centuries. Over time, they were gradually stripped of resources and assets by the state rather than the market. The state forced bands onto tiny reserves inadequate for sustenance. The state managed the fisheries and restricted Indigenous access through the granting of licences. The state managed logging and hunting in the interests of white rather than Indigenous hunters and loggers. "Indians" in early British Columbia could not register, pre-empt, or lease land, or register mineral or water claims, nor could they hire lawyers to defend such claims. Lutz's is a searing indictment of a whole series of state interventions, at all levels of government, that limited the economic, political, and civil rights of Indigenous peoples. "With every act that affected Indians and non-Indians differently, governments redefined race to the disadvantage of Aboriginal People." And across Canada, as John Tobias remarks, "the legislation to remove all legal distinctions between Indians and Euro-Canadians actually established them."[23] Nineteenth-century legislators lacked the capacity to administer assimilation on the ground but – increasingly into the twentieth century – sterner enforcement of fish and game laws, along with more effective provision of schools and welfare, would have a more pronounced effect on traditions.

State racialization came into full and free flow in nineteenth-century Canada whenever property relations were deemed illiberal. Chinese people, who began to immigrate about the middle of the century, were understood as a threat to liberal property relations, and so they were stripped of political rights. The British Columbia legislature deprived Chinese and "Indians" of the vote before and after Confederation, and the federal government followed suit. Chinese immigrants were likely to be men, so they did not form family households but often bunked together in warehouses put up by companies that imported them for labour. They were believed to hoard their wealth for an eventual return to China, so that every penny paid them left local circulation. Their property relations were too dense and complicated for officials like tax collector Noah Shakespeare in Victoria, who led the Anti-Chinese Association there. Settler society feared the competition of such men who could work for lower wages because they lived more cheaply and were taxed less effectively. Thus, concerns about protecting liberal property relations and equalizing the burdens of citizenship fuelled state racialization. Confronted with taxpayer revolt against sloppy and clientelist tax collection, officials scapegoated the Chinese as tax evaders. Stripped of their political agency, Chinese immigrants could be better subjected to a series of legislative restrictions, most notoriously a head tax to make Chinese immigration prohibitively expensive, a ban on their employment in the public service, and a curtailment of "white" employees in establishments run by people of Chinese descent. Much of the anti-Chinese legislation aimed at preventing vices attributed to Chinese Canadians, such as tax evasion and opium addiction, from taking hold in the population as a whole.

By contrast, Canadians of African descent, who came to British North America in the tens of thousands around mid-century, were understood to emulate rather than threaten liberal property regimes. Each colony had its own history: slavery was moribund in the Canadas, Nova Scotia, and Prince Edward Island before imperial legislation to abolish it in 1834. There was a great deal of popular racializing and bigotry, often formalized as local legal restrictions on access to such services as schools, shops, and theatres, or in different rates of conviction and incarceration. Blacks served on juries in some colonies but not all. But Canadians of African descent kept their vote and their political standing, and the state did not aggressively racialize them as a mechanism for managing the larger population.

Things got worse before they got better. By the end of the century, theories of race were becoming more concerned with biology than with property. The liberal project of rule was, increasingly, eroded by a racialized project of rule, a return to the old insistences that some peoples were naturally unable to govern themselves and were resistant even to the benefits of education. The new biological essentialism was widely applied to immigrants of all shapes and colours, according to a sliding scale of supposed ability to adapt to healthy northern climates. It was also applied to the emerging Canadian cities, where slums counteracted the healthy climes and threw up a proletariat that seemed to have, according to the *Journal of Commerce,* "the brutality of the untamed savage" about it.[24] Ordinary working men and women resisted liberalism and required assimilation no less than did Indians on reserves.

Organized labour posed perhaps the biggest threat to liberal relations at the end of the nineteenth century. The great strength of a liberal conservatism founded on relations of property was that it directed peoples' energies towards the private rather than the public sphere. Passion was thereby transformed into interest, and people advanced themselves primarily by acquiring land – unless the political obstacles to successful development of land propelled them into the public sphere, as occurred in Upper Canada, Prince Edward Island, and Western Canada in the early, middle, and later decades of the century. Labour, it was increasingly recognized, was also a kind of property, one that working men sold on the marketplace, but it was one that encouraged collective rather than individualized mobilization. Liberals saw in that collective mobilization of labour a threat to public order. When capitalists banded together, they looked like a fashionable club; when labourers banded together, they looked like a criminal combination in restraint of trade, according to their critics. Over the century, a growing proportion of public resources was devoted to suppressing public disorder and violence through an expanding police apparatus, and that project always overlapped with the suppression of strikes and demonstrations by working men. The state often doubled as employer as well as regulator of labour – as when it built canals at mid-century – and laws such as the 1845 Act for the Preservation of the Peace near Public Works served to both entrench a police presence and trample agitation for better-than-starvation pay. But working people made up too much of the wider public to be ignored, and many had the right to vote, especially those skilled labourers who often brought ideological focus to workplace confrontations. They were gradually building common ground with other propertied groups that shared their distrust of big business, including farmers. The profound ambivalence of Canadian statesmen towards the claims of organized labour can be seen in the 1872 legislation that made collective bargaining legal and most collective action illegal. Industrial organs such as the *Canadian Manufacturer* insisted that any picketing amounted to a threat of violence, while price-setting combines had no such flavour of violence about them. Statesmen generally accepted the argument. They introduced toothless legislation against "unduly" uncompetitive business collaboration. In practice, despite nods to the theoretical legitimacy of workers' claims, time and again local employers and officials confronted with a strike would plead for armed troops to restore order. In February 1886, when the Massey implements company in Toronto was hit by a strike by about 400 workers, city authorities sent police to confront the strikers, only to call them back after aggrieved strikers convinced a sympathetic mayor, William Howland, that they had no intention of damaging property and resented seeing their own tax dollars so used. But many strikes were too bitter to be so easily defused and led to armed repression, a trend that increased from the turn of the century when labour militancy grew more powerful and effective. Strikes escalated into "miniature civil wars" that were, inevitably, won by the combined forces of capital and the state, whether army deployment actually occurred or was merely threatened.[25]

At the turn of the century, the great "social question" in Canada was the apparent polarization of society into workers and capitalists. Each side complained that the state sided with the other. Middle-class reformers looked to the state to mediate, as a neutral umpire, and perhaps to overcome extremes of class wealth and class poverty that became more entrenched year by year and that equally offended middle-class mores. But there seemed few grounds for optimism. If the state was not merely a crude instrument for bourgeois class interest (as Marxists argued it was), neither did it stray very far from something like class interest. J.W. Bengough, a late-Victorian intellectual, captured public sentiment with a series of cartoons that showed statesmen in cahoots with industrialists, each piling their own financial burdens atop the struggling labourer, or myopically trying to investigate "monopoly" in the nooks and crannies around the gigantic face of a businessman. The cultural capital of businessmen was high and, indeed, everywhere could be heard arguments for bringing "business methods" to public administration.

William Lyon Mackenzie King had a solution. As deputy minister of labour from 1898, King, who did graduate research in industrial relations, championed forced arbitration of industrial disputes to show how the state could lead industry and labour towards harmonious progress. His arguments had a venerable pedigree in the notion that the state epitomized intelligent purpose, a theory put forward by the German philosopher G.W.F. Hegel in the early nineteenth century. Hegel's theories of political rationality had been upended but hardly banished by Karl Marx (when he made the state a mere cover for economic interest), and they continued to enjoy considerable purchase in academic departments of politics and philosophy. By the end of the century, the emergence at Canadian universities of social science departments, nurturing expert advisers and qualified civil servants, seemed to promise a solution to the social problems and polarities confronted by the state. At least that was the hope. King eventually moved into electoral politics and became minister of labour under Laurier, whereupon he pushed through the new Combines Investigations Act in 1907, which insinuated the state as a mediator between capital and labour. But his regulatory regime proved unequal to easing the rising social and economic tensions of the early twentieth century. The polarized camps only gradually accepted bureaucratic mediation; both expected better outcomes from conflict.

Academic credentials notwithstanding, Mackenzie King remained an old-fashioned liberal who worried about the decline of liberalism in Canada in the face of female suffrage, socialism, nationalism, and monopoly capitalism. The ideological vacuity that André Siegfried noticed in Canadian party politics was inadequate to such challenges. Groups that reasoned from property and self-interest to enter the liberal public sphere used their newfound legitimacy to denounce those agencies. Whereas liberals believed there could be no higher good than a balance of power between competing interests, the new groups rejected that agonistic view of politics in favour of a robust public good that must trump mere interest. Women sought the vote both as a right and as a means to make politics moral; they rejected liberal relativism. Marxists wanted a dictatorship of the proletariat. Such projects often shared an appeal to facts to overcome the politics of interest and opinion. Even as it mediated between competing interests, knowledge advanced itself as a privileged interest, one with a particular affinity for the good of the whole – a claim that businessmen had previously tended to monopolize.

Liberal politics were limited by choice, albeit a choice rooted in natural necessity. No one could dictate anyone else's best interests; that's why no individual or group could govern authoritatively for anyone else without some form of check in place. Academics began to reject such limitations; they advanced themselves as a class by insisting that if they were properly empowered by the state, a robust public good could be both known and implemented. Income taxes, for example, feared by Victorian liberals such as Goldwin Smith as "inquisitorial," became practical new instruments of fairness. The change reflected a process of social and political professionalization. Many early-nineteenth-century politicians had been trained as liberal professionals, especially as lawyers, but they were often, like John A. Macdonald, apprenticed rather than university trained, at a time when there were as many legal cultures as political, ethnic, and social divisions in a given community. By century's end, academic education had become the norm, and powerful professional organizations policed standards of entry and comportment. The result worked to diminish yawning gaps between elite physicians and humble general practitioners, for example, or those trained abroad versus at home, and to create more homogenous and consolidated professional cultures anchored upon rigorous knowledge that, professional mouthpieces argued, wanted only proper respect and application to transform society for the better.

The new ideas provoked a reconceptualization of civil society. For liberals, the boundary between the state and civil society was akin to a border between civilized nations, something to be negotiated diplomatically. Liberal statesmen believed that a moderate state required them, as far as possible, to respect the autonomy of civil society. Social scientists were far less committed to an autonomous civil society. They advocated the use of state powers to scrutinize and reconstitute private life so as to reconcile private and public purposes. From that perspective, the boundary between state and society was not a border but a frontier; beyond it lay unreconstructed, sullen, and radical elements, which continually threatened to spill out into public life and overturn political and social relationships that the state sought to congeal. Mature liberal society, it turned out, was bedevilled with frontiers at its very core. Postliberal academics began to insist that the state must extend its authority into these reaches.

The state was infiltrating new places. Even "nature," the antithesis of the Hobbesian state, could no longer be understood except in statist terms. It became "natural resources," to be managed for the benefit of national prosperity. The more the reluctant northern land obstructed those aims, the more it had to be reconstructed, whether by canals and railways or by scientific conservation. Science, to liberal Canadian politicians, offered mechanisms for developing resources, and from 1841 they had begun to sponsor a Geological Survey of Canada that would identify coal fields badly needed for industrialization. Scientific officers predicted that the Prairies could be made into fertile agricultural land, and they developed new agricultural techniques, such as breeding hardier strains of wheat suited for northern climates, on the Dominion Experimental Farms created from 1886. Dominion fish hatcheries began about the same time, as did national parks and notions of forest conservation – reversing early environmental theories that advocated clear-cutting in order to improve the climate (by letting the sun's rays reach the earth). Natural and human agency interacted dynamically; the demanding northern climate would create a hardy northern nation more able to impose its will on its environment.

Early environmental thinking reflected liberal politics; a particular environmental feature was only as valuable as the industry or the interest that advocated its claims. Companies justified their right to pollute by arguing that a few dead fish should not stand in the way of progress. The need of municipalities for clear drinking water ceded to the need of other municipalities to dump untreated sewage into waterways, where treatment was costly. The liberal state could no more take the view of a beleaguered environment than it could take the view of a beleaguered public good: either position would have amounted to paternalism, a return to the top-down, centralized, and knowledgeable state that Adam Smith had so effectively decapitated. But as the trees and fish ran out, as rivers choked into stagnant pools, as workers perished in industrial accidents, and children died from water-borne filth diseases, the arguments – from scientists as well as reformers – in favour of a public good not reducible to prosperity, one that could be sustained only by the state, began to trump the blusterings of industrialists and the timidity of liberals.

4

The People's State in the Twentieth Century

Whereas state growth in the nineteenth century tended to be a covert, apologetic process, the growth of the people's state in the twentieth century was flamboyantly celebrated as a triumph of collective reasoning and intervention. A Georgian ode that captured this once and future spirit appeared in a radical pamphlet written in Toronto in 1887, and in a conservative plea for reform of New Westminster's finances in 1891:

> What constitutes a State?—
>
> Men, high-minded Men,
>
> With Powers as far above dull brutes endued,
>
> In forest, brake or den
>
> As beasts excel cold rocks and brambles rude;
>
> Men, who their Duties know,
>
> But know their Rights, and knowing, dare maintain,
>
> Prevent the long-aimed blow,
>
> And crush Corruption, while they rend the chain:
>
> These constitute a State.[1]

Such a state reflected lofty ambitions, rather than liberalism's more restrained checks and balances, and an increasing ability to put private life into the service of those ambitions. The state and business seemed in thrall to one another, mutually saturated – state and domestic life far less so. But war and depression would tip the balance, forcing state and household into intimate dialogue with one another. Public opinion would remain the primary interface between state and society, but in new ways. The liberal project to govern through property as a proxy for opinion, one that amplified agency and insulated people from direct state action, was abandoned; like religion, it was losing too much ground among the urban, unpropertied classes. In refusing to emulate their betters, those classes seemed to refuse reason itself; they would need to be governed more directly, by propaganda and by reform of domestic life, seen as the seedbed of reason. Opinion could no longer be shaped by a few daily hours in the schoolroom. That remained important of course, and public schooling continued to expand. But if the rest of the day was spent in squalor and a state of malnutrition, education could not build up a rational, self-interested working class. Paradoxically, direct reconstruction of everyday life became a precondition of a liberal state. Welfare legislation and darker, more coercive processes of intervention evolved together. The state never abandoned its commitment to extending market-oriented behaviour, but it learned to privilege personal rights over property rights, developing new kinds of identity politics and techniques of governance in the process.

Reforming the Liberal State at the Turn of the Century

By 1900, the state and the market served as organizing principles across Canada. Conceptually they pulled in opposite directions – towards and away from formal, centralized control – but in practice that polarity amounted to convergence. Everywhere that anyone grew, mined, made, bought, or sold anything, the state was always a partner to the transaction, providing the security of property that made ownership and exchange stable. It set the rules for commercial transactions, regulating, encouraging, or discouraging them with bounties, tariffs, taxes, royalties, consolidation, and monopolization, and by specifying limits to concentration, dictating when contracts reigned supreme and when they could be trumped by legislation, and specifying civil or criminal penalties for breach of the rules. Where the state was not regulating, it was actively trading, building, or subsidizing. The accepted patterns for intervention followed a conception of the public good that remained tethered to the marketplace. It wasn't that people couldn't conceive of a conflict between market and public interests but, rather, that authorities were expected to behave like economic agents when they pondered the common good, because the kinds of goods that coincided with market logic were the most likely to produce efficient results. Reformers made the most successful arguments for state intervention, even in moral matters, when they argued from property. Classic Victorian liberals considered the market at least as good as the state at maintaining justice and morality. The market provided the best forum for agency and free choice, and the state largely catered to that function – smoothing obstacles, upholding contracts, punishing criminality.

So long as crime exists, so long will pundits denounce the state's failure to repress it. A huge upswing in population and urbanization during the "Laurier boom" at the turn of the century made people acutely worried about rising crime levels. Violence, theft, and the like were zealously targeted by policemen on the beat, but white-collar crime and collusion between businessmen and officials, while they drew much editorial criticism, were harder to repress. Montreal was ground zero for corruption at the turn of the twentieth century (and the twenty-first), with commissions of investigation indicating widespread larceny. But corruption imbued every level of government, whether federally – where Sir Hector Langevin, longtime Tory minister of public works, retired in disgrace from public life in 1896 and spent his remaining years "behind his drawn curtains on Rue Saint-Louis,"[2] – or provincially – where railway and resource scandals seemed ten a penny. Yet reform movements seemed inevitably to decline into what economist and humorist Stephen Leacock mocked in his parody of Arcadia (read Montreal) as "the great fight for clean government": a veil for more plunder. The boundary between state and enterprise served primarily to let one blame the other for misdeeds. Intractable problems were nominally transferred back and forth with scant practical change.

The state was far less intimately engaged with private households. The great nineteenth-century project to found that interface on education had accomplished much and it continued apace, but it never succeeded in inculcating middle-class values through the population as a whole. Dropouts began to worry legislators as a problem that could not simply be left to parents or schools. In 1908, the federal Parliament passed a juvenile delinquency law aimed at rehabilitating children in institutions that were quasi-educational and quasi-penal. Children perplexed legislators because, if property constituted the cage of the modern state, children slipped easily between the bars, having no property to protect. And children, it became clear, were not an anomaly of the system but were the core governing problem. Children without property became adults without property. The boys stole, the girls became sexualized, and both drank too much; such was the discovery of juvenile courts. Boys seemed too impatient for property, while girls had the opposite problem, one shared with potlatching "Indians": they gave away their most prized possession too cheaply, impoverishing and demoralizing themselves in the process. Small wonder, given these converging prejudices, that Indigenous women made up a disproportionate number of juvenile cases. Drinking, too, reflected the distortion of market incentives and the need for new techniques of governance less reliant upon presumed rationality. But if education and market incentives failed as instruments of governance, what was left?

Liberalism now had ideological competitors. The state was at the heart of many radical theories that powerfully challenged the liberal order at the turn of the century. They usually posited a producerist outlook and shared class consciousness. The classic liberal state, taking its cue from Thomas Malthus's 1804 essay on population, perceived as its great enemy a pauperism that was collective primarily in statistical terms. But by the end of the century, Marxist theorists challenged liberal individualism when they argued that whole social classes were disadvantaged by contemporary state structures and the social and economic relations that they congealed. In an industrialized, urban society, the new threat to the state and the nation was that the new radical consciousness would lead these classes to rise up and overturn the state, whether by economic means, through unions, or by means of socialist political parties that focused more directly on the state. The basis of economic reasoning shifted from individual morality to sociological categories. Socialism could emerge as a serious presence in Canada only with the rise of cities and industrial labour forces, and by the turn of the century the necessary conditions were in place. Left-wing political movements were rich, diverse, and quarrelsome, but together they seriously challenged the underpinnings of the liberal state. Queen's University professor and government adviser O.D. Skelton published a PhD dissertation in 1911 warning that state reforms were needed to mitigate capitalism and ward off socialism in Canada. By 1918, Skelton was advocating a "wiser social order" with a whole series of state interventions, including labour exchanges, technical education, and the expansion of state-regulated insurance for sickness and old age as well as unemployment. Capitalism had a new enemy and needed new techniques of government to do battle against it.

Liberalism's enemies were physical as well as ideological. Classic liberals believed that people learned how to become rational and self-interested citizens and to participate in a civil, fruitful rational public sphere. By the early twentieth century, confronted with recalcitrant, unreconstructed populations, reformers wondered whether there might be deeper obstacles to rationality. They began to see identity as more hardwired than they had understood, perhaps even as something biologically determined. In 1912, McGill University pathologist J.G. Adami debunked the claim that acquired characteristics were not transmitted to the next generation, providing evidence of fetal exposure to alcohol, syphilis, tuberculosis, and lead poisoning to suggest that children could be born incapacitated by their environment. This was fearful news in an age of scant environmental protection. Environment here meant some sort of relationship between locality and household, the emphasis depending on one's political priorities. Some reformers focused on alleviating poverty, others on improving public hygiene, still others on attacking immorality. Either way, a new politics of identity replaced the old property politics and fuelled demand for well-baby and other public health clinics. Prohibition of alcohol was briefly passed, though it quickly relapsed into state supervision of liquor sales in most jurisdictions.

Identity and environment were conjoined. In the nineteenth century, when people spoke urgently of "the environment" they meant the cold, northern climate and landscape; by the early twentieth century, they meant the slums that characterized old and new, Eastern and Western cities alike. The state had many problems in early-twentieth-century Canada, but perhaps none so pressing as that of the modern city. The Victorians had worried about how to govern opinion in the city, showing sporadic concern for sporadic epidemics. By the turn of the century, as dirt, disease, and disorder seemed to threaten whole communities, epidemic disease became hardwired in projects of government. A key turning point was the terrible smallpox epidemic in Montreal in 1885 that killed thousands of people, provoked open fighting in the streets, and revealed – to fascinated worldwide audiences – the state's inability to govern population in the Dominion's greatest city. The lofty state as an expression of humanity's higher purpose was brought down to earth by sewage – an intrinsic problem of sociability itself that plagued even the most upright, propertied neighbourhoods. Of such problems was the modern, postliberal state constructed.

It was constructed at the municipal level first. New theories and experiences of collective social behaviour transformed state institutions across the country, but the higher the political authority, the more attenuated were those effects. The municipal state was the most directly implicated by the new environmental problems and the new late-Victorian technological fixes, and it was also the most easily reconstructed. Municipal governments lacked the obvious and effective trappings of statehood. Too much corruption, debt, disease, dearth, and death shadowed the scattershot efforts of dilettante aldermen and councillors, who were elected for much shorter terms (usually a year) than provincial and federal politicians, on primitive platforms that bore no resemblance to elaborate provincial and federal party campaigns. The threat of epidemic disease had always provided grounds for drastic state intervention into market and domestic life through such measures as quarantine, forcible cleansings, or mass burials. Such interventions often sparked violent resistance that, to liberal reformers, seemed worse than the epidemics they were supposed to prevent. Over the course of the nineteenth century, a sporadic, unfocused effort to arrest epidemics was gradually transformed into a permanent bureaucracy that, thanks to improvements in hygienic science, could act much more precisely and effectively, all the while teaching people to be clean and orderly. The new municipal apparatus of public health – which came under provincial oversight in the late nineteenth century – took a very broad interest in public life, zealously used its power to appropriate and destroy dangerous property, and pushed up municipal spending. Sanitary inspectors issued lists of "necessary" improvements justified by statistical tables of preventable mortality and morbidity that could not be countered by traditional arguments for balancing budgets. The mayor of Montreal declared in 1874 that the $600,000 needed for better drainage was but a "feather" in the balance against the character and interests of the city and the health and lives of people in it. The cry that babies were dying for lack of sewers was unanswerable. So were the lawsuits that propertied businessmen began to initiate, blaming municipal negligence for foul-smelling refuse or flooded drains that injured their businesses and their health. Municipalities never granted the full wish list of public health reformers, but hygiene-inspired bureaucracy, intervention, and taxation all expanded inexorably.

Problems of sewage, water supply, and road building, all extraordinarily expensive, led the new municipal state but were seconded by a host of other new services, including lighting, gas, electricity, streetcars, and telephones. Such things could not be provided by market competition. They required long-term monopoly contracts but, time and again, the monopolies abused their contracts, taking too much money and providing too little service. Politicking made matters worse: aldermen won elections by promising services, and the result was sky-high debt. Developers lobbied and bribed their way to getting expensive city services in newly built streets, and then departed with huge profits, leaving municipalities and householders to shoulder unsustainable civic debts. The city, reformers decided, should abandon politicking and be remodelled as the New Westminster reformer urged, "as much as possible, in the nature of boards of directors of incorporated business companies." Small, appointed committees named by elected councils would insulate municipal government from the perils of democracy; thus could the public and the private be made to dovetail.

Larger municipalities had begun to take over the supply of water in the mid-nineteenth century, but often found it as difficult as earlier private investors had to ensure enough water to run factories, supply homes, and extinguish fires.

Gas companies were famously expropriated by civic authorities in Birmingham and Philadelphia, and the spectre of
municipalization loomed in Canada as well, following years
of bickering over prices and the quality. So municipalities
thought hard about protecting the "public good" when
they negotiated with streetcar companies beginning in the
1860s. In Toronto, exasperation with prices, service, and
anti-unionism in the street railway company led city council
to annex the company; in Montreal, the streetcar company
warded off municipalization by appointing a prominent
provincial politician as president. Similar problems and
negotiations followed the introduction of electrical power
to Canadian cities. Sometimes, provincial politicians protected the private utility companies, as in British Columbia
and Quebec; sometimes they nationalized them, as in Ontario. Municipal governments there led the call for public
ownership of electrical power; their leader was Adam Beck
who was simultaneously mayor and member of the provincial legislature for London. Beck pushed through the legislation in 1906 to create a provincial power commission,
and for twenty years he built Ontario Hydro into one of
the world's most successful power companies. Beck played
provincial and municipal authorities against one another
to make his commission largely independent of electoral
politics.

New business forms and new kinds of knowledge powered
the municipal reform movement. Experts were increasingly
called upon to narrate and integrate the data of progress
and poverty: to identify and classify municipal prosperity –
both public and private – and the calculation of life and
death that revealed the slums occupying municipal heart-
lands: traditional city cores or, in new Western towns, near
the railway stations. They filled pages of newspapers and
new municipal journals and appeared before municipal
conventions. S. Morley Wickett, PhD, university lecturer,
entrepreneur, and mouthpiece for the Canadian Manufacturers Association, typified the new sociology. He advised

mayors, banded together in a Union of Canadian Municipalities, that better accounting would help them defeat the
monopolies: "What do we care whether the Committee on
'Markets, Licenses and Health,' as such, spends $1,000,000
a year or not? But we do care a great deal how much it has
cost to preserve the health of the community; how much
to operate the markets, and how much to superintend licenses."[3] Cost-benefit analysis was news to the mayors, who
immediately championed the reform. The emergent political scientists peppered their technical tracts with a lofty
rhetoric all their own; in 1889 they launched *Toronto University Studies in Political Science* with a study of townships that
began with the remark, "The State, with all its constituent
parts and all its activity, can be studied in the same spirit as
the biologist brings to the observation of the animal organ-
ism, or the mathematician to the manipulation of numbers,
i.e., with absolute impartiality, with a complete suppression
of all other motive than the ascertainment of truth."

These were big changes that could go forward only with
the concurrence of lawyers. At the turn of the century, professors of law and politics vehemently disputed whether the
rule of law was best upheld in the legislatures, the courts,
or the administrative bureaucracies accreting around commission forms of government: municipal commissions,
railway commissions, and so forth. Corruption discredited
machine-style party governments, but the courts offered no
reassuring correctives. As litigation accumulated at a dizzy-
ing pace around such problems as the taxation of railways or
utilities, it seemed ever less obvious that judges could get to
the facts as they came to each case de novo, and ever more
obvious that leaving such powers in judges' hands cancelled
out the experience and expertise of the commissions. If a
railway alleged confiscatory taxation, was a judge really the
best arbiter as to the true value of the corporation's stock?
Adam Shortt, founder of the influential school of political
economy at Queen's University in Kingston, began the transition to a career in the civil service in 1904 to address precisely that question. Important turn-of-the-century law firms

developed stables of lawyers who found that they served clients' interests best by negotiating with commissioners and other kinds of officials, rather than by litigating. As those lawyers drove up workloads, state bureaucracies expanded. A sea change in legal culture, thus, underpinned the emergence of the modern administrative state and a vast new lobbying industry that transferred individuals back and forth between private and public employment.

Business still led knowledge in ways that insurance exemplified. Insurance companies were a bugbear at the Union of Canadian Municipalities because they forced municipalities to improve their facilities, against fire for example, without ever seeming to reduce premiums. In the name of shareholder profits, they forced up local public spending, even as they demanded exemption from municipal property taxes on the grounds that they served a public good, according to formulae that were (in the words of Thomas Bradshaw, director of the Imperial Life Assurance Company) "mathematically determined and governmentally required."[4] That was in 1913; by 1916, Bradshaw was overseeing Toronto's finances. Insurance constituted a shadow state, where risk to life and property was calculated and managed with a precision that officials might envy. Insurance companies partook of what the philosopher Michel Foucault called "governmentality": non-government institutions that exercised disciplinary and regulatory powers, disseminating the logic of rule into civil society – albeit according to commercialized, bureaucratized logic initially developed in private companies. The state was something of a latecomer to that logic: mutual aid societies, for example, had already been forced to remake themselves in the image of insurance companies. In the hands of a Bradshaw or a Wickett, the calculus of life, health, and profit became a program of rational measurement susceptible to expert management, with business and academic credentials here operating almost interchangeably. Businessmen taught state officials how to govern or donned a different hat to do the work themselves.

But officials found ways to force the costs of insurance back into the private sphere, using government not to distort the marketplace, but (as they saw it) to prevent a skewed marketplace from distorting the public sphere. Insurance provided a means to cope with the swathes of victims that industrial capitalism left in its wake. Labour had always been hard, dangerous, and uncertain, often seasonal. But the move to urban factories and breadwinner households made work more precarious, and the sheer numbers involved ramped up the social and fiscal costs of unemployment, injury, and bereavement to levels that municipal and provincial authorities began to resent. A workplace injury was an uncomfortable exception to the rule of marketplace justice. The family might experience a workplace injury as an unpredictable catastrophe, but from the perspective of insurance underwriters and social investigators, injuries were more or less statistically predictable. Actually, few knew better than the coal miners employed by the Dunsmuirs in British Columbia that they worked at some of the most unsafe mines in the world, or that Premier Dunsmuir was unlikely to take up their cause. From mining catastrophes of the 1890s and 1900s emerged a growing consciousness that blood on the rock face indicted not nature but capitalism and the governments that purportedly regulated it. Canadian workers challenged the hegemony of the marketplace, and governments began to heed their complaints.

Labour carried the new statism into provincial legislatures. In Manitoba from 1891 and Ontario from 1892, universal male suffrage – excluding some categories of "Indians" – enfranchised working men. Both provinces harnessed machine-party government and ostentatiously Protestant rhetoric to a provincial rights campaign. The rejection of Catholic state schooling was one consequence in most provinces; another was the advent of pro-labour legislation. Ontario in particular had a prosperous mixed economy with a lot of wealth to be shared out (more wealth than in the Maritime provinces where the fights were, as a consequence, much more bitter), and it made some of the most important innovations. In 1913, an Ontario Royal Commission chaired by Sir William Ralph Meredith gave its final report on employers' liability for employees' injuries. Meredith found employers and workers in agreement that existing case law set in 1837, which required that workers bear the risk of injuries, was outdated and unjust; rather, the risks should be understood as "risks of the industries," and the cost should be borne by employers (who could pass the increased costs of labour on to consumers). Only legislation could have that result. By Meredith's reasoning, the state was already intervening to manage industrial relations, but blindly and inefficiently. The Ontario Workmen's Compensation Act of 1914 was an innovation taken up in other provinces, including Nova Scotia in 1915, British Columbia and Manitoba in 1916, and Alberta and New Brunswick in 1918.

This new mode of reasoning was soon extended to unemployment, which was taken up by another Ontario Royal Commission in 1916. The chief commissioner, Sir John Willison, discovered that unemployment had economic rather than moral causes; it was "but a phase of a movement alternating between inflation and depression, which is a characteristic of modern industry." In a market economy, especially one like Ontario's, which was subject to international pressures, recessions would occur and, although individuals could not prepare against them, states could, by planning, work in advance to "replace the lessened private demand. It is desirable," Willison continued, "that Governments should more fully recognize the large extent to which their activities are industrial. Public expenditures should, therefore, be based on sound business principles, and governed by the actual requirements of communities rather than by political considerations, and other uneconomic influences."[5] And, arguing that unemployment was more demoralizing than was scientific state intervention, he recommended that a provincial Labour Commission be created to study economic statistics and create labour offices (following recent British example) to match workers to available jobs; eleven such offices were established in Ontario within a couple of years. Innovation in Ontario again led the nation, as the federal government sponsored employment offices across most of Canada.

Industry pooled risk all the time, so why shouldn't the state? What were mid-Victorian laws on bankruptcy protection or limited liability but ways of reducing business risks? The new programs merely expanded the pool. The strength of the argument lay in the observations that the state was already deeply implicated in the economy and needed merely tweak its workings. Such arguments did not always go in labour's favour, and laws were regularly flouted. In 1899, Wilfrid Laurier rejected the arguments of his deputy minister of labour, William Lyon Mackenzie King, that the Grand Trunk Railway should reinstate strikers after a strike. And in 1925, by which time King was prime minister, his government refused to mediate in a fierce labour dispute in Cape Breton (where the massive British Empire Steel Corporation was imposing double-digit wage cuts on destitute mining communities), on the grounds that labour was, after all, a provincial matter. The state remained an unreliable ally to labour – unreliable under Laurier who remained a Victorian liberal, unreliable under the deeply conservative Robert Borden, and all the more unreliable under Mackenzie King as tempers polarized anew in the 1920s.

But even the federal state was being reconstructed from the bottom up. John A. Macdonald had thought that if a state did not tax its population directly, it could go a long ways towards avoiding painful public debate about the relationship between the state, the citizen, and the property that they more or less shared. Indirect taxes, such as the National Policy tariff, sheltered his government from the vigilance of local ratepayers, while he shrugged off complaints that it drove up prices, insisting that it created jobs. But by the mid-1890s it was becoming harder to hide the

state behind the tariff. From the very beginning of agricultural settlement in Western Canada, settlers, who faced
hardships in districts where crops grew only slowly and
unevenly, blamed their economic stagnation on taxes and
state-set high prices for goods and transportation of goods,
which transferred their wealth to central Canadian pockets.
Their complaints peaked in the early 1920s, as a collapse
in commodity prices and soaring freight rates prompted
powerful regional protest movements, amplified by provincial governments and by a new federal Progressive Party
that briefly held the balance of power. Atlantic Canadians
also built up a Maritime Rights Movement around such
complaints in the 1920s. There was little to be gained from
blaming a reluctant land for your troubles; blaming the government held out better prospects. Regionalist sentiment
with a strong statist bias hardened into economic theory:
a "staples" theory of economic development, advanced by
Harold Innis at the University of Toronto, that insisted on
the importance of the Canadian state in knitting together
the different economic regions and mitigating the effect
of the international market.

Meanwhile, mounting evidence pointed to the impact of
taxation on domestic life. Tax politics intensified from the
1890s as the cost of living rose, provoking commissions of
inquiry. But whereas Macdonaldian commissions solicited
public opinion, twentieth-century investigations were informed by scholarly data, as new methods of social investigation mapped poverty and raised its political profile. H.B.
Ames was a businessman, politician, and reformer who was
worried by growing popular agitation against economic inequality in Montreal and decided to measure the discrep-
ancy between family incomes and the cost of lodging, food,
and clothing in working-class Montreal. His findings of dire
poverty, published in 1897, lent momentum to the urban
reform movement. Canadian reformers also drew upon
American scholarship to show, for example, that regressive
consumption taxes, such as the tariff, appropriated 3 per

cent of savings among the wealthy and 75 to 90 per cent of savings from the poor. Here was evidence of massive state intrusion in domestic life that made the rich richer and the poor poorer, and confounded the supposed morality of the marketplace. Somehow the state had to neutralize that distortion.

It was the work of modern social science to discover, around the turn of the century, an interventionist state that was always already reconstructing society in covert ways. It was the ambition of modern social science to make those covert workings visible and to subject them to rational, informed control from above, overturning government by opinion from below. Such processes were underway when the First World War broke out; they were hugely amplified by the war. Canada passed income tax legislation in 1917 as a triumph of wartime solidarity and sacrifice, of popular will over elite interest. But social investigators had begun to realize that income tax was none of those things; jurisdictions that taxed income were growing wealthy upon it and most income taxes were paid, as one study in Saint John, New Brunswick, revealed in 1916, by "wage earners and men with small and fixed salaries such as clerks and other officials, many of whom find it difficult on the stipend they receive to maintain their efficiency and reasonable standard of living."[6] Economic biases continued to riddle structures of government in complicated ways before, during, and after the Great War.

Still, the war transformed the relationship between state and society. The Conservative government of Robert Borden mobilized the economy and the population in an extraordinary war effort. But, having once subordinated profits and privacy to patriotic public ideals, statesmen found they could not impose a return to liberal relations of priority. Never again would the federal state be able to shrug the great social questions of the day off to lower jurisdictions. Liberalism proved too thoroughly discredited to survive the challenges of the 1930s and 1940s.

War, Depression, and Welfare

Nineteenth-century British liberalism had triumphed as a reaction to the corrupt, tax-eater state that resulted from decades of war with France and the United States. In 1914, the pendulum swung the other way, as military defence trumped civil and economic liberties. Britain fought many late-Victorian wars but none so desperately or so close to home as the Great War. Canadians were not so immediately threatened by the European war and, as a consequence, their state commanded nothing like the British consensus that it strove to emulate. Canada's commitment to imperial defence had always been controversial. No single policy could command the consent of the whole population of Canada, and ambitious politicians only deepened the divisions by appealing to them. Laurier tried to find compromises, such as sending a voluntary contingent to the South African War in 1899 or creating an all-Canadian navy in 1910 rather than paying for British dreadnoughts. But the divisions seemed only to grow as Borden's election in 1911 reduced French-Canadian political influence and enhanced the imperial connection. In 1914, Britain declared war on Germany on Canada's behalf, but Borden pledged Canada to full commitment to the Allied effort, and the final price tag reflected that: between 1913 and 1918 the national debt rose from $463 million to $2.46 billion. The Canadian government put more than half a million people into uniform, made them a professional, effective fighting force, and it sustained an efficient, productive imperial munitions board as the core of a managed wartime economy. It enacted conscription and the mobilization and enfranchisement of women, and it provided medicine and support for soldiers and their families. It created a National Research Council to harness science to the war effort. It also passed a War Measures Act to give it extraordinary powers of public security, and it spied on and interned purported enemies. Another new wartime expedient, income tax, also remained in place after the war. It did not replace the tariff – Borden had campaigned and won the election in 1911 on a protectionist platform – but Borden reformed the civil service so as to replace cronyism with merit and expertise and to make the state less partisan and more impersonal in its workings. He similarly turned his Conservative Party government into a "Union" government that recruited some Liberals. Borden began to unravel the cronyism that John A. Macdonald had so carefully ravelled, but the result was Liberal political hegemony for most of the twentieth century.

Public debate about state intervention was enriched by the new experiences and new voices. By stoking public-spiritedness, the state was able to demand extraordinary sacrifices from ordinary people. This was not an appeal to rational, economic self-interest, but an appeal to cast such things aside for higher purposes; there was nothing rational about death on the battlefield. Recruitment, victory loans, war bonds, and other forms of public devotion were solicited, using all the resources of modern public opinion. Above all, these appealed to masculinity, like the Montreal poster that contrasted a hockey game with an injured soldier: "Why be a mere spectator when you should play a *man's* part in the real game overseas?" "The Happy Man Today is the Man at the Front," declared another for the Royal Highlanders. The soldier's masculinity lay not only in picking up a bayonet but in using it to defend the family: Whistler's mother figured on one poster for the Montreal Irish Canadian Rangers Overseas Battalion, alongside the words "fight for her," while other posters asked women to persuade their men to sign up.[7] In such posters, the state hitched the modern cultural industries to lofty public purpose. But a masculinity so aroused could not be simply retired at the end of the war, especially not a war vividly commemorated by the artists, writers, and film-makers that media baron Max Aitken, Lord Beaverbrook, sent to the European front, over the objections of timid Canadian politicians.

Governments could hardly send men to die for the family if they did not take the family's claims seriously themselves. Politicians had to ensure that soldiers' families did not suffer inordinately from the absence of the family breadwinner, and they began to take an interest in the struggles of ordinary housewives. Discovering serious hardship among soldiers' families, legislators introduced a separation allowance for families whose head of household was overseas. Over time, a handful of officers and clerks in the pay and record office in Europe ballooned to 2,841 employees by September of 1916; at home, the bureaucracy responsible for paying families stood at 625 by early 1917. But there were gaping cracks in the system. Widows and disabled fathers dependent on combatant sons weren't initially recognized for separation allowances: Mr. and Mrs. John Grant of Sault Ste. Marie both "died of want" in 1915 before the Canadian government got around to recognizing their claims. And, discovering that soldiers regularly failed to send any part of their salary to support their families, amidst much trembling at the danger to patriarchal authority, officials began to pay part of soldiers' salaries directly to their families in 1916.

Still, many families experienced a calamitous decline in income that the national government was not well placed to remedy. Charities had begun to organize themselves "scientifically," so as to rationalize spending and cut off spurious claimants. Bureaucrats had no such expertise or mandate. So the government created a national charity, the Patriotic Fund, headed by H.B. Ames, to investigate such cases and allocate resources. Its proponents celebrated this triumph of voluntarism as part of what distinguished a liberal country like Canada from an authoritarian regime like the Kaiser's. But voluntarism ultimately proved inadequate against the Kaiser's methods and, in 1917, Borden began forcibly to conscript soldiers to fill depleted ranks. Support for the Patriotic Fund declined precipitously, especially in Quebec, where a deeply divisive conscription crisis ignited political tensions.

Soldiers' families considered payouts an entitlement, not a charity, and they deeply resented the interference of social workers who scrutinized their behaviour and docked their payments for waywardness. Hardship often worsened as the soldiers returned home. The government provided for disabled veterans but made scant provision for the able-bodied: a War Service Gratuity averaging about $240 per head, $35 for new clothing, and the unemployment offices. Veterans demanded more, but the Canadian government, already shockingly in debt, refused anything more than paltry winter relief, around $5 million, administered by the Patriotic Fund. Mackenzie King promised better terms in the election campaign of 1921, but once in office his government refused to honour any such commitment to "state paternalism." Veterans found themselves poor, unemployed, and surrounded by people who had grown affluent in their absence. That contrast found a focus and a scandal in Sir Joseph Flavelle, the chair of the Imperial Munitions Board, who had roared "To hell with profits!" but had also profited from selling bacon to soldiers.

Postwar economic and political tensions were already running high, especially in Western Canada, where radical industrial organizations made considerable headway in resource towns and camps. In the aftermath of the Russian Revolution of 1917 (which Canada sent soldiers to repress), many in authority saw scant difference between support for a strike and Bolshevism. In December 1918, Prime Minister Borden expanded the quasi-military Royal North West Mounted Police (RNWMP), adding 1,200 men, as an alternative to unionized municipal police officers, who seemed too sympathetic to strikers. Matters came to a head in Winnipeg in 1919 when highly skilled workers joined with unskilled compatriots to initiate a general strike. Eventually about thirty thousand workers walked off the job, and sympathy strikes erupted across Canada. Police infiltrators depicted the strike as an attempt to overthrow the Canadian government. Authorities crushed the strike, put ringleaders on trial for sedition or deported them outright, and introduced changes to immigration laws – which already provided for denial of entry or deportation for those of a revolutionary persuasion – by proscribing those who advocated the destruction of property or assumed the functions of governments (as the Winnipeg strike committee had done in taking over basic municipal functions when city workers walked out). Later that year, the RNWMP was further expanded to become a national police force and secret service and was renamed the Royal Canadian Mounted Police (RCMP). Critics like J.S. Woodsworth, a Methodist minister turned labour politician, objected to the government's spending eight times more on the new force than on unemployment.

By the early 1920s, the interface between state and society had changed irrevocably. Property rights were a casualty; they could harmonize public and private goals in peace but not in war. You couldn't send people far away to die for property as a way of life when they had no personal knowledge of that way of life. Governments dismantled property restrictions on the vote and espoused the language of democracy. They had to address public opinion in new ways, initially to win the European war, later to stave off communism and socialism. Unfortunately they understood public opinion as fraught, fragile, and easily undermined. They accused communists and socialists of secretly infiltrating civil society and agitating to overthrow governments, effectively importing violence deep into the heart of civil society. Here was one last frontier to justify state growth and repression. Socialism and communism, tolerated when peaceful, were outlawed when they advocated violence – a reasonable balance, but one tainted by the tendency to read violence, at will, into almost any left-wing movement, and to blame radicalization upon foreigners: "Immigration is war," stormed one conservative pundit in 1920.[8] Amidst a postwar economic downturn that heightened regional and class tensions, the emerging security state worked to decapitate radical and labour movements into the 1920s and 1930s by means of jail sentences, deportations, and occasional killings.

But opinion, as David Hume had so long ago remarked, cannot simply be coerced; it must also be wooed. Now it had to be wooed in comparison with regimes that advocated collectivist ideals. If communist countries provided for their sick and their poor, it ill behooved capitalist countries to let theirs die on street corners. Transnational left-wing movements powerfully stoked popular demand for a welfare state.

The earliest welfare legislation was aimed at women. Even as the federal government maintained a harsh line with male householders, provincial governments were directing new funds towards their dependants. The experience of the nineteenth century had been that the male-breadwinner model left many "innocent" victims in its wake, and the war confirmed that discovery. A new maternalism infused political discourse, as women, newly enfranchised at the end of the war, refused to let domestic concerns fade. Organizations like the National Council of Women advocated women's rights and needs, and many men, especially those connected to the churches, seconded their efforts on behalf of the family. The war, with its massive haemorrhage of young men, provoked a new concern over birth rates and healthy childhood. Reformers demanded state institutions of health and welfare, including well-baby clinics and free milk outlets, institutions designed at keeping children healthy within the home. They insisted that the family was a public institution as much as it was a private one. One journalist summed up the discovery in 1918: "Home and State are seen by even the most short-sighted to be an Indivisible Whole."9 Five provinces passed laws in favour of mothers' allowances. Mothers' allowances aimed primarily at restoring the male breadwinner household. Women could now devote themselves to their true vocation, raising children, rather than competing with men for paid employment or sending the children out for work. The sums allocated were not enough to sustain families outright – the state had no intention of making charity redundant or encouraging women-led households – but could help to make ends meet.

Another trend that drove the new concern for welfare was a legislative feedback loop. The state could not ignore the ways that innovative legislation made subsistence harder for struggling families. In the nineteenth century, poor families usually sent older children to work, rather than mothers, who were needed to run the household. Now, laws forbade child labour and insisted that children attend school (even Quebec mandated school attendance from 1943). But mothers were forced into the workforce. State officials tried to harmonize the commercial and moral incentives that made the family such a reliable partner to social order, but every intervention seemed to undermine those incentives and alter family relations. Similarly, if the federal income tax made it harder for middle-class savers and investors to squirrel away money to see them through hard times, then the state had to bear some responsibility for aiding them in hard times. The effect of tax rates upon marriage rates was another preoccupation that forced its way to national consideration. The more governments taxed and regulated populations, the more they had to ponder poverty as a problem of national as well as domestic economy.

Social welfare expanded primarily as part of a spending spree by provincial governments flush with royalties on resources and corporate taxes in the 1910s and 1920s. Some passed minimum-wage laws, but no legislature directed public money towards male breadwinners. Provincial and federal governments alike refused to extend base welfare or unemployment payments to able-bodied men for fear of destroying market incentives. Welfare remained a municipal responsibility. The one exception was old age pensions, which were foisted upon a reluctant Mackenzie King by two Western labour MPs, J.S. Woodsworth and A.A. Heaps, during a political deadlock in the mid-1920s. The elderly had always constituted a large proportion of the institutionalized poor in almshouses, asylums, and workhouses. Still, the new pensions would be rigorously means-tested to relieve only utter destitution, at an extremely low level.

There was no entitlement to relief, according to the purveyors of the new welfare programs. And yet entitlement seems to have been the consequence. People who received aid from the state came to believe that the state owed it to them. The mores of legislators were not passed on friction-free with the laws and resources; ordinary people had their own views, and the new negotiations amplified them. Rigid criteria of eligibility were liberalized in practice, as officials responded to the wrenching stories of poverty before them. Centralized officials constantly tried to rein in their counterparts in the field, a trend seen in other departments such as Indian Affairs or Veterans' Affairs. People circumvented the law in ways that suited their own sense of social justice, and they defended their choices and their lives eloquently in submissions to officials, associations, and newspapers. They drew powerfully from alternative narratives articulated by feminists, socialists, unions, and farmers' organizations.

Welfare for the poor was one political hot potato; welfare for the rich was another, even if it went by different names. Politicians and railways still colluded industriously. The Canadian Pacific Railway was completed in 1886 with a guaranteed monopoly, but that monopoly was broken one year later by a Manitoba premier, John Norquay, courting the vote of farmers who complained bitterly of ruinous freight rates and a lack of branch lines. He had no money to subsidize a new railway, but did promise to guarantee railway debts. Contractors drawn by these terms began to build the Canadian Northern Line. By 1901, they had a new deal with the Manitoba government: in return for further assistance, they offered a rate of ten cents per hundred-weight of wheat shipped. (In 1897, the CPR had halved its own charge to fourteen cents, in return for a federal subsidy to build a line through the Crow's Nest Pass.) This was a risky offer, but, after all, investors could not lose any money, thanks to the provincial guarantee, and contractors predicted, accurately, that rather than pay the Northern's debts, the Manitoba government would relax its policy on rates. Thus did Manitoba succeed in lowering the cost of railway transport. But when Laurier decided he, too, wanted the political capital to be made from transcontinental railway building and supported a new Grand Trunk, excess competition, financial downturn, and the spectre of bankrupt provinces and banks led to nationalization of the two new lines as the Canadian National Railway, headed by Sir Joseph Flavelle, which began its new life with $1.3 billion in debt. The railways were too important to fail and served as the first experiments with federal Crown corporations. The state could not stop at mere investment; it had to ensure that the investment served public purposes and, in so doing, entangled itself in spiralling disputes between regions and corporations. The federal government again followed a trajectory laid out by local governments, as negotiations over financial support led to negotiations over rates and prompted the creation in 1903 of a Board of Railway Commissioners that, into the 1930s, was still trying unsuccessfully to find technical, expert criteria for resolving what amounted to irreducibly political problems.

A railway was never just a railway but a series of economic relationships. Creating a new railway broke down grain monopolies, but also boosted Eastern financial interests. The Canadian Pacific Railway was closely connected with the Bank of Montreal, the Canadian Northern Railway with the Canadian Imperial Bank of Commerce, and those involved branched into other investments. Mid-century critics reckoned that twenty-five directors of the Royal Bank of Canada held over 240 directorships between them, thirty Bank of Montreal directors held 220 directorships, and so on. Federal and provincial regulations that aimed at segregating such institutions as banks and trusts from one another instead provoked "legally independent but incestuously connected financial institutions, in which corporate conflict of interest reigned supreme and self-dealing was the norm rather than the exception."[10] Such men also took public office. Louis-Joseph Forget was a stockbroker and financier, chairman of the Montreal Stock Exchange, first French-Canadian director of the CPR, and an active partner in navigation, power, and railway companies, as well as a Conservative Party organizer, MP, and newspaper publisher, most famous for consolidating many of his interests into what became one of the most important companies in the country, Montreal Light, Heat & Power, in 1901 (eventually nationalized in 1964 as Hydro-Quebec). His partner in that enterprise, Sir Henry Holt rose from CPR office boy to president of the Royal Bank of Canada, and also served the Conservative Party and occasional government commissions. Holt was the unpopular face of capitalism; the audience at a sporting event cheered when informed of his death. Sir John Aird was president of the Canadian Bank of Commerce in 1928 when Mackenzie King asked him to chair a Royal Commission to advise whether the state should involve itself with the new broadcasting industry; there was considerable surprise when Aird recommended a national broadcasting agency to regulate the industry and provide public-interest content. This agency became the Canadian Broadcasting Company, or CBC, which later governments divided into separate broadcasting and regulatory bodies. Communication technologies seemed like railways: vital means of spanning Canada's distances and ensuring a modicum of political and cultural cohesion. Bankers were national powerbrokers; the Bank of Canada, created in 1934, scarcely restrained them.

Provincial control of natural resources prompted other collusions. As good, accessible farmland began to run out in the early twentieth century, land-hungry settlers and their legislators propelled new railways into new regions and annexed Indian reservation lands unilaterally, justifying such grabs with reference to wartime food needs, or postwar veteran resettlement needs, or simply the value of wheat over "weeds." Meanwhile, corporate onslaught of such resources as pulp and paper, mining, and oil and gas development fuelled new state alliances. Frank Cochrane could mine

and develop northern Ontario, and then, as first a provincial then a federal minister, pass pro-mining legislation
and send monies for schools, roads, and railways to northern Ontario. Scholars describe the wholesale handover of
resources and policy agendas to industrial interests as an
abnegation of responsible government. Some businessmen-
statesmen operated locally; others, like Lord Beaverbrook,
rose to imperial heights.

The political capital of businessmen still stood high at
the onset of the Great Depression of the 1930s. Overpro-
duction, crop failure, and an international credit crunch
combined to create an unprecedented crisis across the
country. Prices dropped precipitously (wheat fell by 57 per
cent in 1930 alone), prompting mass layoffs. Municipal governments could not sustain the hundreds of thousands of
unemployed, nor could, in turn, provincial governments.
Hopes turned to Ottawa. Electors ousted King in 1930, in
favour of R.B. Bennett, a wealthy lawyer and businessman,
inheritor of the Eddy Match Company fortune, who promised that business methods would set government and the
economy back on track. Among his emergency measures
were a new commonwealth tariff, a wheat marketing board,
emergency relief for farmers, increased federal payments
to the old age pension so that poorer provinces could now
afford the scheme (though New Brunswick and Quebec remained outside), and $20 million injected into provincial
and municipal unemployment payments. It seemed like a
lot, but it was entirely inadequate to the situation.

By the middle of the 1930s, people wondered if they were
witnessing the end of conventional politics and economics.
Edward Beatty, president and chairman of the CPR, advocated a return to all-party union government that would
save popular opinion from itself, and he fought a losing
battle on behalf of private industry as a way of life. Howard
Robinson, a dominant figure in publishing and utilities in
Saint John and erstwhile Maritime Rights advocate, called
for such drastic cuts to public spending as to discredit

himself. Academic expertise, if it wished to ease rather than inflame social tensions, would increasingly distance itself from such business expertise as this. New policy instruments were desperately needed as all levels of government verged on fiscal collapse and began to cut back on welfare despite the unabated demand. Hunger marches turned violent. After 1932, unemployed men were forced into federal relief camps cobbled from old logging camps and run by the military wing of the government – a move intended to prevent the "Reds" among them from spearheading revolution. In 1935, organizers led a protest march first to Vancouver and then on to Ottawa. A federal cut of 20 per cent to relief payments ensured public sympathy for the marchers, who were well treated wherever they paused. Bennett sent in the RCMP to stop them in Regina, and a bloody riot ensued, with 128 arrests. But the press and public did not believe Bennett's claim that the intervention was necessary to stop a soviet-style revolution. Nor did they accept his too-little, too-late conversion to a new social conscience – inspired by F.D.R. Roosevelt's New Deal – that would mean, as Bennett explained, "government intervention. It means Government control and regulation. It means the end of laissez-faire." But his promises – including minimum wage and maximum workday and workweek hours, as well as unemployment insurance – all fell outside federal jurisdiction and were overturned by the Judicial Committee of the Privy Council.

Bennett was stung from the political middle by the success of populist and leftist politicians promising more drastic remedies. In Alberta, an evangelical preacher, William Aberhart, rode into the premier's office with a ringing denunciation of the "fifty big shots" who had reduced the country to disaster, and a scheme to nationalize the "unearned increment" that increased property values brought to land by paying out state dividends in the form of credit to consumers, so as to revive consumer spending. The scheme soon collapsed, but Aberhart's Social Credit Party governed

Alberta for many more years, with a growing gap between populist rhetoric and quiet accommodation with business. On the left, the Cooperative Commonwealth Federation formed in 1933 from combined workers' and farmers' organizations. It advocated all of Bennett's welfare measures and much more, ultimately declaring its commitment to replace capitalism with a "full programme of social planning." The emergence of the CCF on the national stage in the 1930s, its growing public support (documented in the new science of polling during the early 1940s), helped push the mainstream political agenda to the left more effectively than had earlier regional protest parties.

Amidst the clamour and the chaos, the public, or at least 45 per cent of it, looked to the familiar, pudgy features of Mackenzie King to preserve what was worth preserving and reform what had to be reformed. Back in office in 1935, King eased the tariff, propped up farmers, and began to address the staggering relief payments and the jurisdictional boundaries that inflicted those payments on municipal and provincial governments. But new structures of social governance would require a new constitutional arrangement, and there the reforms lost momentum. The provinces might want more federal money, but they did not want to cede powers to the central state. In vain did a National Employment Commission declare an end to classic liberalism in Canada and a new standard for a "humanitarian state" that would ensure "at least minimum standards of survival for its people." The Royal Commission on Dominion–Provincial Relations (the Rowell–Sirois Commission) of 1937–1940, therefore, brought the full resources of academic scholarship to bear on the problem and tried to bury traditional political economy in a barrage of facts and analyses. The commissioners noted that state responsibility for relief had traditionally been minimal, beginning at $1 million in 1867 and rising to $250 million at the time of reporting, but, they declared, such fallbacks as "temporary retreat to the family homestead" no longer sufficed. They revisited the reasoning behind Confederation to insist that a centralization of powers at Ottawa was both necessary and orthodox, and they advocated federal responsibility for unemployment and old age pensions, both too important and complicated to be left to lower governments. The federal government should also centralize taxation and redistribute the income, assuming provincial debts. Historian Douglas Owram describes the Commission's report as "a mature statement of the creed of modern social and economic planning."[11]

Recalibrating Public Opinion and Civil Society

The emergence of modern planning helps to explain why laissez-faire liberalism succumbed to such events as war and depression, which it had shrugged off over the previous century. The expansion of universities in Canada created a body of self-styled experts and white-collar workers who demanded a place in government by appointment rather than election. Many of these "experts" entertained a low opinion of popular knowledge – now vested in women (except Quebec until 1940) and working classes – and drew on sociology and psychology to explain popular error. Political truths in the nineteenth century were what the political nation forged from debate and consensus; those of the twentieth century were manufactured from statistical analysis and dispassionate observation. A non-interventionist government did not need expert advice. It took information in the form of public opinion (and private lobbying) and then tried to balance competing interests. An interventionist government, by contrast, needed facts and expertise beyond the merely public. A symbiotic relationship emerged between public-minded intellectuals and government authorities seeking their expertise. The Depression worked to enhance the claims of the experts insofar as it was a new and national phenomenon, and resulted from causes that individual workers and farmers could not have been expected to foresee. Economists could identify those national causes and could advise governments how to act against them. British economist John Maynard Keynes insisted as early as 1923 on the need to make "regulation of the standard of value to be the subject of *deliberate decision*. We can no longer afford to leave it in the category of which the distinguishing characteristics are possessed in different degrees by the weather, the birth-rate, and the Constitution, – matters which are settled by natural causes, or are the resultant of the separate action of many individuals acting independently, or require a Revolution to change them."[12] To transfer the economy from "natural causes" to "deliberate decision" necessarily placed it under the control of the state, the highest manifestation of collective political purpose. Keynesian economics – the theory of counter-cyclical spending – provided a more refined content to an interventionist framework that was already developing. At first, expert knowledge was concentrated in the statistics division, far from the corridors of power, and served to inform public opinion rather than direct it. But as King brought political economists like O.D. Skelton into public office, he created an efficient civil service.

Civil servants and scholars were natural allies behind the new knowledge. Nineteenth-century public servants drew upon party patronage for their appointments and legitimacy; their twentieth-century counterparts drew upon objective knowledge. Warrants to authority abhor a frontier much as nature abhors a vacuum; they will always encroach upon any line drawn in the sand. Liberal distinctions between circumstances that individuals could and could not control were just such a line. The notion of "disaster" mediated between those distinctions, standing for extraordinary moments when nature swamped reasonable human precautions. But nature and disaster alike were being incorporated into larger schemes of bureaucratic mastery and governing laws, much in the way that the insurance industry had been founded upon the statistical mastery of risk; indeed, insurers ever inserted themselves into these conversations, as they sought to maintain profits amidst escalating risks. If the crisis could be measured, then it could be managed, and chance could be tamed. The realization occurred at a moment when statesmen and bureaucrats seemed better managers than did businessmen.

The transition was not smooth or linear, and divisions between old-style liberals and new-style Keynesian monetarists in and out of government remained. Seeing a shift in political power from the public and the legislature to the bureaucrat and the social scientist, Harold Innis, dean of political economy at Toronto during the interwar years, denounced the Rowell–Sirois Commission's reports as approximating "state socialism." Frank Underhill, a leftist historian at Toronto, welcomed more intervention and took the line that it was consistent with classic liberalism because only the state could guarantee the access to opportunity of choice that liberal theories presumed. But Underhill, too, was troubled by the "new Machiavellianism" of the new managerial class in government and industry. Its proponents treated public opinion as just another factor to be managed rather than as the underpinnings of political authority; the self-styled elite used the "'opinion industries' – press, school, radio, etc." to manufacture public opinion and make "the basic democratic process of government by the consent of the governed a subject for mockery amongst the sophisticated."[13] Slick management of public opinion, often by hired advertising gurus, characterized twentieth-century political discourse. Confronted by hard times in Nova Scotia, for example, long-time premier Angus Macdonald sustained traditional laissez-faire liberalism by nurturing an anti-modernist Scottishness designed to attract tourist dollars while romanticizing poverty and underdevelopment. Corporate and statist ideologies and projects found new ways to dovetail in the brave new world of democratic politics.

And yet public opinion was nobody's poodle. It resided in powerful institutions, including national political parties, local charitable societies, unions, and a range of organizations in between. The expansion of the franchise brought the concerns of ordinary citizens for access to food, shelter, hygiene, and medicine more thoroughly into the public arena.

Commodification strengthened rather than weakened political content; families dining on mustard sandwiches while surrounded by advertisements for material happiness were radicalized. Veterans had supposedly fought for the good life and the manly ideal; when they complained that the breadwinner ideal eluded them en masse, politicians slowly but finally moved to prop it up. "Once a soldier, always a man," declared one wartime poster in favour of rehabilitating disabled soldiers. Having elevated rights, dignity, and national spirit over property during the Great War, politicians couldn't force the genie back into the bottle.

The old arguments – that people's rights were best protected when property was protected, and the bigger the property the better – rang hollow. The confrontations were often most powerfully experienced locally, in towns dominated by such powerful corporations as BESCO or General Motors. Western Canadian municipalities cut their teeth in struggles with corporations, such as the CPR and HBC, that owned huge tracts of valuable land and fought against taxes and schools all the way to the Judicial Committee of the Privy Council. Amidst such confrontations were communitarian and statist political ideologies hammered out at the grassroots level. Thus, for example, the *Edmonton World*, vehement critic of the local property franchise (which accorded extra votes for more valuable property), in 1910 articulated an alternative theory of municipal property and its entitlements: "The man who pays a street car fare becomes by that act a patron, a contributor, and a part owner in the same. The patron of every other utility is in the same position. But the non-resident property holder who is not a patron is not a contributor, and therefore not an owner. Consequently the resident who lives in a shack down on the flats is more entitled to a vote on the question of how these utilities should be conducted than the Hudson's Bay Company which owns three million dollars' worth of land."[14] Such confrontations led to the articulation of rich and vigorous conceptions of state-sustained community life.

The decline of the old two-party monopoly on public life gave rise to genuinely independent movements in all regions and among all classes, nurturing a much more varied and heterodox social life. Take the community chest by way of example: charitable organizations in a given town or city, confronted with growing state funding for the poor and the sick, began to organize themselves collectively so as to raise and distribute their funds "scientifically." They carefully scrutinized potential donors and recipients, and they approached problems of security of food, shelter, hygiene, and medicine as practical problems rather than as inroads upon an ideologically freighted distinction between state and society. Organizations of the sort brought together business elites, state actors such as social workers, and volunteers from all walks of life, who, in collaboration, developed their own rationality and culture of intervention. The more complex models of human agency and understanding, replacing the rational liberal actor with a desiring consumer who was prey to fashion and opinion, extended the scope of governmentality ever more expansively and intimately and ensured that "the work of governing and the activity of social citizenship" constituted one another as mirror images.[15] People came to this new culture gradually. Charlotte Whitton, who founded Canada's pre-eminent national welfare council and served as mayor of Ottawa, warned against the collapse of public and domestic boundaries: "the walls of the home have been knocked down: all its members roam in and out of a community into which it has merged, and the public authority ranges at will through all its traditional intimacies and sanctities."[16] Jane Wisdom, an early social worker from New Brunswick who trained at McGill and then in New York, initially opposed state allowances for mothers, believing charities much better placed to manage domestic problems. She worked in Halifax in the aftermath of the explosion, later moving to Montreal, where she spent nearly two decades. Over time, Wisdom became an outspoken advocate of state-sponsored welfare, and she ended her career as the first municipal welfare officer in Nova Scotia.

Canadians and Americans shared the traditions of a vibrant and engaged civil society and the terrible shocks that the Great Depression inflicted upon those traditions. But their responses differed. In the United States, public opinion stretched, but did not rupture, the two-party political framework. In Canada, the constitutional straitjacket prevented the two dominant political parties from delivering the kinds of welfare reforms that the public demanded. While Liberal and Conservative politicians squabbled, temporized, and investigated, the CCF grew provincially and nationally, and it proved a marvellous conduit for bringing progressive public opinion into national debates about the role of the state in welfare. This was not the work of the CCF alone; rather, alliance with the CCF amplified pressures emanating from provincial premiers and organized labour.

The emerging social economy, with its broad mix of public and private agencies and concerns, was not universally benevolent; far from it. Relinquishing property as the main mechanism for social and political engineering, and beginning to think harder about intrinsic identities, reformers perpetuated many Victorian prejudices, newly garbed in science. Scientists, doctors, and social scientists, anxious to prove their worth and engineer national progress, began to identify biological constituents to social problems such as poverty, lunacy, and criminality. They built a powerful movement around eugenics: a movement to control birth rates so as to reduce the social damage done by indiscriminate breeding among "unfit" people – who were defined primarily by race, class, and by the new fad for intelligence tests (also designed to discriminate by race and class). The more that society as a whole learned about poverty as a social category, the more intrusive became the means for managing it. A wide range of eugenics programs were introduced across Canada, but it was Alberta that carried eugenics the furthest. Provincially as federally, new parties staked political platforms on these new social attitudes, and in the provincial arena they were able to form governments. Thus, in 1928, a government headed by the United Farmers of Alberta (the association with cattle breeding was not incidental) introduced a program of eugenics that forcibly sterilized hundreds of people. In practice, the criteria and safeguards, under the supposed scrutiny of a professor of philosophy, were so lax that a young girl might be institutionalized and sterilized simply because her mother declared her troublesome. In other jurisdictions, she would likely end up in juvenile detention.

Eugenics was only one result of the new marriage between science, morality, and the coercive powers of the state. The same attitudes and projects reshaped immigration policy, as theories of racialized unfitness were used to keep specified "races" outside of Canada. Chinese immigration, long repressed by an exorbitant head tax, was prohibited outright from 1923. An active Black lobby in eastern Canada prevented any such block ban on Black immigration to Western Canada, although dark-skinned people were stopped at the border by doctors who claimed to find all sorts of invisible incipient diseases. But the First Nations were the most thoroughly smeared by science. Tuberculosis, rampant among the poor everywhere, was especially visible among Indigenous people, because they were concentrated on reserves or in residential schools with designated medical inspection. As a consequence, the prevalence of the disease was racialized – invoked as proof positive that the Native peoples of Canada were dying out, biologically unequal to the demands of the modern world. Fatalism of this sort and lack of political accountability justified the exclusion of Indigenous people from early state sanatoria – until better treatments, empty beds, and the prospect of redundancy prompted medical superintendents to admit them. When, in the 1940s, doctors and officials began to wonder whether poverty and malnutrition were the causes of tuberculosis and population decline rather than the other way around, their immediate instinct was to reduce rather than improve diets, so that they might test the theory and advance scientific knowledge.

Where people were governed by irresponsible authority, scientists threw their energies behind grasping and enhancing that authority, rather than querying its premises or effects. As they took control of political apparatus, progressive politicians implemented the advice of scientists, deploying the state's growing powers of social engineering. After mid-century, a civil rights movement would begin to reverse the worst excesses – though eugenics remained public policy in Alberta until 1972. Indeed, the civil rights movement shared some biases with the statist reform projects, including a preference for abstract definitions of human identity and intolerance for local complexity. Marching in tandem with the new biological theories of poverty were new sociological theories of poverty that investigated it as a function of environment. But well-meaning reformers still grasped at crude, destructive projects of assimilation. From the 1940s, they pursued slum clearances, aimed at Toronto's Cabbagetown; Montreal's Molasses district; Vancouver's Chinatown (where the project was narrowly averted); and, most infamously, Halifax's Africville, where irregular records of property holdings facilitated the process of removal and destruction. Social engineering and military modernization dovetailed insidiously in projects to relocate Indigenous communities to the High Arctic and rebuild or create Arctic cities, so as to assert Canadian sovereignty around new Alexandrias of the north – projects that undermined long-standing ways of life. State officials and experts jointly developed an ethos of centralized planning aimed at imposing simple structures on a complex world, an ethos that anthropologist James Scott describes as "seeing like a state," often with calamitous results for local populations.

The Heyday of the Welfare State

The experience of the Second World War altered some aspects of the new statist social economy, while confirming others. Once again, the Canadian state roused public sentiment to put the country onto wartime footing; once again government intervention and managerialism of the war effort, the economy as a whole, and the welfare of combatants and non-combatants alike, set new standards that would not be easily forgotten once the war was over. Discarding Borden's imperial enthusiasms, interwar Canadian statesmen pursued diplomatic isolation, and after 1931, for fear of military entanglements, they used their new powers of independent foreign policy to undermine the League of Nations. But when a "great and clear call of duty," came in 1939, King fulfilled long-standing promises and led Canada into war. He tried to reduce political polarization and casualties by concentrating efforts on research and the production of weapons, training for the air war, and mediating between Britain and the United States economically and diplomatically. One small but representative example: at one American university, the chair of the physics department was a British national who, being foreign born, could not enter laboratories conducting war research. Canada solved the problem by giving him a nominal position with the National Research Council. The NRC, like other state agencies, had stultified between the wars, but during the Second World War it expanded to employ thousands, as scientists across the country joined the war effort; after the war it remained an important institution, organizing and centralizing Canadian science. C.D. Howe, a wealthy businessman turned Liberal cabinet minister, oversaw arms production within a "centrally directed economy" and stayed on in cabinet after the war to oversee the return to a peacetime regulative state. Canada spent about $18 billion on the war (fifteen times its annual peacetime expenditure on the eve of war), about a fifth of it as a direct gift to Britain.

One consequence of the effort was economic integration between the United States and Canada. The apparently endless debates about Canada's place in the Empire ended, replaced by debates about the Americanization of Canada's economy, culture, and politics. As for direct military contribution, Canada put more than a million people into uniform – twice as many as in the previous war – and suffered fewer military deaths (42,000, down from 54,000). French Canadians again remained aloof from a war that seemed too imperial and remote. King did not entirely avoid a popular crisis over conscription, but he did mitigate it. Other tensions intensified, prompting internment and confiscations of property, on distinctly slender evidence; most egregiously, even Canadian-born citizens of Japanese descent were interned purely on racial grounds. This was, in miniature, a land grab all over again; economic opportunism ever follows closely behind political disempowerment.

At the end of the war, as the wartime controls began to be eased, many people feared a return to the bitter postwar class politics of the 1920s. In Britain, a government commission chaired by William Beveridge, head of the London School of Economics, began planning for "cradle to grave" welfare. His report, published in 1942, became an international bestseller. Mackenzie King created an Advisory Committee on Reconstruction that had as its research secretary Leonard Marsh, a Beveridge-trained social scientist at McGill University, who recommended an extensive statist program of social welfare. The Liberal government, which had already introduced a federal program of unemployment insurance in 1941 (at a moment when unemployment was almost non-existent) initially rejected the report, but, as the CCF rose in the polls, it began to pass welfare legislation, including family allowances in 1945 and universal pensions in 1951. Quebec churchmen and officials objected to the family allowances, fearing they might cause rural depopulation. Consequently, federal officers distributed them directly to that province's population, their first such direct interaction. Family allowances dramatically altered Aboriginal economic relationships; in the North, they sustained families being forced by compulsory schooling into fixed settlements. The fact that they were paid to all Canadians, regardless of race, religion, region, or franchise, reflected the new attempt to depoliticize state payouts and remove all local discretion over their operation. One expert observed, "We soon found an increasing resistance on the part of the public to the idea that any person, social worker or not, should presume to decide who is a deserving case and who isn't a deserving case. We got to the stage where people began to demand that legislation be written down in specific terms to provide as a matter of right certain benefits to people under clearly defined conditions that were prescribed in the law rather than left to the judgment of some individual." The profits and perils of modernity were pooled, swamping the wise or foolish choices of individuals. Under such conditions, welfare was a right of the modern citizen, as King himself observed during the parliamentary debates in 1944, echoing his earliest views: "If need is not the individual's fault but the fault of the industrial system, the State must overcome it one way or another." Still, businessmen demanded that social insurance be run on an actuarial basis so as not to transfer wealth from rich to poor.[17]

King withstood growing public demand for health and hospital insurance (polls in 1944 showed that clear majorities supported a national health-care plan), but in Saskatchewan a CCF provincial government, braving medical opposition, introduced hospital insurance in 1947 and complete health insurance in 1962. The other provinces followed Saskatchewan's example more or less quickly and completely (schemes in British Columbia and Alberta, for example, were means-tested), and the federal government offered national funding for hospital insurance from 1957 and complete health insurance in 1967.

Between the early 1930s and the late 1960s, social spending at all levels of government together increased thirtyfold, while spending on education increased fiftyfold and on health care nearly a hundredfold. Transportation and general government also grew, but more slowly. The period from 1965 to 1971 saw tremendous expansion in welfare provision – not only universal health insurance, but also social assistance, unemployment assistance, pensions, and a guaranteed income supplement. An expanding tax bureaucracy underwrote the largesse. Income tax became an inquisitorial, effective, mass imposition. Income tax never earned the federal government more than $50 million before 1940; by the mid-1950s it stood at $1.5 billion, doubling each decade after that to reach $12.7 billion in the mid-1970s (accounting for almost half of total federal revenues). Much remained to be negotiated, but a basic orientation towards welfare had been established within the Canadian state. If the state was still a cage that worked to congeal political and economic structures, it was also committed to a certain amount of redistribution of resources within that cage. Postwar prosperity facilitated the change. Canada and the United States spent less on welfare than European governments, trusting rising employment and wages to equalize economic conditions. There was less squabbling over state resources in Canada than in the United States because Canada spent far less on its military establishment, so that ideological opponents to state intervention found fewer allies during the golden age of state expansion.

There were variations upon this general theme across Canada. Underdeveloped regions had less state presence, and in small, resource towns, welfare might be managed through company stores. In the north, the Hudson's Bay Company trading post often provided the only shop in a village. Welfare cheques received at these stores, which doubled as post offices, could be spent nowhere else. The notion of an independent state remained elusive under such conditions. During the 1930s in Newfoundland (which had Dominion status from 1907), merchants generally provided fishing families with credit in hard times;

the state became involved only when, as international sales slumped, merchants began to refuse credit to poorer families. In Battle Harbour, the lone local government official opened an account with the local merchant to extend a very small amount of credit to those poor families (which he then milked to his benefit). When angry fishing families threatened to break into company stores to seize supplies, officials had to extend relief because they couldn't defend the stores. The state remained a bit player in such confrontations between merchants and inhabitants. Its attempts to diversify the economy, both before and after Confederation in 1949, made few inroads and changed little for coastal communities. Other provinces also sponsored economic development and diversification with mixed to modest success, even when equipped with the vast sums that the oil industry spawned in Alberta from 1947. In recent years, Atlantic Canadian scholars have rebutted centralist narratives that blamed underdevelopment on the backwardness of the people themselves and replaced them with analyses of the institutional and political "pull" of central Canada as an example of internal colonialism.

Organized labour grew in numbers and militancy during the 1940s and achieved political gains. In 1944, the federal government, temporarily responsible for labour under the War Measures Act, passed an order of the Privy Council, PC 1003, that legalized and even entrenched labour unions as the legitimate means of bargaining. Employers could no longer refuse to recognize them, and workers had to support them as the basic bargaining unit, their wages docked for their support. The federal regulatory regime was dismantled at the end of the war, but provincial versions soon replaced it. Thus institutionalized, unions also experienced the postwar years as a golden age, with increased membership and political influence. But they also relinquished some of their radicalism in a process that some describe as "statization" of workers' movements. The labour movement became more intertwined with government and political-party bureaucracies and more internally bureaucratized itself. Leftist scholars have argued over whether this amounted to success or failure, according to whether they saw genuine working-class interests translated into state policy and state structures, or a growing distance between unions and more radical working-class interests. By the end of the century, as hard times returned, unions seemed to many people to be divorced from local grassroots concerns, representing a narrow and self-interested swathe of the public. Older ideas of hardy individualism had never disappeared, and they revived amidst an attack on the mounting tax burdens and a "culture of entitlement" among unionized workers, public sector workers, and welfare recipients.

By the end of the 1960s, even the wealthiest governments were running out of money. The cost of schooling in Ontario, for example, still financed locally on property taxes, was spiralling upwards by as much as 20 per cent per year, leading to property tax increases of 25 to 50 per cent. In other provinces, the "limits to affluence" had long since been felt, and everywhere politicians and bureaucrats began to consider how to rein in the growing statism, even before the economic downturn of the 1970s made cutbacks a necessity and gave rise to neo-conservatism with its ideological anti-statism.

The numbers no longer added up as they had done. The welfare state was sold to the Canadian public in much the same way as public education had been sold a century before: as a means of pooling the risks and costs of protecting one's property and oneself in a harsh world. The middle classes bought into the welfare state because it served their interests; their modest holdings were increasingly insufficient to buy them modern health care or security in the face of old age or unemployment. The field of medicine provides an example: A century earlier, the middle classes had been well able to afford the services of general practitioners, and they eschewed hospitals as deathtraps. Hospitals existed primarily to give nursing care to the poor; doctors could do little for patients. That changed when the advent of antisepsis pushed surgery into operating theatres, while new hospital-based therapies expanded their clienteles. Radium for cancer, iron lungs for polio, and kidney transfusions for diabetes were three expensive new therapeutic technologies that could be provided only in hospitals and could be paid for only with state subventions. Hence the attractions of pooling risks and expenses through the intermediary of the state. But the costs of medical care soon outran predictions. Expensive new technologies continued to pile up, driving costs ever higher; and more life events became highly medicalized – like childbirth or old age. Moreover, labour costs grew explosively. Charitable hospitals relied on voluntary or near-voluntary labour from medical and nursing students, as well as the "honorary" consultants who took a few hours out of their lucrative practices to oversee medical and surgical care; once these people became state employees, they demanded and received decent salaries. Politicians could face hard choices in other areas of welfare spending, but seemed as unable as the early municipal councils to defy medical prescriptions.

Health care continually ramped up the costs of welfare but it did, at least, improve health in measurable ways, as Canadians began to outlive Americans. Other programs seemed less effective even as they, too, prompted apparently boundless demand. Early ambitions to eradicate poverty faded. J.K. Galbraith, a Canadian-American economist, argued that governments should shift their focus from growth to redistribution. But others pinpointed a "culture" of poverty that prevented the poor from benefitting from growth. Studies of welfare identified much that was arbitrary and unfair about its workings, including disincentives for work. Governments began to experiment with "workfare" programs to push reluctant jobseekers into the workforce. Intense focus upon the distinctive qualities of the poor worked to dismantle the social solidarity that had made pooling risk so attractive in the first place. The propertied classes grew increasingly resentful of spiralling taxes and public indebtedness. As expenses grew disproportionately to resources, fights over those resources became fiercer.

The construction and expansion of the welfare state in Canada required extraordinary feats of diplomacy between provincial authorities responsible for social welfare and federal authorities, who alone had the resources for those programs. Complicated calculations of "equalization payments" redistributed money to poorer provinces. But interprovincial diplomacy broke down as resources diminished. The provinces demanded more money and powers than the federal government was willing to concede, and every confrontation led to a debate about the constitution. Quebec now led the challenge to the federal state. Sensitive to the anti-statism of powerful Catholic interests, that province's government was long the least interventionist. But many Catholics themselves were relinquishing ideological anti-statism and joining in the heterogeneous construction of social citizenship. During the Quiet Revolution of the 1960s, Quebec's government "caught up" and surpassed the other provinces. Its new programs to reformulate, among other things, power, pensions, and pedagogy, became the envy of other premiers. But its efforts to develop special programs to reflect the special political and cultural profile of the province were blocked by a constitution that successive governments fought to overturn, beginning with a throne speech, in December 1966, that promised "to strive to the utmost to achieve a new constitutional order, which will be the instrument, not of an artificial unity, but of a true alliance between two co-equal peoples."[18] Federal politicians such as Lester Pearson fought just as hard for an unhyphenated Canadian identity, and people began to wonder if the country could survive such supercharged confrontations.

An expanding state investment into culture, seen as a national solder, deepened the developing divisions. If religious or class values could not promote unity, then perhaps shared institutions of culture could. The early commitment to a national broadcaster led the Canadian government to provide for Canadian oversight and content in television and film, and to begin to invest in older cultural activities such as ballet, theatre, and writing – including poetry, novels, and academic scholarship – through such new organizations as the National Film Board, the Canada Council for the Arts, and the Social Sciences Research Council. In the early 1960s, Prime Minister John Diefenbaker reduced the overt control of cultural production and, instead, brought in regulations specifying minimum Canadian content requirements for television, later applied to radio. But rather than producing a one-nation narrative, the expanding cultural industries of the 1960s used state sponsorship to put forward regionalized or gendered or racialized postcolonial perspectives that exploded Canadian nationalism into apparently incommensurable pieces.

At the end of the 1960s, politicians in Ottawa and in Quebec grew further apart, as Quebec nationalists began to agitate for separation from the rest of Canada. There was an inevitable logic to the devolution of powers from Ottawa to the Quebec provincial state that seemed to lead towards dissolution. The Liberal premier of Quebec, Jean Lesage, observed, "We had started to tear the sheet, the fabric of the country, about half way. What do you do when you reach that point? Do you keep ... the fabric half torn? Or do you tear it all the way?"[19] Separatist movements formed, some espousing violent revolution, though their murder of a popular Quebec politician, Pierre Laporte in 1970, appalled many nationalists. A more moderate branch of sovereigntists captured the provincial government in 1976, although its referendum in favour of negotiating sovereignty association failed in 1980. Few were reassured; there would clearly be further such campaigns in Quebec's future.

The Balance of Rights and Interests in the Late Twentieth Century

Elected prime minister in 1968, Pierre Trudeau sought a solution in constitutional reform. First, there was the repatriation of the constitution. The Supreme Court had replaced the Judicial Committee of the Privy Council as the final court of appeal in 1949, but any amendment of the constitution still had to receive the assent of British Parliament. To alter the constitution so as to shift all legislative authority to Canada, Trudeau needed the consent of all the provincial premiers. When he tried to argue that no such consent was stipulated anywhere, the Supreme Court responded that, even if it was not *legally* necessary, it was *constitutionally* necessary – a meaningless formulation that Trudeau accepted with blistering fury. Second, Trudeau wanted to introduce a charter of rights to guarantee the liberal rights of individuals to equal and fair treatment before the law and, at the same time, help to block any and all demands for special status and special treatment. Confronted with a resurgence of secular nationalism in Quebec, Trudeau responded much as Lord Durham had: reinvigorated liberalism would rein it in. While they might support repatriation, the provinces remained suspicious of centralizing tendencies in the particular plans that he proposed. As for a charter of rights, the provinces saw nothing in it for them; it would check their authority in their own jurisdiction. Quebecers felt they had adequately guaranteed civil rights by means of a provincial charter passed in 1975.

There was little tradition in Canada of the kind of liberal rights talk that Trudeau espoused. Canadian politicians had cloaked themselves in talk of "the rights of the British subject" from the earliest extension of British authority over Quebec, but those rights were the traditional and historical rights of groups rather than the abstract individual rights of the American constitution. Rights talk in Canada tended to describe group rights, such as the rights of a province or a religious or linguistic community. Abstract, individualized human rights were too absolute for Canadian politicians, who preferred shades of grey and jurisdictional negotiations. Canadian diplomats and politicians enthusiastically joined the new multilateralism in international affairs, helping to launch the United Nations and its peacekeeping projects to empower middle-power countries. They were slower to subscribe to such rights-based UN projects as a declaration of universal human rights (which, in fact, Canadian scholar John Humphreys helped to formulate). They filtered rights talk through the various institutions and jurisdictions of Canadian public life. But the horrifying genocides of the Second World War and the unravelling of empires generated a new, international discourse of human rights that ultimately found purchase in Canada. On the one hand, state-imposed impediments to civil liberties were challenged in the courts with growing success; on the other hand, access to social programs, many of them unevenly distributed, became an entitlement.

State immigration policies exemplify the change. Canadian attitudes to immigration fluctuated between welcoming large numbers of immigrants to settle, labour, and boost the economy, and opposing certain kinds of immigrants deemed to threaten Canadian economic standards and cultural mores. The fact that many of these potentially dangerous immigrants were British subjects – from Hong Kong or India or the Caribbean, for example – forced Canadian policymakers to veil the overt racism in some of their laws, such as the Continuous Passage Act in force between 1908 and 1947 that prohibited would-be immigrants from stopping en route to Canada, effectively shutting the door against immigrants from India. Through the 1950s and into the early 1960s, the responsible department maintained the position that some peoples were simply "unsuitable" by reason of their "peculiar customs, habits, modes of life or methods of holding property" (from the Immigration Act of 1952). But pressures were mounting to repeal the racist policies. Inside Canada, members of targeted immigrant groups demanded the same rights as those of preferred identities, and they made common cause with other voices and organizations in Canada, including Quebec nationalists, in criticizing an excess of Britishness; they were helped by a decline in British immigration at the end of the 1950s. From without, transnational authorities and rights organizations also put pressure on Canada to reform. In 1962, new legislation began the process of replacing ethnic with technical and economic criteria as the basis for admission. Racial and class biases were not erased but decades of more liberal immigration policies substantially reconstructed the country's population and made it much more diverse.

Lester Pearson refined immigration criteria in the later 1960s, but the change was initiated during Progressive Conservative John Diefenbaker's stint as prime minister, and it reflected a personal opposition to discrimination based on "colour, creed or racial origin." Of German descent, Diefenbaker had advocated bills of rights long before he entered the Canadian Parliament, but was successful only when he became prime minister. He was at the forefront of an early Canadian civil rights movement, which began between the wars and gathered steam after the Second World War in response to the increasingly repressive character of the Cold War state. War on communism did not bring out the same divides as previous wars had. Quebec's priests and politicians joined far more enthusiastically in this war than previous ones, and legislation there went furthest towards outright criminalization of communism in the Padlock Law of 1937. But everywhere Canadians expanded a bureaucracy of surveillance and repression, with a broad mandate that encompassed leftish activities among labour unions, immigrants' organizations and help centres, university and high school student unions, and even such housewives' organizations as the Ladies' Auxiliary of the Mine, Mill and Smelter Workers Union of Sudbury, whose Tupperware parties it infiltrated. State officials genuinely feared that the institutions of civil society were being overtaken by international revolutionaries, but they also found it useful to demonize unions and leftist critics with the slur of communism. A Housewives Consumers Association active in the late 1940s that petitioned the government to continue its wartime price controls was politely greeted by the minister of finance in 1947, but turned away in 1948 on the grounds that "the primary purpose of these delegations was to foster Communistic propaganda." As one member, Mrs. A.C. Latham of Moose Jaw, exclaimed, "You can't raise your voice in protest about anything anymore without having a charge of Communist levelled at you."[20] The range of legitimate political dissent narrowed alarmingly.

More worrisome to state officials than the communist infiltration of civil society was the possibility that the state itself might be infiltrated. The vetting of people even marginally connected to the civil service became a large-scale project with an ever-broadening mandate and a whole branch devoted to "character weakness." The apparatus of surveillance extended to sexual behaviour according to a whole series of pretexts: that the same species of weak character that led to homosexuality also led to communism; that people engaging in illegal sexual activities such as sodomy were more easily blackmailed by communists to give up state secrets; and that aberrant sexuality threatened the stability of the traditional family, which remained the state's most reliable ally in maintaining liberal democracy.

Early civil liberties organizations were restrained by the fear of being associated with aberrant sexuality and communist organizations, but they were never entirely silenced and gradually broadened, by the late 1950s and early 1960s, into a civil rights movement, mutually sustained by and sustaining a reinvigorated union movement. Even as Diefenbaker pushed through his Bill of Rights, public opinion was outpacing state action. Diefenbaker's bill was a federal law that could affect only federal legislation, but it did enter the realm of practical politics when, for example, it was used to overturn that part of the Indian Act that prohibited "Indians" from drinking alcohol off the reserve. When the case came to the Supreme Court in 1969, the 6–3 judgment reflected the perplexities of rights versus traditions in Canada. The dissenting judges refused to overturn such a venerable law, either for fear of the threat to legislative supremacy or because they believed that "Indians" did require special legislation.

The campaign for a right to drink reflects the trajectory of rights talk in postwar Canada. At the end of the Second World War, it seemed shocking that Indigenous veterans, who had freely imbibed overseas, should be prohibited from joining their comrades in veterans' clubs. Even people who had no right to vote had an obvious right to consume. This was the flip side of those slick marketing campaigns that managed public opinion, but it also reflected long-standing consumer movements demanding a "right" to cheap necessities, among other claims – demands that had been given powerful new impetus by the government's management of prices during the war. Advertising and consumerism provided the template for "normal" Canadian identity and for the exercise of personal agency. The mixed social economy of welfare officials drew upon that template to forge a new and consensual project of assimilating immigrants to Canada by teaching them how to shop and consume in "Canadian" ways, and they extended that program to Indigenous peoples of Canada, still all too obviously unassimilated. Prominent public figures and Indigenous fraternal groups began to demand repeal of the prohibition, and they totted up provincial successes (permitted by enabling federal legislation) by the early 1950s, even as the campaign moved on to end the humiliating and infantilizing political restrictions more generally, including disenfranchisement, which was overturned in 1960.

Canadians everywhere were debating these points. In 1967, a report from the University of British Columbia denounced the historical mistreatment of Indigenous peoples. In 1968, Pierre Trudeau was elected prime minister on a platform that carried human rights to new heights. If the category of "the Indian" required illiberal legislation to prop it up, then the whole rickety structure should be dismantled, and Indians should become unhyphenated Canadians, as should francophones, anglophones, and whoever else came to the country's shores. Trudeau's White Discussion Paper of 1969 promised to revoke the Indian Act and establish legal equality. He lost that battle. Trudeau forgot that the treaties were historical and legal documents and couldn't be repealed without suppressing the legal agency of the signatories. From 1973, the Canadian government began to negotiate land claims directly. But Trudeau remained convinced that the war (against special status not just for "Indians" but as a political and legal strategy in Canada) could still be won by a charter of rights. And, during one final round of constitutional hearings and diplomacy, Trudeau achieved what had seemed so impossible: constitutional reform. In 1982, the British North America Act of 1867 was revised, and the constitution was patriated. But the discretion of the newly empowered Canadian Parliament, would, along with other legislatures, be checked by a Charter of Rights and Freedoms.

The Charter was a political game changer and, for our purposes, an effective state changer. It has empowered ordinary people to challenge legislation, and it has largely forced legislative bodies to "Charter-proof" their laws, anticipating and preventing head-on confrontations. Above all, Section 15, which guarantees equality rights, has proved a bonanza for rights-based challenges to existing state provisions and services. Take the case of Sandra Lovelace Nicholas. If the paradigmatic citizen pushing at the boundary between civil society and the state at the turn of the century was an H.B. Ames, and at mid-century a Jane Wisdom, the late-twentieth-century example might well be Lovelace Nicholas. A Maliseet woman, in 1977 she petitioned the United Nations to protest human rights violations in Canada including the section of the Indian Act that deprived women who married non-Aboriginal men of their Indian status (by contrast men could not lose their status by marriage). There could be little doubt that this was a sexist law, but Indigenous women were powerless to overturn it. With a Charter, everyone knew that that section of the Indian Act would be overturned. A three-year delay was built into the original legislation, and, in 1985, Parliament repealed the relevant section of the Indian Act. Lovelace Nicholas was eventually named to the Senate – the first Indigenous woman so appointed. Other legislative overhauls reflect other kinds of Charter challenges. Enforcing Sunday closure of shops and denying pregnant women access to unemployment insurance were ruled not to violate the Bill of Rights, but were overturned as discriminatory under the Charter of Rights. Nova Scotia was told that delays in building French-language schools breached the rights of francophones in that province, the Quebec government that long hospital waiting lists violated patient rights in that province. The Charter has enabled the increasingly ethnically and religiously diverse population to demand more liberal services and institutions than the government's official policy of multiculturalism tended to provide. Governments can defy the Charter by invoking the opt-out "notwithstanding" clause, but the public pressure in favour of conforming to the Charter is so great that the clause is almost unusable for most governments most of the time, the one great successful exception being Quebec's insistence on French-language use in that province. Its imposition of French-language schooling on families not already in the English-school system strains to the breaking point conceptions of individual rights to free expression, and it continues to be challenged in the highest courts. Quebec politicians have successfully created a special legal status for Quebecers, one that they can sustain only because they have popular support, that is, because Quebecers believe that their historical identity trumps liberal rights. So long as they choose to maintain their position amidst fierce national debates on the subject, so long will they enjoy a special status that is all the stronger for residing in popular opinion rather than constitutional formulations. Trudeau's Charter also failed to overturn the category of Indian, because (to his surprise) Indigenous activists negotiated the inclusion of existing "Aboriginal" rights. Courts and politicians continue to argue as to what constitutes Aboriginal rights, and Indigenous activists have had setbacks, but the Charter, and participation in the debates leading up to the Charter, strengthened the modern renaissance of Indigenous peoples in Canada, in particular their access to hunting, fishing, and other resources. Some of these victories have come from careful reconsideration of old treaties, others from a more expansive understanding of the relationship between rights and culture. The Charter has strengthened groups that previously lacked sufficient influence to inform and shape legislative debates.

Some politicians argue that the Charter dramatically transformed parliamentary sovereignty by "judicializing" politics and subordinating legislatures to unelected judges. Others point out that the courts are constituted by legislators who can change their rules and their composition, brandishing the same kinds of threats that have historically kept the unelected Senate more or less in line. Negotiations between the government and the Court tend to sidestep Parliament in favour of the cabinet and the prime minister's office (where judicial appointments are made, for example), but this only exaggerates the trend toward the centralization of power in the executive branch of government that has characterized Canadian political history more generally. Not without cause has the Canadian state been described as a "friendly dictatorship."

The Charter explicitly applies to governments but not to private relations and contracts, so the Supreme Court is regularly asked to distinguish between state and non-state entities. The answer is often a matter of degree; how much funding does the government contribute, for example, and how much control does it exercise? The answers can change over time. In 1990, faced with a protest against mandatory retirement (on the grounds of age discrimination), the Supreme Court declared that universities, not being state agencies, were not governed by the Charter. But in 2012, when two students protested that an academic punishment – inflicted because they had said rude things about a professor on Facebook – breached their Charter rights, the highest provincial court ruled that the university was indeed subject to the Charter.

The Charter has reframed old problems in new ways. In matters of sexual politics, for example, the Charter has reinforced Pierre Trudeau's efforts to get the state out of the bedrooms of the nation. Among his earliest political acts in Ottawa was the decriminalization of homosexuality and contraception. He also ruptured the link between vagrancy and prostitution; after 1972, the act of "soliciting" sex (after 1985 "communicating") justified arrest. Activists fought these laws by appeal to the Charter, claiming on the one hand the right to free expression, and on the other hand that the laws against prostitution unduly threatened a right to life, liberty, and security of the person. The sex itself was legal but the trade – the use of bawdy houses or living on the avails of prostitution – remained illegal. Sex workers argued that they could not protect themselves, leaving them vulnerable to predators. The legal challenges continue to perplex and discomfit legislators as judges have shown increasing sympathy for sex workers, persuaded, no doubt, by their atrociously high murder rates. Their plight reflects the biases that continue to plague a legal apparatus supposedly sworn to equal justice for all. Police, judges, and juries discount their complaints and their testimony on the grounds of character. Notoriously, when one woman complained in 1997 that Robert Picton had kidnapped and tried to kill her, the Crown stayed charges on the grounds that the woman was not a sufficiently credible witness. Freed, Picton resumed his serial killings of prostitutes. Public opinion, and consequently the state, cling to an insidious logic that sexualized women (a category that can stretch from sex workers to rape victims to politicians with cleavage) are ipso facto untrustworthy witnesses and threats to public morals, and so cannot speak up in their own defence. In a world where women sit at the bench, such logic cannot survive judicial review. Since the 1960s, organized feminist groups have made effective use of such state instruments as Royal Commissions and the Charter of Rights to get more women into the apparatus of government. The basic human rights of gay, lesbian, bisexual, and transgendered peoples, who also suffer from discrimination and disproportionate mortality, are also becoming more openly debated and defended.

Charter cases have also defined the state's powers of intervention into civil society. As well as working to rein in the state, by limiting the use of search and seizure for example, rights activists have also sought to expand the state's mandate to push equality ever further into civil society on a variety of fronts. In 1997, the Supreme Court ruled in favour of hospital translation services for deaf people, for example, and in 2012 in favour of intensive special education for those with learning disabilities (apparently reversing a 2004 decision to refuse special treatment for autistic children). A key question at stake is whether or not the Supreme Court could, or should, hardwire certain expenses into provincial budgets. The provinces strenuously insist that, in an age of scarce resources, allocation is a matter of politics, not rights. Half a century's experience of the welfare state has taught them that pleading poverty is the only reliable way to check demands for more rights and resources. The marketplace no longer exemplifies justice, but it still informs reasoning about justice and, sometimes, supplies a bottom line.

Property was excluded from the Charter of Rights on the understanding that it was adequately protected by the common law. Some consider this a major failing. But if the Charter does not apply to business and contractual relations, other kinds of legal conventions have done much to constitutionalize economic relations, especially the GATT (General Agreement on Trades and Tariffs), which provides general rules for reciprocal trade relations among the member countries (23 in 1947, 153 in 2008 under the umbrella of the World Trade Organization), and the special Canadian-American trade deals: the Auto Pact of 1965 and the North American Free Trade Agreement (NAFTA) of 1994. But special permission to breach the GATT was given in the case of not only Auto Pact but also agricultural subsidies and controls, sustained on the insistence of the United States, that remain deeply controversial among the member nations.

NAFTA (and the Canadian-American trade agreement that preceded it), marked the end of Macdonaldian protectionist economic policies in Canada. Economic nationalism ran high through most of the twentieth century. American companies created branch plants in Canada so that their products could be manufactured within the tariff wall, but those plants were controlled by and sent their profits largely to American headquarters, and most of their research and development spending occurred in the United States. The arguments for greater Canadianization of the Canadian economy ramped upwards during the 1960s as Canadians, rather than American or British expats, began, increasingly, to fill academic positions in Canadian universities and to make arguments for greater Canadianization in all reaches of Canadian life. The 1970s in particular saw a spate of nationalist and statist interventions into the Canadian economy, such as the creation of the Canada Development Corporation in 1971 and Petro Canada in 1975. The Conservative government elected in 1984 reversed these policies and sold off its stakes in these corporations at the same time as it pursued freer trade with the United States. It responded to pressure from cultural workers to exempt Canadian cultural industries from the open market, but, in practice, had already come round to the view that market success should be the primary criterion for identifying the Canadian culture that it would protect. Attempts to defy market pressures were continually denounced as elitist rejection of popular taste and inappropriate use of taxes paid by the many. The alliance between highbrows and statists, which had long sustained such institutions as the CBC and the NFB, gave way under the onslaught of populist cultural producers determined to seize a share of the state's bounty for themselves, leaving those institutions with no clear mandate in relation to the logic of the marketplace.

NAFTA comes close to providing the kinds of protections for property that the Charter provides for people. For example, it prohibits "discriminatory" expropriation of foreign-held investments without compensation at fair market value. The effect of NAFTA is to create a "right" to property that does not exist explicitly elsewhere in Canadian legislation and to push legal disputes over that property from legislatures to international panels that do not accommodate political concerns. Whereas the Charter permits the breach of rights where infringement can be "demonstrably justified," no such breach is recognized in NAFTA. NAFTA also permits companies to sue the Canadian government; previously they had had to act through political channels. In 1997, when the Canadian government banned the import and interprovincial transport of a gasoline additive, MMT, a company that produced the additive in Canada sued on the grounds that the act amounted to expropriation of their Canadian factory. Canada backed down, rescinded the legislation, and paid the company millions of dollars in compensation. The full implications of NAFTA, as of the Charter, are still being worked out, but there can be little doubt that they have altered the way that the state operates, and limited its ability to play umpire between individuals and corporations.

Even without NAFTA, the globalization of markets and capital has helped corporations to challenge and defy national standards of regulation and taxation. When one bank throws caution to the wind and engages in high-risk but enormously lucrative investments, other banks tend to follow, and they have proved themselves adept at arguing for lighter regulation so that they can better compete with counterparts abroad. Canadian banking interests lobbied for deregulation and mergers to keep them on par with American banks. Those kinds of pressures in favour of international competitiveness have tended towards lessening taxation and regulation on corporations. Canadian banks did not get the deregulation that they requested and, in retrospect, some of those bankers have breathed sighs of relief. John McCallum, one-time McGill University professor, subsequently chief economist at the Royal Bank of Canada, and proponent of a merger with the Bank of Montreal, later recalled, "The mentality of the day within the bank was that it wanted to grow up fast, kick global butt and grow up ... Having observed the financial crisis, I became completely converted to the view that Mr. Chrétien was right [and] that bank mergers were bad for Canada."[21] McCallum was disingenuously praising a government that he subsequently joined, and further evidence of regulatory restraint is scant. The profits garnered by the five top Canadian banks in the early decades of the twenty-first century were extraordinary: in 2007 they earned nearly $20 billion in profits between them, with McCallum's RBC topping the list at $5.5 billion. In 2014 RBC profits were closer to $9 billion. Canada remains, as it has always been, open to business and especially to big business, according to terms that are continually being renegotiated according to an international repertoire of possible choices.

The Canadian government still faces confrontations between big business and petty traders in such industries as fishing, farming, and logging, as its imperial forebears once did, and it often shows the same bias for deep pockets and lobbying power. In agriculture and fisheries, for example, state investment promoted economic concentration. By the mid-1980s, state subsidies accounted for 34 per cent of farmers' gross receipts, and the one-third of farmers who operated large farms accounted for 87 per cent of all production.[22] In the fisheries, that bias resulted in the near eradication of the cod in the once seemingly limitless Grand Banks. Local fishermen had long warned of decline among fish stocks, blaming the destructive new techniques of factory fishing, but economists and National Research Council–sponsored scientists developed complicated statistical models and theories that privileged the more "efficient" industrial methods. State-sponsored fishing and agriculture reflected the process of modernist reconstruction seen in other projects for improvement. Canadian companies, especially resource extraction companies, also exert similar pressures on a global scale. Canadian mining companies, for example, are at the forefront of a hemispheric mining boom, developing above a thousand different mining projects in Latin America in any given year, straining local environments and state capacities in the process.[23]

Business interests swagger in ways not seen for a century. "Business methods" challenge "the public good" as a mechanism for delivering public services, and they commandeer social science knowledge more efficiently than in the past. Private interests sponsor think tanks, often with government partners, to ensure that evidence supporting their interests – for example, downplaying the risks and highlighting the benefits of oil and gas development or salmon farming – appear prominently before the public. They draw on American-style, anti-statist ideologies to apply continual pressure upon Canadian authorities to favour downsizing and privatization in all aspects of collective life – ranging from deregulating industries and dismantling the remnants of protectionism, to introducing market incentives into health care and education. Left-leaning organizations support think tanks of their own, such as the Canadian Centre for Policy Alternatives (established in 1980), whose importance has grown as unions have lost some of their political weight. Critics complain that the race to the regulatory bottom threatens environmental protections and workplace safety, and may be blamed for such disasters as the Lac-Mégantic derailment that destroyed the town's centre. These critics advocate a robust public good, one that can encompass long-term considerations that elude commercial logic, such as flood protection or the prevention of environmental degradation. Both sides draw heavily upon science to prove their point – in think tanks, government departments, and universities – with considerable crossover between them. Both sides accuse the other of undiluted patronage and corruption and promise they will purge government of collusion; neither seems able to do so.

Governments can slant the debate by privileging scientific research that supports economic development and cutting funds for the rest. In the emerging world of "post-expertise," heartfelt conviction often trumps scholarly studies. Downsizing, thus, tends both to fulfil and to confirm neoconservative arguments. Liberal Prime Minister Jean Chrétien and his finance minister and successor as prime minister, Paul Martin, responded to such pressures when they cut government spending during the 1990s and early 2000s, so that it fell from 53 per cent of GDP in 1992 to 36 per cent in 2006. The latter figure is less than what Britain or France spend and close to what the United States spends. Still, at the end of the twentieth century, slightly more than one in a hundred Canadians worked for the federal government, twice the rate of a century earlier. When other levels of government are added, the figure is closer to about one in thirty Canadians, with provincial and municipal governments providing for 40 per cent and 20 per cent of the employment respectively. Canada's remains a big state, though at the low end for industrialized countries. Its social welfare investment also remains at the low end.

The size and scope of the state reflects popular attitudes towards it. Large numbers of Americans believe, viscerally, that too much government is "the principal obstacle to their personal fulfillment."[24] Their northern neighbours have been far less suspicious of government. Canada has been described as the most "politically correct" of nations,[25] suggesting an optimistic view that official and popular standards of morality, justice, or perhaps civility can approximate one another, with the state disciplining and censoring contrary opinions by means of human rights tribunals and laws against hate speech. Accusations of a left-wing, statist bias in Canadian courts, media, and universities proliferate in right-wing blogs and newspaper columns. Canadian economists, on the other hand, have tended to share the laissez-faire leanings of their American counterparts, as have a great many political scientists, many of them educated in the United States. The "Calgary School," in particular, has jocularly promised that "we will not cease from mental fight, till we have built a Hayekian Jerusalem in Canada's green and pleasant land."[26] It invokes classic liberal hostility to being "overgoverned" on matters such as hate speech or the mobility of capital and labour, but it has also learned to deploy the language of "the people" in new ways against itself. Without resorting to the blatantly sexist and racist language of the past, conservatives build populist protest parties on the language of purported "special interest groups," who have used the state to restrict the freedom of the people as a whole.

Canadian social democrats have formulated a wide variety of responses to this renewed language of classic liberalism. Philosophers such as Charles Taylor, James Tully, and Will Kymlicka have debunked classic theories of individual autonomy with new theories of collective culture and identity that have won international plaudits. Other scholars point to the many ways in which prejudice and exclusion continue to infuse and shape public life and to limit the formal and informal agency of visible minorities and women, who, for example, compose 10 per cent and 25 per cent respectively of Canadian parliamentarians at the time of writing – well below their respective proportions in the wider population. The critique of power extends beyond identity to material conditions. Whereas disparities in wealth shrank during the middle decades of the twentieth century, they began to expand after 1980, as redistributive tax policies were overturned, leaving a shrinking proportion of very wealthy people owning a growing proportion of the country's wealth. Wealthy individuals and corporations have successfully lobbied for lower corporate and personal taxes (top marginal rates have fallen almost by half since 1971), and they have moved profits into offshore shell companies and trust accounts worth billions annually, according to the advocacy group Canadians for Tax Fairness. The effect is compounded by severe job cuts in Revenue Canada. Without fiscal reform, Canada is in danger of becoming the kind of plutocracy that progressive-era social reformers feared and fought with admirable effectiveness. But Canada, too, is a tax haven, serving to widen those polarities on a global scale. Canada has signed many tax treaties designed to encourage Canadian investment abroad by exempting it from local taxation in those countries, but the effect upon those low-income countries is inadequate state revenue for even the most basic public services, such as sanitation or education.

Into the twenty-first century, the growing influence of Western Canada in Ottawa, and especially the small-state liberalism that has long characterized Alberta political discourse, gave a powerful impetus towards government downsizing. Stephen Harper's Conservative government has shown nostalgia for the traditional fiscal-military state, with policies apparently aimed to redirect spending away from social services and towards military defence, a move that also provides for the suppression of vaguely defined threats to public order within Canada. In the wake of the 9/11 attacks on the World Trade Centre and some egregious human rights violations in its wake, the potential for a return to the old fear-and-loathing campaigns and repressions kept civil rights activists awake at night; they saw not Jerusalem, but Sparta looming on the horizon. Indeed, the downsizing was highly selective: spending on law and order increased by $2.5 billion during the first six years of Harper's government. Social spending was being pushed back upon provincial governments in ways that Stephen Harper justified as a return to Canada's 1867 constitution. Macdonald predicted that direct taxation would weaken social spending. Knowing better, so to achieve the same effect, Harper devolved much of the escalating costs of law and order onto the provinces. Quebec alone responded by increasing social spending and avoided the rise in economic inequality seen elsewhere in Canada over the last quarter century. Quebec also jailed a smaller percentage of its population than do other provinces. But servicing its debt cost the province 10 per cent of its budget.

The Canadian state has never been either unambiguously repressive or free; it has always existed in a space between the two, a space defined as much by comparison with other regimes as by the stories that Canadians have told themselves about who and what they are. But the definition of freedom is irrevocably and paradoxically freighted with statism. To return to the language of Michael Mann, whereas early states had "power over" society, modern states have "power through" society. In such a world, there can be no real freedom from the state that is not also freedom from civil society and the dense network of institutions that interweave the two. The opposite of the organization of consent is not freedom but a gun. Government by consent transformed both state and society. The early modern state could mobilize violence against subjects and enemies, but it could not get ordinary citizens to do very much at its behest. In the modern state, because ordinary citizens believe that they have a measure of control over the apparatus of government, they cooperate more extensively with it and involve it in projects of self-fulfilment. The mixed economy of private and public welfare characterizes nearly all aspects of social, cultural, and economic activity, and it has generated trust and legitimacy for the state.

The state bolsters that trust by the extensive use of advertisement and propaganda. It has also had to forego some of its earlier powers of repression. State violence still occurs, of course, both domestically and internationally, but is rarely performed before the eyes of Canadian voters. Criminals are no longer executed, and prisoners' civil rights are upheld by state watchdogs as well as by such rights-based organizations as Amnesty International. Canada sends soldiers around the world to wage war and keep peace at the behest of transnational organizations such as NATO and the UN. But soldiers retain a whiff of frontier violence about them and, without close civil supervision, may run amok, as seen in Somalia in 1993, when a youth caught stealing was tortured to death by Canadian soldiers. Anti-war activists warn that military and paramilitary values, if nurtured, may rebound upon Canadians, resulting in harsh repression of Canadians at home. They point to public protests violently put down by riot police. Police forces in Canada can still summarily kill people that they think pose a lethal threat to the public or to themselves, and hundreds of people have died at their hands, possibly more than the 710 that were judicially executed before the death penalty was eliminated in 1976. Such violent interventions have provoked public outrage, government inquiries into police wrongdoing, and occasionally reforms. So, too, have such other casually lethal practices of law officers as the "starlight tour," whereby the police drive intoxicated persons to the outskirts of town, leaving them to walk back, sobered, or to die where they were dumped.

Most victims of the "starlight tour" have been Indigenous and male. The same casual racism among law enforcement officers has permitted an "epidemic" of deaths among Indigenous women, who are five times more likely than other women to be murdered and whose deaths are more likely to remain unsolved. The trust and legitimacy that characterizes most Canadians' relationship with their state does not characterize relations between Indigenous peoples and the state. With some notable exceptions reflecting numerical superiority, as in Nunavut, the Canadian state still comes perilously close to governing over rather than through Native peoples. The active delegitimization of popular opinion and political forms, practised for many decades, has been replaced by efforts to nurture the self-government of Indigenous peoples according to their own traditions and processes of selection, but past policies are not so easily negated and legitimacy is often very fragile. Criticism of a policy inevitably becomes criticism of a political form when that form is innovative and the stakes are high. Internecine quarrels at Kettle and Stony Point in Ontario, for example, delayed a long-overdue return of land appropriated for military training during the Second World War, as competing Chippewa and Potowatomi communities each claimed to be the rightful recipient. Perplexed federal authorities hemmed and hawed, and the result was violent altercation at Ipperwash Park in 1995. Cottagers were not the only local residents dismayed by the violence long before it turned fatal.

When blockades and barricades go up, government and media spokesmen insist on the contrast between law and criminality, legitimate state-sanctioned violence and illegitimate non-state violence. But no such binary exists. Communities are fractured and multifarious, and intermediaries on both sides regularly claim more authority and deploy more violence than either formal rules or community norms genuinely afford them. Some commentators celebrate Warrior Associations as representing "timeless Indigenous values,"[27] while others decry them for entrenching drug trafficking and gun violence on reserves. Meanwhile, the effect of such rhetorical polarization is to destabilize politics – and nowhere more so than on reserves, where rival political factions suddenly find they have national audiences for their mutual recriminations. The closest that contemporary Canada has come to armed uprising occurred in 1990 at Kanehsatà:ke, the former Sulpician mission north of Montreal, when persisting tensions over unresolved land claims erupted into a military stand-off. In the lead-up to that confrontation, rival claimants included a hereditary chiefs association that distrusted the elected chief, George Martin, and an association of Mohawk Warriors quickly assembled by Warriors from Kahnawà:ke and Akwasasne, that would, at the height of the confrontation, chase Martin off the reserve. A few days later, three federal and three provincial negotiators could not find common ground with the fifty-four Mohawk negotiators who claimed to represent the various interests and factions on reserve. In the end, the barricades went down and a deal was eventually done around the land, but the incident had far-reaching effects. The Canadian army, ignoring incitements to violence from many quarters, kept the peace, so that public opinion turned against the Warriors and for the Canadian government. But that public opinion also swung in favour of better redress of long-standing Indigenous grievances. Meanwhile, at Kanehsatà:ke, both policing and governing became harder to sustain in the aftermath of the confrontation. Accusations of unlawful violence, in short, tend to ramp up violence rather than restrain it. Occupations and blockades are not a new tactic and are not likely to disappear so long as the ownership of land is under dispute. Authorities would do better to emulate Macdonald's negotiated resolution of occupation in 1870 than his bloody resolution of 1885. Governments and protesters alike must woo broader public opinion if there is to be any lasting settlement, a fact recognized by Innu Chief Daniel Ashini, who was arrested and jailed multiple times for protesting and occupying military installations at Goose Bay: "If we have any power at all in Canada as colonized peoples, it is through our ability to win the hearts and minds of the general non-Aboriginal population, to put pressure on government people who make the policies that affect us and to take our issues to international publics."[28]

Other social groups also suffer from state discrimination. Black people are more likely to be shot by police, and they are jailed disproportionately to their population. But Indigenous incarceration rates are even higher. The dysfunctional interface between Indigenous peoples and the state is exacerbated by the state's control over the very definition of an "Indian." Take, for example, the legislation, passed in 1985, that restored Indian status to women who married non-status men. It created tensions on reserves by expanding the populations eligible for federal grants, and it confirmed earlier legislation that deprived children of Indian status after two generations of intermarriage – the "second-generation cut-off rule." At age eighteen, these children are suddenly cut off from the resources available among their communities. Such distinctions in regard to legal identity and social security create confusion and hardship, as evidenced by one press report from 2009: "In one case, a couple with a sick child from a New Brunswick reserve ended up living on the streets of Halifax while their baby received care at the IWK Health Centre. Because the baby is considered non-Native, the First Nations and Inuit Health would not cover the costs. And because the family lived on a reserve, the province would not help the family. The parents used what money they could scrape together to take their baby to Halifax, and they did not have any money for accommodations or meals, so they lived on the streets in Halifax while their baby was receiving treatment."[29] The state remains a very blunt instrument for intervening into domestic arrangements and defining identity.

A mixed social economy of Indigeneity exists in Canada, whereby Aboriginal activists, state officials, and Aboriginal officials negotiate a whole range of political, economic, and cultural practices and institutions that are both public and private. But, like the public sphere in Quebec, this mixed social economy is to some degree distinct within the broader Canadian public sphere, and as a consequence the state has only a limited mandate from the Canadian public in regard to Indigenous affairs. A welfare-oriented interventionist state rests on social solidarity, but it remains only semi-constructed. Indigenous peoples across Canada have fought hard to have their claims recognized by the Canadian state and judiciary, and have secured no mean successes, no small degree of independent sovereignty, but the wholesale project of creating new statist forms that would integrate with existing statist forms, remains elusive. The Royal Commission on Aboriginal Peoples, created in 1991, exemplifies the difficulties: it proposed that the 542 Indigenous bands in Canada be reorganized into perhaps sixty distinct nations – defined by language, history, and geography – that would exercise core jurisdiction, alongside cross-national forms of negotiation and solidarity for broader shared questions ranging from resource exploitation to education. Indigenous response was sceptical, reflecting not only concerns over the price of such constitutional overhaul and disillusionment with previous failed overhauls, but also the pattern of Indigenous history, which has tended towards small and autonomous units of government. Frameworks for collective association beyond the merely local – grand confederacies and councils – never disappeared and sometimes gained new strength in dialogue with colonial officials and courts. But without stable links between personal and collective identity, such associations still rest upon consensus rather than coercion. They may fragment as opinions fragment – as, for example, when a dissenting person or village creatively claims an alternative tribal identity. The complicated, entangled histories of mobility, adoption, kinship, and alliance, of matrilineal versus patrilineal claims of descent, all lend legitimacy to such alternative claims. The state has laboured to attach fixed political identities to discrete groups situated in discrete locations. But the constructions of such broad ethnic or geographic labels as "the Stó:lo" or "Nunavik" do not fix civic identities and political imaginaries in the way that Western constitutional forms seem to require.

Still, to say that a political imaginary does not command consensus or that people have overlapping and competing identities and loyalties does not single out Indigenous identities from other identities. Such categories may be constructed, but they are not imperial fantasies imposed from above; they have become dialogical, subject to negotiation, and that negotiation is an important sign of progress. There is, of course, a danger that such negotiations may become politically or epistemologically lopsided. Anthropologist Paul Nadasdy observed such an outcome in conversations between the Kluane people of the southwestern Yukon and state-sponsored bureaucrats and academics, as they collectively tried to work out policies for hunting and conserving Ruby Range sheep. Bureaucrats and academics consistently overruled local conventions of knowledge with tendentious claims to more "scientific" standards. Still, reinforced by such scholars, Indigenous communities have found mechanisms to restore a measure of dialogical balance, forcing officials to heed local wisdom and experience. Slowly, not at all steadily, the lessons of contact continue to trickle upwards to moderate state rigidities.

If, as suggested earlier, "the work of governing and the activity of social citizenship" genuinely mirror one another, then the process of private and political negotiations over welfare, enterprise, resource management, and all the other concerns that bridge Indigenous and non-Indigenous lives probably go a long way towards creating a shared experience of governmentality. Perhaps they may, ultimately, precipitate Canadians towards something more genuinely collaborative than has hitherto existed. This collaborative culture will emerge only from broadly based organizations and institutions that can ratchet up the pressure upon the state to find real rather than legal solutions to pressing problems through the continuing contact zone. Canada has long sustained many such organizations, ranging from national entities such as Amnesty International to local ones such as Winnipeg's Indian and Metis Friendship Centre, established in 1951, which has been run by a shifting combination of status and non-status Winnipeggers and has aimed at helping an unhyphenated poor adapt to urban life; or Project North, a Victoria-based interchurch organization, established in 1978, which aimed at generating public support for land title negotiations. The Idle No More movement, begun in 2012 as a protest against unpopular federal revisions to a slew of laws governing Indigenous use of land and resources as well as their political organization, drew thousands of people across Canada to public demonstrations and other kinds of lobbying. Perhaps the powwows that bring crowds and income to reserves, proudly re-enacting and reasserting Indigenous traditions of mutual cooperation and self-government, also help to expand and renew a public identity that will continue to seek positive solutions to age-old problems of collective life in Canada.

If anything distinguishes the recent history of the Canadian state, it is the discovery – one continually reaffirmed with all the technical and cultural resources at our disposal – that we must collectively pursue such solutions. Early modern people did not think that way; their state existed primarily to uphold and protect itself against internal and external enemies. Enlightened, liberal philosophy and the political programs that followed in its wake pursued such questions at one remove, through the government of property. Understanding the state in that way enabled politicians to pursue a public weal oriented towards commercial progress and against the needs, wants, and desires of people without property, who remained largely beyond the pale of liberal governance. So things stood at the start of the century. But two things changed. Those needs, wants, and desires began to be powerfully advocated by unions and socialists, by social reformers and social scientists, always as part of a broader understanding of social and economic interconnectedness. Meanwhile, the state began to demand extraordinary acts of loyalty from the unpropertied and consequently had to incorporate them more fully into the polity. Gradually, the institutions constituting the state shifted from a core focus on property to a core focus on people, a process that culminated in the creation of universal welfare programs and the Charter of Rights and Freedoms. People came to trump property in significant ways.

None of this means that property and people are polarized opposites. Arguments from economic growth still provide the most persuasive guide for state intervention most of the time. Welfare programs define well-being in material terms. To say that property continues to pack a huge political wallop would be an understatement: property remains absolutely central to modern techniques of government and the bigger the holdings, the greater the political influence. But the state is no mere cover for, or conspiracy of, big business. For the state to serve the interests of the wealthy, it had to find ways of engaging with and securing the consent of everyone else as well. A top-down, instrumentalist view of the state (considered only as legitimate as it was useful to securing access to land and other resources) lost ground to a view of the state as constituted by the interests and identities of the whole people, albeit amidst continuing controversies over the meaning of *whole* and *people.* The people's state is one that provides ordinary people with some useful tools for banding together against those who would do them harm. The state at the end of the twentieth century isn't always very good at figuring out how to recognize and negotiate the complex needs, wants, and desires of its extraordinarily diverse citizenship, but it remains committed to the attempt.

Public opinion remains the key interface between the state and society. It constantly remakes itself with all the technologies of the day, technologies that stoke both free speech and state repression simultaneously. The Internet has massively expanded the scope of public debate, anti-state activism, and both commercial and political surveillance. It creates new perplexities and new frontiers in the process. The extraordinary proliferation of Internet pornography, for example, has led officials to throw up their hands and abandon any attempt to police consensual adult sexual relations, even as they must investigate such new non-consensual, commercialized genres as "revenge porn." The Internet has given new life to protest movements because it moves too quickly for easy state surveillance without substantial curtailment of civil liberties. Bureaucrats avidly try to scrutinize and curtail conversations, warning that this new frontier brings new dangers; activists are just as avid to curtail such interventions. The boundary between state and resistance to the state continues to evolve.

Conclusion

For most of human history in the regions that are now Canada, there was no state. Instead, there were non-centralized, non-institutional mechanisms for consulting, circulating, and enforcing norms and opinions. Some of those mechanisms worked to permit greater centralization and unity of purpose during times of crisis, such as war or dearth, while others worked to prevent them from taking institutionalized form. Europeans were shocked to discover just how free people could apparently be, and their own institutions of governance never quite recovered from that shock.

The European states that first sent feelers into Canada were only faintly represented through commercial interests and had little independent power to act. It wasn't clear what European crowns could gain from Canada in the way of wealth or territory, and they tended to refrain from direct exertion until commercial interests and settlers pushed them to intervene more directly. Something close to what a modern libertarian might celebrate as anarcho-capitalism largely reigned in Canada during the early period of contact, but the state hovered in the background as an irresistible theoretical and practical resource. Indigenous peoples sought diplomatic alliances, settlers and traders sought protection or enhancement of property and life, and all looked to the institutions of the European state to help them. Even the large corporations that enjoyed king-like powers always needed more power, more legitimacy, more enforcement than they could summon from their own resources. And so, reluctantly at first but with growing purpose, the British and French governments sent naval and military power and civil infrastructure to Canada, and they clawed back the freedoms and privileges that they had originally conceded to trading companies and the developing landed elite. Initially a place where rule of law was virtually suspended, Canada became a strategic testing ground for violent assertions of sovereignty. And, because British trade not in but around Canada became the most lucrative among the national trading interests competing there, and because British merchants and settlers were the most wealthy, influential, and politically empowered, the British state expanded its involvement in and protection for British trading interests to the point of military supremacy.

Politics and trade were always interlocked: merchants and officials constructed military, diplomatic, and civil apparatuses to enhance opportunities for traders, settlers, and other interests represented in and by their regimes. The big change that occurred was to make their claims something close to equal. Early modern states leaned on corporations for practical purposes but retained principled control over policy and over corporate charters. Politics and constitution making were the highest expression of human purpose; that was why most historians wrote political history. Trade, by contrast, had something mean and petty about it. But Enlightenment philosophers advanced a new vision of commerce as more fully representative of human agency and choice than the political sphere. Such a philosophy served to enhance popular agency and to tame the executive. It drew upon theories of "natural" freedom of barter, exchange, and deliberation, as observed in North America, alongside state-constructed civil liberties. As the public sphere of opinion and debate expanded, a kind of commercial logic infiltrated *raison d'état*, or reason of state, to the point that it seemed as if there could be no reason of state prior to commercial logic, no meaningful sovereignty that was not expressed, ultimately, through trade, with military expressions of sovereignty only a kind of temporary stand-in for commercial power.

The Enlightenment theories of moderate British rule had no small appeal in reference to British colonies in North America, surrounded as they were by fearsomely martial enemies that reflected the extremes of authoritarianism and freedom. But a workable balance of freedom and authority was hard to find. Early modern mercantilism, which subordinated colonial to metropolitan needs, came to seem counter-productive: metropolitan restrictions and military investment impeded or nullified the trade and civil liberties upon which commercial expansion and imperial greatness rested. France gave up the attempt in 1760, leaving the British with, supposedly, a freer field to nurture their trading empire. But the threats to British rule never seemed to let up; borderlands reignited in flames and almost everywhere else local populations threatened to defy British constitutional forms unless they could, somehow, be reconstituted as liberal subjects. The change was most marked in regard to relations between the state and the Indigenous peoples in the interior of the continent. The early modern view was that, whether or not they were sovereign (a delicate theoretical and practical question), Indigenous peoples were autonomous and rational peoples who had to be met on their own terms according to a logic of diplomacy that could trump commercial logic. This understanding gave way to another: that these peoples must be transformed into modern, market-oriented peoples because there could be no autonomous agency or rationality and precious little sovereignty on any but market terms. And, more generally, as the state's authoritarian powers of governing over people declined in favour of infrastructural powers of governing through them, the reconstruction of civic identity in the image of an abstract and rational *homo economicus*, took on

apparent urgency. The fact that Canada was a colony oc-
casioned much of the apparent urgency. The metropolitan
state provided a kind of gold standard of statehood, one
that Canadian officials could only approximate. They could
not achieve the same legitimacy and security – try though
they might – with illiberal legislation that repressed the liberties it supposedly pursued.

The Enlightenment project to restrain tyranny by empow-
ering commercial agency worked better at home than in the
colonies. Both British and colonial states were in the hands
of patrician office holders, bound by shared, elite values. But
British North American patricians owed more to commerce
and land speculation than they owed to birth, descent, or
education and, in any confrontation between tradition and
commerce, it wasn't hard to predict which would win the
day. And whereas the British government was broadly accountable to the population by means of elections, colonial
patricians were, in practice, unaccountable to either the
imperial Parliament or colonial populations. They bent the
rule of law to serve their interests and privileges, abusing
their critics and protecting one another from prosecution.
They defended themselves by insisting on the local population's unfitness for self-government. But they discredited
themselves, and the British government discredited itself
when it tried to uphold them. Within a few years of harshly
repressing violent uprising, Whitehall abandoned them to
their critics, as part of a larger disengagement from British
North American commitments more generally. As liberalizing reformers took control over political institutions in the
mid-nineteenth century, they reshaped the state to make it
responsible to an economically and politically empowered
public, which they laboured to reconstruct through public
education and commercial development.

The liberalizing state in the nineteenth century was dedicated to protecting and enhancing public agency or power,
but it understood that agency primarily in terms of property, as the measure of reason and as the really important

interest at stake most of the time. The result was an alliance of the propertied against the unpropertied, and one that "liberal conservative" politicians, fearful of democracy, worked to expand in the decades after responsible government. They built a confederation on the strength of this consensus but, by the end of the century, their project of rule was unravelling. Property proved too blunt an instrument to negotiate complex social relationships. Moreover, too many people without property were proving impervious to liberal rule. Whether disenfranchised by their class, race, or gender, whether unable or unwilling to gain a foothold in the propertied classes, they seemed to threaten the propertied, especially when they turned to radical alternate theories of governance. Wide-ranging, left-wing movements began to challenge strictly liberal expectations of the state and to insist that it must represent more than simply the interests of the propertied.

The flip side of property was poverty; the focus on the one generated increasing scrutiny of the other, and gradually poverty began to force itself on the national consciousness as a political problem. Schools, families, charity, and market incentives – all of these classic liberal solutions to poverty failed to address it. The early twentieth century reached for a new solution in an alliance between academe and officialdom. The emergence of universities created new categories of experts, inside and outside of the civil service, who brandished new theories and instruments to measure and manage individual, domestic, and national well-being. These experts took upon themselves much of the onus for economic planning, drawing it away from households that proved, in dire times, unequal to the burden. They articulated a conviction that the "rights" of the propertied wouldn't ever be fully safe and the state wouldn't ever be stable without security for those without property, and that Victorian mechanisms to restore the decaying distinction between propertied and unpropertied only increased the precariousness of the system as a whole. Academics and bureaucrats initially clung to "business methods" to legitimate their arguments, but, amidst the cataclysms of the early to mid-twentieth century, they grew increasingly distrustful of the increasingly strident business classes and began to advocate a more autonomous public good, often defined in terms of its distance from commercial logic.

Slowly but steadily these new political and social interests turned the ship of state around to make it socially engaged, intimately involved in the negotiation of everyday life. The idea of the state – as power, as legitimation – was and remains too attractive not to be dragged into all the kinds of disputes that the flesh is heir to. The state's growing interest in and power over private life lurched between efforts to nurture and relieve families and efforts to institutionalize or deport those it deemed threatening or unfit for citizenship. Hard times during the interwar years made for hard choices. Postwar prosperity permitted freer distribution of public resources, as well as nurturing a civil rights movement that gradually began to rein in the worst of the state's excesses. The introduction of a Charter of Rights and Freedoms reflected these developments, and its effect has been to further involve the state in everyday life. Canadians ardently pursue freedom *from* abusive state interventions, such as censorship or unreasonable confinement, but they also pursue freedom *to* achieve personal security and fulfilment, and they insist that the state second their efforts. The state emerged largely in response to the demands of ordinary people, who sought protection from violence; security in the means of their subsistence; and food, lodging, or medicine in time of crisis; and who also built up institutions to make themselves heard in public debates. Populist politicians converted popular need into elite consolidation, but reforms in favour of accountability and transparency have sometimes reined in corruption (though an old-fashioned, Tammany Hall–style populist may still nudge things the other way). Non-state organizations could supply many needs, but popular demand for sustenance or protection, over time, exceeded what market forces or charity could provide. The fact that those market forces were often, in fact and in popular imagination, ostentatiously American owned tended to strengthen the hand of the statists. Time and again, fear of the Americanization of important, newly developing institutions such as schools, railways, and media precipitated statist intervention.

Can we read into this story any logic peculiar to the state, any sense of what it means to see like a state? Such language is fallacious: the state is a process more than an institution. It is a shifting series of mechanisms and places to negotiate interests and identities that exist, first, in the wider social world. An older view of the state as disseminating something from "state central" doesn't work. The state is made up in the field, ad hoc, as much as it is made up at the political centre. Teleology is a necessary principle to understand the theory of the state but a bad guide to its actual operations. The modern state is too big to have singularity of purpose or agency, and the boundary between state and non-state remains fuzzy. A new study of the Winnipeg General Strike exemplifies the argument. The authors note that the strike was seen as a moment when civil society challenged the sovereignty and legitimacy of the state and was violently routed as a consequence. But here "state repression" needs a series of qualifiers.

In fact, large tracts of the "state" were either technically neutral (the provincial government, which held the monopoly on criminal prosecutions) or predisposed towards a negotiated settlement (the City of Winnipeg, represented by Mayor Gray). Even the federal government, represented by the acting Minister of Justice Arthur Meighen and Labour Minister Gideon Robertson, had to be prodded along – now willingly, now with misdirection – so that onlookers would be convinced that the *state* had ordered the prosecutions of the Strike leaders. Who held the prod? The shadowy Citizens' Committee of 1000 and the former boy-mayor of Winnipeg, Alfred J. Andrews.

But it wasn't enough to embody the state; Andrews had to embody the public as well. "Having started its own newspaper, and having tried to *be* 1000 citizens, the Citizens understood that if they chorused loudly in the public sphere, the federal government would hear the 'public' applauding all action against the Strike, including iffy Criminal Code prosecutions" (that the anti-strike *Winnipeg Free Press* repudiated). An orchestrated campaign of telegrams followed.[1] As this example shows, every time we use the word "the state" we are taking a shortcut and making a mystification of social and political relationships that closer study can and should debunk. The question of what warrants the invocation of state authority – when the claim is legitimately made and when it is not – must ultimately come down to local circumstances and cannot usefully be summed up in a short overview. One person can claim to be an important agent of the state; whether or not that claim is or becomes true can depend on their powers of persuasion.

Persuasion, intersubjectivity, consensus: all these features characterize the modern state, and they owe something of their current legitimacy to the examples provided by the earliest forms of governance in Canada. Authority is constantly renegotiated at all levels according to a wide range of claims to warrant. Defiance is always possible and may or may not lead to outlaw status, depending on those powers of persuasion. Abortionist Henry Morgentaler persuaded juries that abortion was not a criminal matter for state repression. Because juries refused to convict, legislators had to change the law of the land. Jury nullification of this sort dates back to the Conquest. Other kinds of laws are regularly flouted for a variety of reasons. The state does act to congeal social, economic, and political relationships, but it does not petrify them.

Nonetheless, having a state in place does frame some choices and determine certain outcomes. People expect violence to be repressed and property to be secure, and to that end they tolerate a large apparatus of repression and the commandeering of large proportions of that same property. But so multifarious is the state that it isn't possible to insist upon any one bias in its evolution. Big states probably privilege big business, but grass-roots organizations that command state resources may tend to fight those privileges. And there is a logic of devolution, not just of agency within civil society but even within the state itself, down to something like grass roots. During the period between the wars, a time of extraordinary state proliferation, one Royal Commission counted 7,000 taxing authorities in Saskatchewan alone, or one for every 137 people, as compared to one per 450 in Ontario and one per 285 in Nova Scotia. At that time, the logic of devolution was one of specialization, but more recently the logic of devolution has led regional or provincial leaders to advocate the formation of independent new states, such as a sovereign Quebec or a sovereign Atikamekw First Nation in northern Quebec. At some point, the differences between the claims of the state and the claims of the individual may converge. We are not at that point, but it seems clear that, over time, the claims of individual right and of state warrant have grown closer together, a process that finds fullest expression in and through the Charter of Rights. Conservative scholars denounce the Charter precisely for that reason, because it devolves power away from legislatures.

Canadian history is characterized by contrapuntal melodies of freedom and coercion, centre and periphery, liberality and illiberality. It is Bach, not Beethoven: the dissonance cannot resolve into a glorious harmony of joy. Canadians want vastly different things from their state and their society. They cannot even agree on the differences between freedom and coercion. One person might see in the short account provided here an evolution from freedom through extremes of repression to something approximating the greatest freedom possible within a stated society; all those differences between peoples in Canada, long the occasion for repressive legislation, have more recently encouraged a politics of multiculturalism and a willingness to experiment with new kinds of devolution of powers and even sovereignty. Another person might see a growing corporate influence on the state as the central plotline. Still another, perhaps our libertarian, might call it a transition from an autonomy that was possible under a limited state to a tyranny of the majority within an all-too-powerful state. Discourse about the Canadian state will always be enveloped by a language of "failure" among those who seek ultimate legitimation for their beliefs or for something called "Canada." But that discourse may be no good guide to the success of the Canadian state as a mechanism for negotiating collectively. And, at bottom, if the state is nothing else, it remains, in principle, a pledge to negotiate collectively in ways that can never entirely be reduced to an army or a marketplace.

Notes

Introduction

1 Theda Skocpol, "Bringing the State Back In: Strategies of Analysis in Current Research," in *Bringing the State Back In*, ed. Peter B. Evans, Dietrich Rueschemeyer, and Theda Skocpol (Cambridge: Cambridge University Press, 1985), 4.

Chapter One

1 R.G. Thwaites, ed., *The Jesuit Relations and Allied Documents: Travels and Explorations of the Jesuit Missionaries in New France 1610–1791*: vol. 2, *Acadia 1612–1614*, 71; vol. 7, *Québec, Hurons and Cape Breton 1634–1635*, 19; Chrestien Le Clercq, *New Relation of Gaspesia*, trans. William F. Ganong (Toronto: Champlain Society, 1910), 242.

2 Quoted in Ter Ellingson, *The Myth of the Noble Savage* (Berkeley: University of California Press, 2001), 29.

3 Michel de Montaigne in *The Essays of Michel de Montaigne*, trans. Charles Cotton (London: Reeves and Turner, 1877), 255.

4 Quoted in Wendy Wickwire, "Stories from the Margins: Toward a More Inclusive British Columbia Historiography," in *Myth and Memory: Stories of Indigenous-European Contact*, ed. John Sutton Lutz (Vancouver: UBC Press, 2007), 137.

5 Quoted in Daniel K. Richter, *Facing East from Indian Country: A Native History of Early America* (Cambridge, MA: Harvard University Press, 2001), 148.

6 Theodore Binnema, "Allegiances and Interests: Niitsitapi (Blackfoot) Trade, Diplomacy, and Warfare, 1806–1831," *The Western Historical Quarterly* 37, no. 3 (2006): 330.

7 Michael Mann, *The Sources of Social Power: A History of Power from the Beginning to A.D. 1760*, vol. 1 (Cambridge: Cambridge University Press, 1986), 37, 67.

8 Bruce Trigger, *The Children of Aataentsic: A History of the Huron People to 1660* (Montreal: McGill-Queen's University Press, 1976), 55.

9 Quoted in Carole Blackburn, *Harvest of Souls: The Jesuit Missions and Colonialism in North America, 1632–1650* (Montreal: McGill-Queen's University Press, 2004), 86.

10 George M. Dawson, "The Haidas," *Harper's New Monthly Magazine* 65 (August 1882): 407.

11 Jon Parmenter, *The Edge of the Woods: Iroquoia, 1534–1701* (East Lansing: Michigan State University Press, 2010), 155.

12 Thomas Hobbes, *Leviathan* (Oxford: Oxford University Press, 1946), 86.

13 Roy Porter, *The Creation of the Modern World: The Untold Story of the British Enlightenment* (New York: Norton, 2001), 209.

14 Quoted in Peter Linebaugh and Markus Rediker, *The Many-Headed Hydra: Sailors, Slaves, Commoners, and the Hidden History of the Revolutionary Atlantic* (Boston: Beacon Press, 2000), 68.

15 Quoted in Robert Launay, ed., *Foundations of Anthropological Thought: From Classical Antiquity to Early Modern Europe* (New York: John Wiley, 2010), 155.

16 Baron de Lahontan, *New Voyages to North-America* (1703; reprint, Chicago: A.C. McClurg, 1905), ii, 421.

17 Richard White, *The Middle Ground: Indians, Empires, and Republics in the Great Lakes Region, 1650–1815*, 2nd ed. (Cambridge: Cambridge University Press, 2010), 52.

Chapter Two

1 Quoted in Janice E. Thomson, *Mercenaries, Pirates, and Sovereigns: State-Building and Extraterritorial Violence in Early Modern Europe* (Princeton: Princeton University Press, 1994), 43.

2 Peter Pope, *Fish into Wine: The Newfoundland Plantation in the Seventeenth Century* (Chapel Hill: University of North Carolina Press, 2004), 29–30.

3 Lauren Benton, *A Search for Sovereignty: Law and Geography in European Empires, 1400–1900* (Cambridge: Cambridge University Press, 2010), 158.

4 Bernard Durand, "Royal Power and its Legal Instruments in France, 1500–1800," in *Legislation and Justice*, ed. Antonio Padoa-Shioppa (Oxford: Clarendon Press, 1997), 292.

5 André Vachon, "The Administration of New France," in *Dictionary of Canadian Biography*, vol. 2 (Toronto: University of Toronto Press, and Quebec: Presses de l'Université Laval, 1969), xviii.

6 Pope, *Fish into Wine*, 255.

7 Yves F. Zoltvany, "Michel Bégon de la Picardière," in *Dictionary of Canadian Biography*, vol. 3 (Toronto: University of Toronto Press, and Quebec: Presses de l'Université Laval, 1974), 60.

8 J.F. Bosher, "Government and Private Interests in New France," *Canadian Public Administration* 10, no. 2 (1967): 250.

9 Peter N. Moogk, *La Nouvelle France: The Making of French Canada: A Cultural History* (East Lansing: Michigan State University Press, 2000), 72.

10 Naomi Griffiths, *From Migrant to Acadian: A North American Border People 1604–1755* (Montreal: McGill-Queen's University Press), 30.

11 Harold Innis, *The Fur Trade in Canada* (1930; rev. ed., Toronto: University of Toronto Press, 1956), 112–13.

12 Moogk, *La Nouvelle France*, 83–5.

13 Louise Dechêne, *Le Peuple, l'État et la Guerre au Canada sous le Régime français* (Montreal: Boréal, 2008), 286.

14 John Hector St. John de Crevecour, quoted in Elizabeth Mancke, *The Fault-Lines of Empire: Political Differentiation in Massachusetts and Nova Scotia, c. 1760–1830* (New York: Routledge, 2005), 10.

15 Quoted in James B. Collins, *The State in Early Modern France* (Cambridge: Cambridge University Press, 1995), 121.

16 Nancy Christie, "'He is the master of his house': Families and Political Authority in Counterrevolutionary Montreal," *William and Mary Quarterly* 70, no. 2 (2013): 346.

17 Quoted in John Clarke, *Land, Power, and Economics on the Frontier of Upper Canada* (Montreal: McGill-Queen's University Press, 2001), 47.

18 André Lachance, *La justice criminelle du roi au Canada au XVIIIe siècle: Tribunaux et officiers* (Quebec: Presses de l'Université Laval, 1978) and *Crimes et criminels en Nouvelle-France* (Montreal: Boréal, 1984).

19 Frank Trentmann, "The 'British' Sources of Social Power: Reflections on History, Sociology, and Intellectual Biography," in *An Anatomy of Power: The Social Theory of Michael Mann*, ed. John A. Hall and Ralph Schroeder (Cambridge: Cambridge University Press, 2006), 290.

20 P.J. Cain and A.G. Hopkins, *British Imperialism: Innovation and Expansion, 1688–1914* (London: Longman, 1993), 41.

21 Simcoe quoted in J.K. Johnson, *Becoming Prominent: Regional Leadership in Upper Canada, 1791–1841* (Montreal: McGill-Queen's University Press, 1989), 120; Craig quoted in Gilles Gallichan, *Livre et politique au Bas-Canada, 1791–1841* (Sillery, QC: Septentrion, 1991), 60.

22 David Hume, "Of the First Principles of Government," in *Essays* (London: John Long, 1742).

23 Quoted in F. Murray Greenwood, *Legacies of Fear: Law and Politics in Quebec in the Era of the French Revolution* (Toronto: University of Toronto Press, 1993), 119.

24 Quoted in Daniel Francis and Toby Morantz, *Partners in Fur: A History of the Fur Trade in Eastern James Bay, 1600–1870* (Montreal: McGill-Queen's University Press, 1983), 23.

25 Quoted in Hamar Foster, "Law and Necessity in Western Rupert's Land and Beyond, 1670–1870," in *Laws and Societies in the Canadian Prairie West, 1670–1940*, ed. Louis A. Knafla and Jonathan Swainger (Vancouver: UBC Press, 2005), 73.

26 Alan Taylor, *American Colonies: The Settling of North America* (New York: Penguin, 2001), 395.

27 Quoted in David Milobar, "The Origins of British-Quebec Merchant Ideology: New France, the British Atlantic, and the Constitutional Periphery, 1720–1770," *Journal of Imperial and Commonwealth History* 24, no. 3 (1996): 373.

28 Quoted in Jan de Vries, *The Industrious Revolution: Consumer Behavior and the Household Economy, 1650 to the Present* (Cambridge: Cambridge University Press, 2008), 67.

Chapter Three

1 See the collection Jean-François Constant and Michel Ducharme, eds., *Liberalism and Hegemony: Debating the Canadian Liberal Revolution* (Toronto: University of Toronto Press, 2009).

2 Brian Young, "Positive Law, Positive State: Class Realignment and the Transformation of Lower Canada, 1815–1866," in *Colonial Leviathan: State Formation in Mid-Nineteenth-Century Canada*, ed. Allan Greer and Ian Radforth (Toronto: University of Toronto Press, 1992), 52–3.

3 Library and Archives Canada, MG 24-B19, Brown Chamberlin papers, Macdonald to Chamberlin, 20 January 1856.

4 André Siegfried, *The Race Question in Canada*, trans. Anon. (1907; rev. ed., Toronto: McClelland and Stewart, 1966), 142–3.

5 Egerton Ryerson, "Proposed School Legislation Suggested in Doctor Ryerson's Special Report on the State of Education in Europe and the United States, 1868," in *Historical and Other Papers and Documents Illustrative of the Educational System of Ontario, 1858–1876*, ed, J.G. Hodgins (Toronto: L.K. Cameron, 1911), iv, 90.

6 Quoted in Bryan Palmer, "Popular Radicalism and the Theatrics of Rebellion: The Hybrid Discourse of Dissent in Upper Canada in the 1830s," in *Transatlantic Subjects: Ideas, Institutions, and Social Experience in Post-Revolutionary British North America*, ed. Nancy Christie (Montreal: McGill-Queen's University Press, 2008), 424–5.

7 Michael Mann, *The Sources of Social Power*, vol. 2 (Cambridge: Cambridge University Press, 1993), 25.

8 Provincial Archives of Nova Scotia, RG34–313: A13, Longard, 13 December 1866; A21, Longard, 10 April 1877; A18, Michael Burgess, 8 August 1870; Victoria *British Colonist*, 8 November 1881.

9 Patrick Joyce, *The State of Freedom: A Social History of the British State since 1800* (Cambridge: Cambridge University Press, 2013), 122.

10 Joseph Howe, *Speech of the Hon. Joseph Howe on Inter-Colonial Railroads and Colonization* (Halifax: Richard Nugent, 1851), 5.

11 Richard White, *Railroaded: The Transcontinentals and the Making of Modern America* (New York: Norton, 2011), 59.

12 Siegfried, *Race Question in Canada*, 35.

13 British *Hansard*, House of Lords, 19 February 1839, 600.

14 Gustavus Myers, *History of Canadian Wealth* (Chicago: Charles H. Kerr and Co., 1914), 265; Michael Bliss, *Right Honourable Men: The Descent of Canadian Politics from Macdonald to Mulroney* (Toronto: HarperCollins, 1994), 22.

15 Union of Canadian Municipalities, W.D. Lighthall Papers, Rare Books and Special Collections, McGill University, MS809 Box 1, file 12 (clippings from 1905), *Municipal World* 1 (1905), 89.

16 Jason Opal, "General Jackson's Passports: Natural Rights and Sovereign Citizens in the Political Thought of Andrew Jackson, 1780s–1820s," *Studies in American Political Development* 27 (2013): 69–85.

17 Quoted in Bill Waiser, "The White Man Governs: The 1885 Indian Trials," in *Canadian State Trials, Volume III: Political Trials and Security Measures, 1840–1914*, ed. Barry Wright and Susan Binnie (Toronto: University of Toronto Press, 2009), 475.

18 Quoted in Frank H. Underhill, *In Search of Canadian Liberalism* (Toronto: Macmillan, 1960), 16.

19 *Hansard*, House of Commons, 14 April 1882, 894.

20 Michel Foucault, *Society Must Be Defended*, ed. Mauro Bertani and Alessandro Fontana, trans. David Macey (New York: Picador, 2003), 33; *Power/Knowledge: Selected Interviews and Other Writings, 1972–1977*, ed. and trans. Colin Gordon (New York: Pantheon, 1980), 101–2.

21 Quoted in Sidney L. Harring, *White Man's Law: Native People in Nineteenth-Century Canadian Jurisprudence* (Toronto: University of Toronto Press, 1998), 51.

22 Peter Jones, *History of the Ojebway Indians* (London: A.W. Bennett, 1861), 243; "Report on the Affairs of the Indians in Canada," *Journals of the Legislative Assembly of Canada 1847*, Appendix T (unpag).

23 John S. Lutz, *Makúk: A New History of Aboriginal-White Relations* (Vancouver: UBC Press, 2008), 254; John L. Tobias, "Protection, Civilization, Assimilation: An Outline History of Canada's Indian Policy," in *The Prairie West: Historical Readings*, ed. R.D. Francis and H. Palmer (Edmonton: University of Alberta Press, 1992), 210.

24 Quoted in Michael Bliss, *A Living Profit: Studies in the Social History of Canadian Business, 1883–1911* (Toronto: McClelland and Stewart, 1974), 74.

25 Ian McKay, "Strikes in the Maritimes, 1901–1914," *Acadiensis* 13, no. 1 (1983): 27.

Chapter Four

1 Sir William Jones quoted in Phillips Thompson, *The Politics of Labor* (New York, 1887), 51, and in *Some Thoughts and Suggestions on Municipal Reform in British Columbia* by W.J. Walker (New Westminster, 1891).

2 Andrée Désilets, "Sir Hector-Louis Langevin," *Dictionary of Canadian Biography*, vol. 13 (Toronto: University of Toronto Press, and Quebec: Presses de l'Université Laval, 1994), 572.

3 *Canadian Municipal Journal* 4, no. 10 (1908): 453–6.

4 Quoted in Albert Luther Ellis III, "The Regressive Era: Progressive Era Tax Reform and the National Tax Association – Roots of the Modern American Tax Structure" (PhD dissertation, Rice University, 1991), II, 354.

5 *Report of the Ontario Commission on Unemployment* (Toronto: King's Printer, 1916), 12.

6 City of Saint John, NB, *Report of the Civic Assessment Commission* (September 1916), 64–5.

7 Canadian War Poster Collection at McGill University: http://digital.library.mcgill.ca/warposters/english/

8 Andrew Macphail, quoted in Daniel Coleman, *White Civility: The Literary Project of English Canada* (Toronto: University of Toronto Press, 2006), 176.

9 Quoted in Nancy Christie, *Engendering the State: Family, Work, and Welfare in Canada* (Toronto: University of Toronto Press, 2000), 112.

10 Gregory P. Marchildon, *Profits and Politics: Beaverbrook and the Gilded Age of Canadian Finance* (Toronto: University of Toronto Press, 1996), 115.

11 Douglas Owram, *The Government Generation: Canadian Intellectuals and the State, 1900–1945* (Toronto: University of Toronto Press, 1986), 242.

12 J.M. Keynes, "Inflation and Deflation," in *Essays in Persuasion* (1923; repr., London: Rupert Hart-Davis, 1951), 104. Emphasis in the original.

13 Frank Underhill, "The Canadian Party System in Transition," *Canadian Journal of Economics and Political Science* 9, no. 3 (1943): 306.

14 *Edmonton World*, 12 December 1910.

15 Shirley Tillotson, *Contributing Citizens: Modern Charitable Fundraising and the Making of the Welfare State, 1920–66* (Vancouver: UBC Press, 2008), 23.

16 Quoted in Ian Mosby, *Food Will Win the War: The Politics, Culture, and Science of Food on Canada's Home Front* (Vancouver: UBC Press, 2014), 61.

17 Expert quoted in Dominique Marshall, *The Social Origins of the Welfare State: Québec Families, Compulsory Education, and Family Allowances, 1940–1955*, trans. Nicola Doone Danby (Waterloo, ON: Wilfrid Laurier University Press, 2006), 76; King quoted in Alvin Finkel, *Social Policy and Practice in Canada: A History* (Waterloo, ON: Wilfrid Laurier University Press, 2006), 139.

18 Quoted in Richard Simeon, *Federal-Provincial Diplomacy: The Making of Recent Policy in Canada* (Toronto: University of Toronto Press, 2006), 89.

19 Quoted in Dale C. Thomson, *Jean Lesage and the Quiet Revolution* (Toronto: Macmillan, 1984), 401.

20 Julie Guard, "Women Worth Watching: Radical Housewives in Cold War Canada," in *Whose National Security? Canadian State Surveillance and the Creation of Enemies*, ed. Gary Kinsman, Dieter K. Buse, and Mercedes Steedman (Toronto: Between the Lines, 2000), 83, 80.

21 *Hansard*, House of Commons, 14 February 2012.

22 Grace Skogstad, "The Two Faces of Canadian Agriculture in a Post-Staples Economy," *Canadian Political Science Review* 1, no. 1 (2007): 26–41.

23 McGill Research Group Investigating Canadian Mining in Latin America: http://micla.ca.

24 Jeff Madrick, *Age of Greed: The Triumph of Finance and the Decline of America, 1970 to the Present* (New York: Knopf, 2011), 124.

25 Stephen Jewell, "Niall Ferguson the History Boy," *The New Zealand Herald*, 6 May 2011; quoted in C.P. Champion, "Putting the Empire Back into Canada," *Dorchester Review* 2, no. 1 (2012).

26 Tom Flanagan (paraphrasing William Blake), letter to the editor, *Literary Review of Canada* (December 2010). Friedrich Hayek's theories inform most contemporary anti-statism.

27 Taiaiake Alfred and Lana Lowe, *Warrior Societies in Contemporary Indigenous Communities*, commissioned research paper (Toronto: Ipperwash Inquiry, 2005), 37.

28 Quoted in *Blockades or Breakthroughs? Aboriginal Peoples Confront the Canadian State*, ed. Yale D. Belanger and P. Whitney Lackenbauer (Montreal: McGill-Queen's University Press, 2014), 150.

29 Quoted in Lisa Perley-Dutcher and Stephen Dutcher, "At Home But Not at Peace: The Impact of Bill C-31 on Women and Children of the Tobique First Nation," in *Making Up the State: Women in Twentieth-Century Atlantic Canada*, ed. Janet Guildford and Suzanne Morton (Fredericton: Acadiensis Press, 2010), 207.

Conclusion

1 Reinhold Kramer and Tom Mitchell, *When the State Trembled: How A.J. Andrews and the Citizens' Committee Broke the Winnipeg General Strike* (Toronto: University of Toronto Press, 2010), 4, 184.

Bibliography

Canadian history is deeply embedded in global history. I cannot include here the full roster of international and theoretical sources on the modern state and note only those that have directly informed the narrative. I also signal in a general way some large-scale general collections with multiple editors and authors:

Canadian Centenary Series. 19 vols. Toronto: McClelland and Stewart, 1963–86.

Dictionary of Canadian Biography. 15 vols. Toronto: University of Toronto Press, and Quebec: Presses de l'Université Laval, 1959–. http://www.biographi.ca/en/index.php

Essays in the History of Canadian Law. 96 vols. Toronto: Osgoode Society for Canadian Legal History, 1981–.

Thwaites, Reuben Gold, ed. *The Jesuit Relations and Allied Documents: Travels and Explorations of the Jesuit Missionaries in New France 1610–1791.* 71 vols. Cleveland: Burrows Brothers, 1896–1901. http://puffin.creighton.edu/jesuit/relations/

The Origins of the Modern State in Europe, 13th–18th Centuries. 7 vols. Oxford: Clarendon Press, 1995–2000.

Oxford History of the British Empire. 5 vols. Oxford: Oxford University Press, 1998–2000.

Oxford History of the British Empire Companion Series. 18 vols. Oxford: Oxford University Press, 2003–.

Chapter One

Beaulieu, Alain. *Les autochtones du Québec: Des premières alliances aux revendications contemporaines*. Rev. ed. Montreal: Fides, 2000.

Bérubé, Harold, Donald Fyson, and Léon Robichaud, eds. *370 ans de gouvernance montréalaise*. Montreal, Éditions Multi-Mondes, 2014.

Binnema, Theodore. "Allegiances and Interests: Niitsitapi (Blackfoot) Trade, Diplomacy, and Warfare, 1806–1831." *The Western Historical Quarterly* 37, no. 3 (2006): 327–49.

— *Common and Contested Ground: A Human and Environmental History of the Northwestern Plains*. Norman: Oklahoma University Press, 2001.

Blackburn, Carole. *Harvest of Souls: The Jesuit Missions and Colonialism in North America, 1632–1650*. Montreal: McGill-Queen's University Press, 2004.

Bohaker, Heidi. "'Nindoodema': The Significance of Algonquian Kinship Networks in the Eastern Great Lakes Region, 1600–1701." *William and Mary Quarterly* 3s 63, no. 1 (2006): 23–52.

Carlson, Keith Thor. *The Power of Place, the Problem of Time: Aboriginal Identity and Historical Consciousness in the Cauldron of Colonialism*. Toronto: University of Toronto Press, 2010.

Clastres, Pierre. *Society against the State*. Translated by Robert Hurley. New York: Zone, 1987.

Deslandres, Dominique. *Croire et faire croire: Les missions françaises au XVIIe siècle (1600–1650)*. Paris: Fayard, 2003.

Dickason, Olive P. *The Myth of the Savage and the Beginnings of French Colonialism in the Americas*. Edmonton: University of Alberta Press, 1984.

Ellingson, Ter. *The Myth of the Noble Savage*. Berkeley: University of California Press, 2001.

Feit, Harvey A. "The Construction of Algonquian Hunting Territories: Private Property as Moral Lesson, Policy Advocacy, and Ethnographic Error." In *Colonial Situations: Essays on the Contextualization of Ethnographic Knowledge*, edited by George W. Stocking, 109–34. Madison: Wisconsin University Press, 1991.

Fenton, William N. *The Great Law and the Longhouse: A Political History of the Iroquois Confederacy*. Norman: University of Oklahoma Press, 1998.

Francis, Daniel, and Toby Morantz. *Partners in Fur: A History of the Fur Trade in Eastern James Bay, 1600–1870*. Montreal: McGill-Queen's University Press, 1983.

Grabowski, Jan. "French Criminal Justice and Indians in Montreal, 1670–1760." *Ethnohistory* 43, no. 3 (1996): 405–29.

Grek-Martin, Jason. "Vanishing the Haida: George Dawson's Ethnographic Vision and the Making of Settler Space on the Queen Charlotte Islands in the Late Nineteenth Century." *Canadian Geographer* 51, no. 3 (2007): 373–98.

Havard, Gilles. *Empire et Métissages: Indiens et Français dans le Pays d'en Haut, 1660–1715*. Sillery, QC: Septentrion, 2003.

Labelle, Kathryn Magee. *Dispersed but Not Destroyed: A History of the Seventeenth-Century Wendat People*. Vancouver: UBC Press, 2013.

Lafitau, Joseph-François. *Customs of the American Indians Compared with the Customs of Primitive Times*. 2 vols. Originally published Paris, 1724. Edited and translated by William N. Fenton and Elizabeth L. Moore. Toronto: Champlain Society, 1974.

Lahontan, Louis Armand de. *New Voyages to North-America*. 1703. Reprint, Chicago: A.C. McClurg, 1905.

Launay, Robert, ed. *Foundations of Anthropological Theory: From Classical Antiquity to Early Modern Europe*. New York: John Wiley, 2010.

Lutz, John Sutton, ed. *Myth and Memory: Stories of Indigenous-European Contact*. Vancouver: UBC Press, 2007.

Manent, Pierre. *An Intellectual History of Liberalism*. Translated by Rebecca Balinski. Princeton: Princeton University Press, 1995.

Mann, Michael. *The Sources of Social Power*. 4 vols. Cambridge: Cambridge University Press, 1986–2012.

Marshall, Ingeborg. *A History and Ethnography of the Beothuk*. Montreal: McGill-Queen's University Press, 1996.

McGhee, Robert. *The Arctic Voyages of Martin Frobisher: An Elizabethan Adventure*. Montreal: McGill-Queen's University Press, 2001.

Mills, Antonia Curtze. *Eagle Down Is Our Law: Witsuwit'en Law, Feasts, and Land Claims.* Vancouver: UBC Press, 1994.

Muthu, Sankar. *Enlightenment against Empire.* Princeton: Princeton University Press, 2003.

Paul, Daniel N. *We Were Not the Savages: Collision Between European and Native American Civilizations.* 3rd ed. Black Point, NS: Fernwood, 2006.

Parmenter, Jon. *The Edge of the Woods: Iroquoia, 1534–1701.* East Lansing: Michigan State University Press, 2010.

Porter, Roy. *Enlightenment: Britain and the Creation of the Modern World.* London: Penguin, 2000.

Richter, Daniel, and James H. Merrell, eds. *Beyond the Covenant Chain: The Iroquois and their Neighbors in Indian North America, 1600–1800.* 1987. Reprint, Syracuse: Syracuse University Press, 2003.

Richter, Daniel K. *Facing East from Indian Country: A Native History of Early America.* Cambridge, MA: Harvard University Press, 2001.

Sayre, Gordon M. *Les Sauvages Americains: Representations of Native Americans in French and English Colonial Literature.* Chapel Hill: University of North Carolina Press, 1997.

Scott, Colin. "Hunting Territories, Hunting Bosses and Communal Production amongst Coastal James Bay Cree." *Anthropologica* 28, no. 1/2 (1986): 163–73.

Sioui, Georges. *For An Amerindian Autohistory: An Essay on the Foundations of a Social Ethic.* Montreal: McGill-Queen's University Press, 1992.

Tennant, Paul. *Aboriginal Peoples and Politics: The Indian Land Question in British Columbia, 1849–1989.* Vancouver: UBC Press, 1990.

Trigger, Bruce. *The Children of Aataentsic: A History of the Huron People to 1660.* Montreal: McGill-Queen's University Press, 1976.

White, Richard. *The Middle Ground: Indians, Empires, and Republics in the Great Lakes Region, 1650–1815.* Cambridge: Cambridge University Press, 1991.

Wicken, William C. *Mi'kmaq Treaties on Trial: History, Land, and Donald Marshall Junior.* Toronto: University of Toronto Press, 2002.

Willmott, Cory, and Kevin Brownlee. "Dressing for the Homeward Journey: Western Anishnaabe Leadership Roles Viewed through Two Nineteenth-Century Burials." In *Gathering Places: Aboriginal and Fur Trade Histories*, edited by Carolyn Podruchny and Laura Peers, 48–90. Vancouver: UBC Press, 2010.

Chapter Two

Allen, Douglas W., and Clyde G. Reed. "The Duel of Honor: Screening for Unobservable Social Capital." *American Law and Economics Review* 8, no. 1 (2006): 81–115.

Anderson, Perry. *Lineages of the Absolutist State*. London: Verso, 1974.

Banks, Kenneth J. *Chasing Empire across the Sea: Communications and the State in the French Atlantic 1713–1763*. Montreal: McGill-Queen's University Press, 2006.

Banner, Stuart. *How the Indians Lost their Land: Law and Power on the Frontier*. Cambridge, MA: Harvard University Press, 2005.

Bannister, Jerry. *The Rule of the Admirals: Law, Custom and Naval Government in Newfoundland, 1699–1832*. Toronto: University of Toronto Press, 2003.

Beaulieu, Alain. "'An equitable right to be compensated': The Dispossession of the Aboriginal Peoples of Quebec and the Emergence of a New Legal Rationale (1760–1860)." *Canadian Historical Review* 94, no. 1 (2013): 1–27.

Beaulieu, Alain, Stéphan Gervais, and Martin Papillon, eds. *Les autochtones et le Québec: Des premiers contacts au Plan Nord*. Montreal: Presses de l'Université de Montréal, 2013.

Beik, William. "The Absolutism of Louis XIV as Social Collaboration." *Past and Present* 188 (2005): 195–224.

Belich, James. *Replenishing the Earth: The Settler Revolution and the Rise of the Anglo-World, 1783–1939*. Oxford: Oxford University Press, 2009.

Belmessous, Saliha. "Être français en Nouvelle-France: Identité français et identité coloniale aux dix-septième et dix-huitième siècles." *French Historical Studies* 27, no. 3 (2004): 507–40.

Benton, Lauren. *Law and Colonial Cultures: Legal Regimes in World History 1400–1900*. New York: Cambridge University Press, 2002.

— *A Search for Sovereignty: Law and Geography in European Empires, 1400–1900*. New York: Cambridge University Press, 2010.

Bosher, John. "Government and Private Interests in New France." *Canadian Public Administration* 10, no. 2 (1967): 244–57.

Boucher, Philip P. "'Revisioning the 'French Atlantic': or, How to Think about the French Presence in the Atlantic, 1550–1625." In *The Atlantic World and Virginia*, edited by Peter C. Mancall, 274–306. University of North Carolina Press, 2007.

Braddick, Michael. *State Formation in Early Modern England, c. 1550–1700*. Cambridge: Cambridge University Press, 2000.

Brewer, John. *The Sinews of Power: War, Money and the English State, 1688–1783*. London: Unwin Hyman, 1989.

Buckner, Philip, and John G. Reid, eds. *Remembering 1759: The Conquest of Canada in Historical Memory*. Toronto: University of Toronto Press, 2012.

— *Revisiting 1759: The Conquest of Canada in Historical Perspective*. Toronto: University of Toronto Press, 2012.

Cain, P.J., and A.G. Hopkins. *British Imperialism: Innovation and Expansion, 1688–1914*. London: Longman, 1993.

Campeau, Lucien. *Les finances publiques de la Nouvelle-France sous les cent-associés, 1632–1665*. Montreal: Bellarmin, 1975.

Cavanagh, Edward. "A Company with Sovereignty and Subjects of Its Own? The Case of the Hudson's Bay Company, 1670–1763." *Canadian Journal of Law and Society* 26, no. 1 (2011): 25–50.

— "Possession and Dispossession in Corporate New France, 1600–1663: Debunking a 'Juridical History' and Revisiting *Terra Nullius*." *Law and History Review* 32, no. 1 (2014): 97–125.

Choquette, Leslie. "Center and Periphery in French North America." In *Negotiated Empires: Centers and Peripheries in the New World, 1500–1820*, edited by Christine Daniels, Jack Greene, and Amy Turner Bushnell, 193–206. New York: Routledge, 2002.

Christie, Nancy, ed. *Transatlantic Subjects: Ideas, Institutions, and Social Experience in Post-Revolutionary British North America*. Montreal: McGill-Queen's University Press, 2008.

— "'He is the master of his house': Families and Political Authority in Counterrevolutionary Montreal." *William and Mary Quarterly* 70, no. 2 (2013): 341–70.

Chute, Janet E. *The Legacy of Shingwaukonse: A Century of Native Leadership*. Toronto: University of Toronto Press, 1998.

Clarke, John. *Land, Power, and Economics on the Frontier of Upper Canada.* Montreal: McGill-Queen's University Press, 2001.

Clark, Henry C. *Compass of Society: Commerce and Absolutism in Old-Regime France.* Lanham, MD: Lexington, 2007.

Cliche, Marie-Aimée. *Les pratiques de dévotion en Nouvelle-France: Comportements populaires et encadrement ecclésial dans le gouvernement de Québec.* Quebec: Presses de l'Université Laval, 1988.

Coates, Colin. *The Metamorphoses of Landscape and Community in Early Quebec.* Montreal: McGill-Queen's University Press, 2000.

Collins, James B. *The State in Early Modern France.* Cambridge: Cambridge University Press, 1995.

Cook, Peter. "Vivre comme frères: Native-French Alliances in the St Lawrence Valley, 1536–1667." PhD diss., McGill University, 2008.

Cornette, Joël. *Le roi de guerre: Essai sur la souveraineté dans la France du Grand Siècle.* Paris: Payot, 1993.

Dechêne, Louise. *Le partage des subsistances au Canada sous le régime français.* Montreal: Boréal, 1994.

— *Le Peuple, l'État et la Guerre au Canada sous le Régime français.* Montreal: Boréal, 2008.

Desbarats, Catherine M. "Colonial Government Finances in New France, 1700–1750." PhD diss., McGill University, 1993.

De Vries, Jan. *The Industrious Revolution: Consumer Behavior and the Household Economy, 1650 to the Present.* Cambridge: Cambridge University Press, 2008.

Dewar, Helen. "Canada or Guadeloupe? French and British Perceptions of Empire, 1760–1763." *Canadian Historical Review* 91, no. 4 (2010): 637–60.

— "Litigating Empire: The Role of French Courts in Establishing Colonial Sovereignties." In *Legal Pluralism and Empires, 1500–1850,* edited by Lauren Benton and Richard Ross, 49–82. New York: New York University Press, 2013.

Dickinson, John A. *Justice et justiciables: La procédure civile à la Prévôté de Québec, 1667–1759.* Quebec: Presses de l'Université Laval, 1982.

— "Reflexions sur la police en Nouvelle-France." *McGill Law Journal* 32 (1986–7): 496–522.

Dickinson, John A., and Brian Young. *A Short History of Quebec.* 4th ed. Montreal: McGill-Queen's University Press, 2008.

Doyle, William. *Venality: The Sale of Offices in Eighteenth-Century France.* Oxford: Clarendon Press, 1996.

Eccles, W.J. *The Canadian Frontier, 1534–1760.* Albuquerque: University of New Mexico Press, 1983.

— *The French in North America 1500–1783.* East Lansing: Michigan State University Press, 1998.

Ferland, Catherine, and Dave Corriveau. *La Corriveau: De l'histoire à la légende.* Sillery, QC: Septentrion, 2014.

Firth, Ann. "Moral Supervision and Autonomous Social Order: Wages and Consumption in Eighteenth-Century Economic Thought." *History of the Human Sciences* 15 (2002): 39–57.

Fisher, David Hackett. *The Great Wave: Price Revolutions and the Rhythm of History.* Oxford: Oxford University Press, 1996.

Fyson, Donald. *Magistrates, Police, and People: Everyday Criminal Justice in Quebec and Lower Canada.* Toronto: University of Toronto Press, 2006.

— "La paroisse et l'administration étatique sous le Regime britannique (1760–1840)." In *Atlas historique du Québec: La paroisse,* edited by Serge Courville and Normand Séguin, 25–39. Quebec: Presses de l'Université Laval, 2001.

Gallichan, Gilles. *Livre et politique au Bas-Canada, 1791–1841.* Sillery, QC: Septentrion, 1991.

Greenwood, F. Murray. *Legacies of Fear: Law and Politics in the Era of the French Revolution.* Toronto: University of Toronto Press, 1993.

Greer, Allan. "National, Transnational, and Hypernational Historiographies: New France Meets Early American History." *Canadian Historical Review* 91, no. 4 (2010): 695–724.

Griffiths, N.E.S. *From Migrant to Acadian: A North American Border People, 1604–1755.* Montreal: McGill-Queen's University Press, 2005.

Harling, Philip, and Peter Mandler. "From 'Fiscal-Military' State to Laissez-Faire State, 1760–1850." *Journal of British Studies* 32 (1993): 44–70.

Hoffman, Philip T. *Growth in a Traditional Society: The French Countryside, 1450–1815.* Princeton: Princeton University Press, 1996.

Horguelin, Christophe. *La prétendue république: Pouvoir et société au Canada, 1645–1675.* Sillery, QC: Septentrion, 1997.

Innis, Harold. *The Fur Trade in Canada.* Revised ed. Toronto: University of Toronto Press, 1956.

Johnson, J.K. *Becoming Prominent: Regional Leadership in Upper Canada, 1791–1841.* Montreal: McGill-Queen's University Press, 1988.

— *In Duty Bound: Men, Women, and the State in Upper Canada, 1783–1841.* Montreal: McGill-Queen's University Press, 2014.

Johnston, A.J.B. *Control and Order in French Colonial Louisbourg, 1713–1758.* East Lansing: Michigan State University Press, 2001.

Kennedy, Gregory. *Something of a Peasant Paradise? Comparing Rural Societies in Acadie and the Loudnais, 1604–1775.* Montreal: McGill-Queen's University Press, 2014.

Kettering, Sharon. "Patronage in Early Modern France." *French Historical Studies* 17, no. 4 (1992): 839–62.

Kiser, Edgar, and April Linton. "Determinants of the Growth of the State: War and Taxation in Early Modern France and England." *Social Forces* 80, no. 2 (2001): 411–48.

Klein, Kim. "Paths to the Assembly in British North America: New Brunswick, 1786–1837." *Acadiensis* 29, no. 1 (2010): 133–57.

Knafla, Louis A., and Jonathan Swainger, eds. *Laws and Societies in the Canadian Prairie West, 1670–1940.* Vancouver: UBC Press, 2005.

Lachance, André. *Crimes et criminels en Nouvelle-France.* Montreal: Boréal, 1984.

— *La justice criminelle du roi au Canada au XVIIIe siècle: Tribunaux et officiers.* Quebec: Presses de l'Université Laval, 1978.

Lanctôt, Gustave. *L'administration de la Nouvelle-France.* Paris: Champion, 1929.

Langford, Paul. *A Polite and Commercial People: England 1727–1783.* Oxford: Oxford University Press, 1994.

Lawson, Philip. *The Imperial Challenge: Quebec and Britain in the Age of the American Revolution.* Montreal: McGill-Queen's University Press, 1989.

Lennox, Jeffers. "An Empire on Paper: The Founding of Halifax and Conceptions of Imperial Space, 1744–55." *Canadian Historical Review* 88, no. 3 (2007): 373–412.

MacMillan, Ken. *Sovereignty and Possession in the English New World: The Legal Foundations of Empire, 1576–1640.* Cambridge: Cambridge University Press, 2006.

Mancke, Elizabeth. *The Fault-Lines of Empire: Political Differentiation in Massachusetts and Nova Scotia, c. 1760–1830.* New York: Routledge, 2005.

Mancke, Elizabeth, and Carol Schammas, eds. *The Creation of the British Atlantic World.* Baltimore: Johns Hopkins University Press, 2005.

Mapp, Paul. *The Elusive West and the Contest for Empire, 1713–1763.* Williamsburg, VA: Omohundro Institute, 2013.

Marshall, Peter, and Glyn Williams, eds. *The British Atlantic Empire before the American Revolution.* London: Taylor and Francis, 2005.

Mathias, Peter, and Patrick O'Brien. "Taxation in Great Britain and France, 1715–1810." *Journal of European Economic History* 5 (1976): 601–50.

Milobar, David. "The Origins of British-Quebec Merchant Ideology: New France, the British Atlantic, and the Constitutional Periphery, 1720–1770." *Journal of Imperial and Commonwealth History* 24, no. 3 (1996): 364–90.

Miquelon, Dale. *New France, 1701–1744: "A Supplement to Europe."* Toronto: McClelland and Stewart, 1987.

Monière, Denis, ed. *La Gouvernance en Nouvelle-France. Bulletin d'histoire politique* 18, no. 1 (2009).

Moogk, Peter N. *La Nouvelle France: The Making of French Canada: A Cultural History.* East Lansing: Michigan State University Press, 2000.

Morgan, Cecilia. "'In Search of the Phantom Misnamed Honour': Duelling in Upper Canada." *Canadian Historical Review* 76, no. 4 (1995): 529–62.

Noel, S.J.R. *Patrons, Clients, Brokers: Ontario Society and Politics, 1791–1896.* Toronto: University of Toronto Press, 1990.

Phillips, Jim. "The Operation of the Royal Pardon in Nova Scotia, 1749–1815." *University of Toronto Law Journal* 42, no. 3 (1992): 3–14.

Pincus, Steven C.A. *1688: The First Modern Revolution.* New Haven: Yale University Press, 2009.

Plank, Geoffrey. *An Unsettled Conquest: The British Campaign against the Peoples of Acadia.* Philadelphia: University of Pennsylvania Press, 2001.

Pope, Peter. *Fish into Wine: The Newfoundland Plantation in the Seventeenth Century.* Chapel Hill: University of North Carolina Press, 2004.

Pritchard, James S. *In Search of Empire: The French in the Americas, 1670–1730.* New York: Cambridge University Press, 2004.

Reid, John G., Maurice Basque, Elizabeth Mancke, Barry Moody, Geoffrey Plank, and William C. Wicken. *Conquest of Acadia 1710: Imperial, Colonial and Aboriginal Constructions.* Toronto: University of Toronto Press, 2004.

Robichaud, Léon. "Les reseaux d'influence á Montréal au XVIIe siècle: Structure et exercise du pouvoir en milieu colonial." PhD diss., Université de Montréal, 2008.

Rushforth, Brett. *Bonds of Alliance: Indigenous and Atlantic Slaveries in New France.* Chapel Hill: University of North Carolina Press, 2012.

Schmalz, Peter S. *The Ojibwa of Southern Ontario.* Toronto: University of Toronto Press, 1991.

Shovlin, John. *The Political Economy of Virtue: Luxury, Patriotism, and the Origins of the French Revolution.* Ithaca, NY: Cornell University Press, 2006.

Smith, Donald B. *Sacred Feathers: The Reverend Peter Jones (Kahkewaquonaby) and the Mississauga Indians.* 1987. Reprint, Toronto: University of Toronto Press, 2013.

Smith, Jay M. "'Our Sovereign's Gaze': Kings, Nobles, and State Formation in Seventeenth-Century France." *French Historical Studies* 18, no. 2 (1993): 396–415.

Steele, Ian K. *Betrayals: Fort William Henry and the "Massacre."* New York: Oxford University Press, 1994.

— *The English Atlantic, 1675–1740: An Exploration of Communication and Community.* Oxford: Oxford University Press, 1986.

Storrs, Christopher, ed. *The Fiscal-Military State in Eighteenth-Century Europe: Essays in Honour of P.G.M. Dickson.* London: Ashgate, 2009.

Taylor, Alan. *The Divided Ground: Indians, Settlers, and the Northern Borderland of the American Revolution.* New York: Knopf, 2006.

Thompson, E.P. "The Moral Economy of the English Crowd in the Eighteenth Century." *Past and Present* 50, no. 1 (1971): 76–136.

Thomson, Janice E. *Mercenaries, Pirates, and Sovereigns: State-Building and Extraterritorial Violence in Early Modern Europe.* Princeton: Princeton University Press, 1994.

Trentmann, Frank. "The 'British' Sources of Social Power: Reflections on History, Sociology, and Intellectual Biography." In *An Anatomy of Power: The Social Theory of Michael Mann,* edited by John A. Hall and Ralph Schroeder, 285–305. Cambridge: Cambridge University Press, 2006.

Trudel, Marcel. *The Beginnings of New France, 1524–1663.* Toronto: McClelland and Stewart, 1973.

— *Histoire de la Nouvelle-France.* Montreal: Fides, 1963.

Weaver, John C. *The Great Land Rush and the Making of the Modern World, 1650–1900.* Montreal: McGill-Queen's University Press, 2003.

Wien, Thomas. "Peasant Accumulation in a Context of Colonization: Rivière-du-Sud, Canada, 1720–1775." PhD diss., McGill University, 1988.

— "Selling Beaver Skins in North America and Europe, 1720–1760: The Uses of Fur-Trade Imperialism." *Journal of the Canadian Historical Association* 1 (1990): 293–317.

Chapter Three

Acheson, T.W. *Saint John: The Making of a Colonial Urban Community.* Toronto: University of Toronto Press, 1985.

Ajzenstat, Janet. *The Canadian Founding: John Locke and Parliament.* Montreal: McGill-Queen's University Press, 2007.

— *The Political Thought of Lord Durham.* Montreal: McGill-Queen's University Press, 1988.

Axelrod, Paul. *The Promise of Schooling: Education in Canada, 1800–1914.* Toronto: University of Toronto Press, 1997.

Backhouse, Constance B. "Nineteenth-Century Canadian Prostitution Law: Reflection of a Discriminatory Society." *Social History/Histoire sociale* 18, no. 36 (1985): 387–423.

— *Petticoats and Prejudice: Women and the Law in Nineteenth-Century Canada.* Toronto: Women's Press, 1991.

— *Colour-Coded: A Legal History of Racism in Canada*. Toronto: University of Toronto Press, 1999.

Baker, G. Blaine, and Donald Fyson, *Quebec and the Canadas: Essays in the History of Canadian Law*. Toronto: University of Toronto Press, 2014.

Baskerville, Peter. *A Silent Revolution? Gender and Wealth in English Canada, 1860–1930*. Montreal: McGill-Queen's University Press, 2008.

Barman, Jean. *The West Beyond the West: A History of British Columbia*. 3rd ed. Toronto: University of Toronto Press, 2007.

Belisle, Donica. *Retail Nation: Department Stores and the Making of Modern Canada*. Vancouver: UBC Press, 2011.

Benedickson, Jamie. *The Culture of Flushing: A Social and Legal History of Sewerage*. Vancouver: UBC Press, 2007.

Bitterman, Rusty. *Rural Protest on Prince Edward Island: From British Colonization to the Escheat Movement*. Toronto: University of Toronto Press, 2006.

Bleasdale, Ruth. "Class Conflict on the Canals of Upper Canada in the 1840s." *Labour/Le travail* 7 (1981): 9–39.

Bliss, Michael. *A Living Profit: Studies in the Social History of Canadian Business, 1883–1911*. Toronto: McClelland and Stewart, 1974.

— *Right Honourable Men: The Descent of Canadian Politics from Macdonald to Mulroney*. Toronto: HarperCollins, 1994.

Bradbury, Bettina. *Wife to Widow: Lives, Laws, and Politics in Nineteenth-Century Montreal*. Vancouver: UBC Press, 2011.

Brown, Desmond. *The Genesis of the Canadian Criminal Code of 1892*. Toronto: University of Toronto Press, 1989.

Brown, Jennifer S.H. *Strangers in Blood: Fur Trade Company Families in Indian Country*. Vancouver: UBC Press, 1980.

Brown, R. Blake. *Arming and Disarming: A History of Gun Control in Canada*. Toronto: University of Toronto Press, 2012.

Buckner, Phillip A. *The Transition to Responsible Government: British Policy in British North America, 1815–1850*. Westport, CT: Greenwood, 1985.

Carter, Sarah. *The Importance of Being Monogamous: Marriage and Nation Building in Western Canada to 1915*. Edmonton: University of Alberta Press, 2008.

— *Lost Harvests: Prairie Indian Reserve Farmers and Government Policy*. Montreal: McGill-Queen's University Press, 1990.

Clarkson, Chris. *Domestic Reforms: Political Visions and Family Regulation in British Columbia, 1862–1940.* Vancouver: UBC Press, 2007.

Cole, Douglas, and Ira Chaikin. *An Iron Hand upon the People: The Law Against the Potlatch on the Northwest Coast.* Vancouver: Douglas and McIntyre, 1990.

Constant, Jean-François, and Michel Ducharme, eds. *Liberalism and Hegemony: Debating the Canadian Liberal Revolution.* Toronto: University of Toronto Press, 2009.

Cook, Ramsay. *The Regenerators: Social Criticism in Late Victorian English Canada.* Toronto: University of Toronto Press, 1985.

Cross, Michael S. "'The Laws are Like Cobwebs': Popular Resistance to Authority in Mid-Nineteenth Century British North America." *Dalhousie Law Journal* 103 (1984): 103–23.

Curtis, Bruce. *Building the Educational State: Canada West, 1836–1871.* London: Althouse Press, 1988.

— "'The Most Splendid Pageant Ever Seen': Grandeur, the Domestic, and Condescension in Lord Durham's Political Theatre." *Canadian Historical Review* 89, no. 1 (2008): 55–88.

— *The Politics of Population: State Formation, Statistics, and the Census of Canada, 1840–1875.* Toronto: University of Toronto Press, 2001.

— *Ruling by Schooling Quebec: Conquest to Liberal Governmentality—A Historical Sociology.* Toronto: University of Toronto Press, 2012.

Dashuk, James. *Clearing the Plains: Disease, Politics of Starvation and the Loss of Aboriginal Life.* Regina, SK: University of Regina Press, 2013.

Den Otter, A.A. *The Philosophy of Railways: The Transcontinental Railway Idea in British North America.* Toronto: University of Toronto Press, 1997.

Di Mascio, Anthony. *The Idea of Popular Schooling in Upper Canada: Print Culture, Public Discourse, and the Demand for Education.* Montreal: McGill-Queen's University Press, 2012.

Dubinsky, Karen. *Improper Advances: Rape and Heterosexual Conflict in Ontario, 1880–1929.* Chicago: University of Chicago Press, 1993.

Ducharme, Michel. *Le concept de liberté au Canada à l'époque des révolutions atlantiques (1776–1838).* Montreal: McGill-Queen's University Press, 2010.

Erickson, Lesley. *Westward Bound: Sex, Violence, the Law, and the Making of a Settler Society.* Vancouver: UBC Press, 2011.

Fecteau, Jean-Marie. *La liberté du pauvre: Sur la régulation du crime et de la pauvreté au XIXe siècle québécois.* Montreal: VLB, 2004.

— *Un nouvel ordre des choses: La pauvreté, le crime et l'Etat au Québec, de la fin du XVIIIe siècle à 1840.* Montreal: VLB, 1989.

Flanagan, Thomas. *Riel and the Rebellion: 1885 Reconsidered.* Toronto: University of Toronto Press, 2000.

Forster, J.J.B. *A Conjunction of Interests: Business, Politics, and Tariffs, 1825–1879.* Toronto: University of Toronto Press, 1986.

Fyson, Donald, and Yvan Rousseau, eds. *Cheminements: L'État au Québec: Perspectives d'analyse et expériences historiques.* Quebec: Centre interuniversitaire d'études québecoises, 2008.

Girard, Philip. *Lawyers and Legal Culture in British North America: Beamish Murdoch of Halifax.* Toronto: University of Toronto Press, 2011.

Greenwood, Murray F., and Barry Wright, eds. *Canadian State Trials, Volume I: Law, Politics, and Security Measures, 1608–1837.* Toronto: University of Toronto Press, 1996.

— *Canadian State Trials, Volume II: Rebellion and Invasion in the Canadas, 1837–1839.* Toronto: University of Toronto Press, 1996.

Greer, Allan. "Commons and Enclosure in the Colonization of North America." *American Historical Review* 117, no. 2 (2012): 365–86.

Greer, Allan, and Ian Radforth, eds. *Colonial Leviathan: State Formation in Mid-Nineteenth-Century Canada.* Toronto: University of Toronto Press, 1992.

Grittner, Colin. "Working at the Crossroads: Statute Labour, Manliness, and the Electoral Franchise on Victorian Prince Edward Island." *Journal of the Canadian Historical Association* 23, no. 1 (2012): 101–30.

Gwyn, Richard. *John A., The Man Who Made Us: The Life and Times of John A. Macdonald. Volume One: 1815–1867.* Toronto: Random House, 2007.

— *Nation Maker: Sir John A. Macdonald: His Life, Our Times. Volume Two: 1867–1891.* Toronto: Random House, 2011.

Harring, Sidney L. *White Man's Law: Native People in Nineteenth-Century Canadian Jurisprudence.* Toronto: University of Toronto Press, 1998.

Harris, Cole. *Making Native Space: Colonialism, Resistance, and Reserves in British Columbia.* Vancouver: UBC Press, 2002.

Harvey, Louis-Georges. *Le printemps de l'Amérique française: Américanité, anticolonialisme et républicanisme dans le discours politique québécois, 1805–1837.* Montreal: Boréal, 2005.

Henderson, Jarrett. "Uncivil Civil Subjects: Race, Reform, and Lord Durham's 1838 Administration of Lower Canada." PhD diss., York University, 2010.

Hodgetts, J.E. *The Canadian Public Service: A Physiology of Government 1867–1970.* Toronto: University of Toronto Press, 1973.

Jackson, James. *The Riot that Never Was: The Military Shooting of Three Montrealers in 1832 and the Official Cover-Up.* Montreal: Baraka Books, 2010.

Kealey, Gregory. *Toronto Workers Respond to Industrial Capitalism, 1867–1892.* Revised ed. Toronto: University of Toronto Press, 1991.

Kelm, Mary Ellen. "Diagnosing the Discursive Indian: Medicine, Gender, and the 'Dying Race.'" *Ethnohistory* 52, no. 2 (2005): 371–406.

Leslie, John. "The Bagot Commission: Developing a Corporate Memory for the Indian Department." *Historical Papers* 17, no. 1 (1982): 31–52.

Little, J.I. *Crofters and Habitants: Settler Society, Economy, and Culture in a Quebec Township, 1848–1881.* Montreal: McGill-Queen's University Press, 1991.

— *State and Society in Transition: The Politics of Institutional Reform in the Eastern Townships 1838–1852.* Montreal: McGill-Queen's University Press, 1997.

Loo, Tina. *Making Law, Order, and Authority in British Columbia, 1821–1871.* Toronto: University of Toronto Press, 1994.

Lutz, John S. *Makúk: A New History of Aboriginal-White Relations.* Vancouver: UBC Press, 2008.

Lux, Maureen. *Medicine that Walks: Medicine, Disease and Canadian Plains Native People, 1880–1940.* Toronto: University of Toronto Press, 2001.

Mackey, Frank. *Done with Slavery: The Black Fact in Montreal, 1760–1840*. Montreal: McGill-Queen's University Press, 2010.

Macpherson, C.B. *The Political Theory of Possessive Individualism: Hobbes to Locke*. Oxford: Oxford University Press, 1962.

Malawani, Renisa. *Colonial Proximities: Crossracial Encounters and Juridical Truths in British Columbia, 1871–1921*. Vancouver: UBC Press, 2009.

McDaniel, Jonathan. "'What is he?' Electioneering and the Emergence of Political Party Allegiance in Canada West and Ontario, 1857–1872." *Historical Discourses* 26 (2011–12): 34–61.

— "Saints and Subversives: The Place of Catholics and the Catholic Church in Upper Canadian Society in the British Imperial Context, 1791–1840." Unpublished paper, McGill University, 2009.

McKay, Ian. *Reasoning Otherwise: Leftists and the People's Enlightenment in Canada, 1890–1920*. Toronto: Between the Lines, 2008.

— "Strikes in the Maritimes, 1901–1914." *Acadiensis* 13, no. 1 (1983): 3–46.

McNairn, Jeffrey L. *The Capacity to Judge: Public Opinion and Deliberative Democracy in Upper Canada, 1791–1854*. Toronto: University of Toronto Press, 2000.

Miller, Bradley. "Emptying the Den of Thieves: International Fugitives and the Law in British North America/Canada, 1819–1910." PhD diss., University of Toronto, 2012.

Miller, James. *Compact, Contract, Covenant: Aboriginal Treaty-Making in Canada*. Toronto: University of Toronto Press, 2009.

— *Shingwauk's Vision: A History of Native Residential Schools*. Toronto: University of Toronto Press, 1996.

— *Skyscrapers Hide the Heavens: A History of Indian-White Relations in Canada*. 3rd ed. Toronto: University of Toronto Press, 2000.

Morton, Desmond. *Mayor Howland: The Citizen's Candidate*. Toronto: Hakkert, 1973.

— *A Military History of Canada*. Toronto: McClelland and Stewart, 2007.

Naylor, R.T. *The History of Canadian Business, 1867–1914*. Montreal: McGill-Queen's University Press, 2006.

Nelles, H.V. *The Politics of Development: Forests, Mines, and Hydro-Electric Power in Ontario, 1849–1941.* Hamden: Archon Books, 1974.

Nelson, Wendie. "'Rage against the Dying of the Light': Interpreting the Guerre des Éteignoirs." *Canadian Historical Review* 81, no. 4 (2000): 551–89.

Nootens, Thierry. *Fous, prodigues et ivrognes: Familles et déviance à Montréal au XIXe siècle.* Montreal: McGill-Queen's University Press, 2007.

Ouellet, Fernand. *Lower Canada, 1791–1840: Social Change and Nationalism.* Translated by Patricia Claxton. Toronto: McClelland and Stewart, 1980.

Palmer, Bryan. *Working-Class Experience: Rethinking the History of Canadian Labour, 1800–1991.* 2nd ed. Toronto: McClelland and Stewart, 1992.

Perin, Roberto. *Ignace de Montréal, artisan d'une identité nationale.* Montreal: Boréal, 2008.

Petitclerc, Martin. *"Nous protegéons l'infortune": Les origines populaires de l'économie sociale au Québec.* Montreal: VLB, 2007.

Piva, Michael. *The Borrowing Process: Public Finance in the Province of Canada, 1840–1867.* Ottawa: University of Ottawa Press, 1992.

Prentice, Alison. *The School Promoters: Education and Social Class in Mid-Nineteenth Century Upper Canada.* Toronto: McClelland and Stewart, 1977.

Ray, Arthur J., Jim Miller, and Frank J. Tough. *Bounty and Benevolence: A History of Saskatchewan Treaties.* Montreal: McGill-Queen's University Press, 2000.

Reid, Gerald F. *Kahnawà:ke: Factionalism, Traditionalism and Nationalism in a Mohawk Community.* Lincoln: University of Nebraska Press, 2004.

Robertson, Ian Ross. *The Tenant League of Prince Edward Island, 1864–1867: Leasehold Tenure in the New World.* Toronto: University of Toronto Press, 1996.

Romney, Paul. *Getting it Wrong: How Canadians Forgot Their Past and Imperilled Confederation.* Toronto: University of Toronto Press, 1999.

— *Mr Attorney: The Attorney General for Ontario in Court, Cabinet and Legislature 1791–1899.* Toronto: University of Toronto Press, 1986.

Rouillard, Jacques. *Histoire du syndicalisme au Québec: Des origins à nos jours.* Montreal: Boréal, 1989.

Rueck, Daniel. "Enclosing the Mohawk Commons: A History of Use-Rights, Landownership, and Boundary-Making in Kahnawà:ke Mohawk Territory." PhD diss., McGill University, 2013.

Ryerson, Stanley B. *Unequal Union: Confederation and the Roots of Conflict in the Canadas, 1815–1873.* Toronto: Progress Books, 1968.

Samson, Daniel. *The Spirit of Industry and Improvement: Liberal Government and Rural-Industrial Society, Nova Scotia, 1790–1862.* Montreal: McGill-Queen's University Press, 2008.

Schammas, Carol. *A History of Household Government in America.* Charlottesville: Virginia University Press, 2002.

Siegfried, André. *The Race Question in Canada.* 1907; revised ed. Toronto: McClelland and Stewart, 1966.

Smith, Andrew. *British Businessmen and Canadian Confederation: Constitution-Making in an Era of Anglo-Globalization.* Montreal: McGill-Queen's University Press, 2008.

Stevenson, Garth. *Ex Uno Plures: Federal-Provincial Relations in Canada, 1867–1896.* Montreal: McGill-Queen's University Press, 1993.

Stewart, Gordon T. *The Origins of Canadian Politics: A Comparative Approach.* Vancouver: UBC Press, 1986.

Stonechild, Blair, and Bill Waiser. *Loyal Until Death: Indians and the North-West Rebellion.* Markham, ON: Fifth House, 2010.

Strange, Carolyn, and Tina Loo. *Making Good: Law and Moral Regulation in Canada, 1867–1939.* Toronto: University of Toronto Press, 1997.

Taylor, Alan. *The Civil War of 1812: American Citizens, British Subjects, Irish Rebels, and Indian Allies.* New York: Vintage, 2011.

Tobias, John L. "Protection, Civilization, Assimilation: An Outline History of Canada's Indian Policy," in *The Prairie West: Historical Readings,* edited by R.D. Francis and H. Palmer, 206–24. Edmonton: University of Alberta Press, 1992.

Treaty Seven Elders, et al. *The True Spirit and Intent of Treaty Seven.* Montreal: McGill-Queen's University Press, 1996.

Underhill, Frank H. *In Search of Canadian Liberalism.* Toronto: Macmillan, 1960.

Van Die, Marguerite, ed. *Religion and Public Life in Canada: Historical and Comparative Perspectives.* Toronto: University of Toronto Press, 2001.

— *Religion, Family, and Community in Victorian Canada: The Colbys of Carrollcroft.* Montreal: McGill-Queen's University Press, 2005.

Vipond, Robert. *Liberty and Community: Canadian Federalism and the Failure of the Constitution.* Albany, NY: SUNY Press, 1991.

Walker, Barrington. *Race on Trial: Black Defendants in Ontario's Criminal Courts, 1858–1958.* Toronto: University of Toronto Press, 2010.

Walker, Glenn. "The Changing Face of the Kawarthas: Land Use and Environment in Nineteenth-Century Ontario." PhD diss., McGill University, 2012.

Walls, Martha Elizabeth. *No Need of a Chief for This Band: The Maritime Mi'kmaq and Federal Electoral Legislation, 1899–1951.* Vancouver: UBC Press, 2010.

Warsh, Cheryl Krasnick, ed. *Drink in Canada: Historical Essays.* Montreal: McGill-Queen's University Press, 1993.

White, Richard. *Railroaded: The Transcontinentals and the Making of Modern America.* New York: Norton, 2011.

Winks, Robin W. *The Blacks in Canada: A History.* 2nd ed. Montreal: McGill-Queen's University Press, 1997.

Wright, Barry, and Susan Binnie, eds. *Canadian State Trials, Volume III: Political Trials and Security Measures, 1840–1914.* Toronto: University of Toronto Press, 2009.

Young, Brian J. *The Politics of Codification: The Lower Canadian Civil Code of 1866.* Montreal: McGill-Queen's University Press, 1994.

Zaslow, Morris. *Reading the Rocks: The Story of the Geological Survey of Canada 1842–1972.* Toronto: Macmillan, 1975.

Zeller, Suzanne. *Inventing Canada: Early Victorian Science and the Idea of a Transcontinental Nation.* Toronto: University of Toronto Press, 1987.

Chapter Four

Alfred, Taiaiake. *Wasáse: Indigenous Pathways of Action and Freedom.* Toronto: University of Toronto Press, 2005.

Bibliography 257

Armstrong, Christopher, and H.V. Nelles. *Monopoly's Moment: The Organization and Regulation of Canadian Utilities, 1830–1930.* Philadelphia: Temple University Press, 1986.

Baillargeon, Denyse. *Un Québec en mal d'enfants: La médicalisation de la maternité, 1910–1970.* Montreal: Remue-ménage, 2004.

Banting, Keith G. *The Welfare State and Canadian Federalism.* Revised ed. Montreal: McGill-Queen's University Press, 1987.

Banting, Keith, and John Myles, eds. *Inequality and the Fading of Redistributive Politics.* Vancouver: UBC Press, 2013.

Banting, Keith, and Richard Simeon. *And No One Cheered: Federalism, Democracy and The Constitution Act.* Toronto: Methuen, 1983.

Belanger, Yale D., and P. Whitney Lackenbauer, eds. *Blockades or Breakthroughs? Aboriginal People Confront the Canadian State.* Montreal: McGill-Queen's University Press, 2014.

Belisle, Donica. "Interrogating the State: Recent Writing in Canadian Women's and Gender History." *Acadiensis* 30, no. 1 (2011): 97–105.

Bliss, Michael. *Northern Enterprise: Five Centuries of Canadian Business.* Toronto: McClelland and Stewart, 1987.

— *Plague: A Story of Smallpox in Montreal.* Toronto: HarperCollins, 1991.

Brodeur, Magaly. *Vice et corruption à Montreal.* Quebec: Presses de l'Université de Québec, 2011.

Brown, Robert Craig, and Ramsay Cook. *Canada 1896–1921: A Nation Transformed.* Toronto: McClelland and Stewart, 1974.

Brownsey, Keith, and Michael Howlett, eds. *The Provincial State in Canada: Politics in Canada's Provinces and Territories.* Toronto: University of Toronto Press, 2001.

Bryden, Penny. *Planners and Politicians: Liberal Politics and Social Policy, 1957–1968.* Montreal: McGill-Queen's University Press, 1997.

Cadigan, Sean. "Battle Harbour in Transition: Merchants, Fishermen, and the State in the Struggle for Relief in a Labrador Community during the 1930s." *Labour/Le travail* 26 (1990): 125–50.

— *Newfoundland and Labrador: A History.* Toronto: University of Toronto Press, 2009.

Campbell, Lara. *Respectable Citizens: Gender, Family, and Unemployment in Ontario's Great Depression.* Toronto: University of Toronto Press, 2009.

Campbell, Robert A. "A 'Fantastic Rigmarole': Deregulating Aboriginal Drinking in British Columbia, 1945–62." *BC Studies* 141 (2004): 81–104.

Carstairs, Catherine. *Jailed for Possession: Illegal Drug Use, Regulation, and Power in Canada, 1920–1961.* Toronto: University of Toronto Press, 2006.

Christie, Nancy. *Engendering the State: Family, Work, and Welfare in Canada.* Toronto: University of Toronto Press, 2000.

Clément, Dominique. *Canada's Rights Revolution: Social Movements and Social Change, 1937–1982.* Vancouver: UBC Press, 2008.

Coleman, Daniel. *White Civility: The Literary Project of English Canada.* Toronto: University of Toronto Press, 1976.

Comacchio, Cynthia. *The Infinite Bonds of Family: Domesticity in Canada, 1850–1940.* Toronto: University of Toronto Press, 1999.

Copp, Terry. *The Anatomy of Poverty: The Condition of the Working Class in Montreal, 1897–1929.* Toronto: McClelland and Stewart, 1974.

Cruikshank, Ken. *Close Ties: Railways, Government and the Board of Railway Commissioners, 1851–1933.* Montreal: McGill-Queen's University Press, 1991.

Dagenais, Michèle. *Des pouvoirs et des hommes: L'administration municipale de Montréal, 1900–1950.* Montreal: McGill-Queen's University Press, 2000.

Edwardson, Ryan. *Canadian Content: Culture and the Quest for Nationhood.* Toronto: University of Toronto Press, 2008.

Epp Buckingham, Janet. *Fighting Over God: A Legal and Political History of Religious Freedom in Canada.* Montreal: McGill-Queen's University Press, 2014.

Fahrni, Magdalena. *Household Politics: Montreal Families and Postwar Reconstruction.* Toronto: University of Toronto Press, 2005.

Farrish, Matthew, and P. Whitney Lackenbauer. "High Modernism in the Arctic: Planning Frobisher Bay and Inuvik." *Journal of Historical Geography* 35, no. 3 (2009): 517–44.

Ferguson, Barry. *Remaking Liberalism: The Intellectual Legacy of Adam Shortt, O.D. Skelton, W.C. Clark, and W.A. Mackintosh, 1890–1925.* Montreal: McGill-Queen's University Press, 1993.

Finkel, Alvin. *Social Policy and Practice in Canada: A History.* Waterloo, ON: Wilfrid Laurier University Press, 2006.

Flanagan, Tom. "From Riel to Reform (and a Little Beyond): Politics in Western Canada." *American Review of Canadian Studies* 31, no. 4 (2001): 623–38.

Forbes, Ernest R. *The Maritime Rights Movement, 1919–1927: A Study in Canadian Regionalism.* Montreal: McGill-Queen's University Press, 1979.

Fourcade, Marion. *Economists and Societies: Discipline and Profession in the United States, Britain, and France, 1890s to 1990s.* Princeton: Princeton University Press, 2009.

Frank, David. *J.B. McLachlan: A Biography.* Toronto: Lorimer, 1999.

Fudge, Judy, and Eric Tucker. *Labour Before the Law: The Regulation of Workers' Collective Action in Canada, 1900–1948.* Toronto: University of Toronto Press, 2004.

Gagan, David. *For Patients of Moderate Means: A Social History of the Voluntary Public General Hospital in Canada, 1890–1950.* Montreal: McGill-Queen's University Press, 2002.

Gagnon, Robert. *Questions d'égouts: Santé publique, infrastructures et urbanisation à Montréal au XIXe siècle.* Montreal: Boréal, 2006.

Gauvreau, Michael. *The Catholic Origins of Quebec's Quiet Revolution, 1931–1970.* Montreal: McGill-Queen's University Press, 2005.

Gidney, R.D. *From Hope to Harris: The Reshaping of Ontario's Schools.* Toronto: University of Toronto Press, 1999.

Glassford, Larry A. *Reaction and Reform: The Politics of the Conservative Party under R.B. Bennett 1927–1938.* Toronto: University of Toronto Press, 1992.

Granatstein, J.L. *Canada's Army: Waging War and Keeping the Peace.* 2nd ed. Toronto: University of Toronto Press, 2011.

— *The Ottawa Men: The Civil Service Mandarins, 1935–1957.* Revised ed. Toronto: University of Toronto Press, 1998.

Guest, Dennis. *The Emergence of Social Security in Canada.* 3rd ed. Vancouver: UBC Press, 1997.

Guildford, Janet, and Suzanne Morton, eds. *Making Up the State: Women in Twentieth-Century Atlantic Canada.* Fredericton: Acadiensis Press, 2010.

Heath, Joseph. *The Efficient Society: Why Canada Is as Close to Utopia as It Gets.* Toronto: Penguin, 2001.

Heron, Craig. *Booze: A Distilled History.* Toronto: Between the Lines, 2003.

— ed. *The Workers' Revolt in Canada, 1917–1925.* Toronto: University of Toronto Press, 1998.

Hubbard, Jennifer M. *A Science of the Scales: The Rise of Canadian Atlantic Fisheries Biology, 1898–1939.* Toronto: University of Toronto Press, 2006.

Humphries, Mark Osborne. *The Last Plague: Spanish Influenza and the Politics of Public Health in Canada.* Toronto: University of Toronto Press, 2013.

Iacovetta, Franca. *Gatekeepers: Reshaping Immigrant Lives in Cold War Canada.* Toronto: Between the Lines, 2006.

Kelley, Ninette, and Michael Trebilcock. *The Making of the Mosaic: A History of Canadian Immigration Policy.* Toronto: University of Toronto Press, 1998.

Kelly, James B. *Governing with the Charter: Legislative and Judicial Activism and the Framers' Intent.* Vancouver: UBC Press, 2005.

Kelly, James B., and Christopher P. Manfredi, eds. *Contested Constitutionalism: Reflections on the Canadian Charter of Rights and Freedoms.* Vancouver: UBC Press, 2009.

Kelm, Mary-Ellen. *Colonizing Bodies: Aboriginal Health and Healing in British Columbia, 1900–1950.* Vancouver: UBC Press, 1998.

Kinsman, Gary, Dieter K. Buse, and Mercedes Steedman, eds. *Whose National Security? Canadian State Surveillance and the Creation of Enemies.* Toronto: Between the Lines, 2000.

Knopf, Rainer. "Populism and the Politics of Rights: The Dual Attack on Representative Democracy." *Canadian Journal of Political Science* 31, no. 4 (1998): 683–705.

Kramer, Reinhold, and Tom Mitchell. *When the State Trembled: How A.J. Andrews and the Citizens' Committee Broke the Winnipeg General Strike.* Toronto: University of Toronto Press, 2010.

Kunitz, Stephen J., and Irena Pesis-Katz. "Mortality of White Americans, African Americans, and Canadians: The Causes and Consequences for Health of Welfare State Institutions and Policies." *Milbank Quarterly* 83, no. 1 (2005): 5–40.

Kymlicka, Will. *Multicultural Citizenship: A Liberal Theory of Minority Rights*. Oxford: Oxford University Press, 1995.

Laycock, David. "Reforming Canadian Democracy? Institutions and Ideology in the Reform Party Project." *Canadian Journal of Political Science* 27, no. 2 (1994): 213–47.

Linteau, Paul-André. *The Promoters' City: Building the Industrial Town of Maisonneuve 1883–1918*. Translated by Robert Chodos. Toronto: James Lorimer, 1985.

Loo, Tina. "Africville and the Dynamics of State Power in Postwar Canada." *Acadiensis* 39, no. 2 (2010): 23–47.

Lux, Maureen K. "Care for the 'Racially Careless': Indian Hospitals in the Canadian West, 1920–1950s." *Canadian Historical Review* 91, no. 3 (2010): 408–34.

Mackenzie, David, ed. *Canada and the First World War: Essays in Honour of Robert Craig Brown*. Toronto: University of Toronto Press, 2005.

Maioni, Antonia. *Parting at the Crossroads: The Emergence of Health Insurance in the United States and Canada*. Princeton: Princeton University Press, 1998.

Marchildon, Gregory P. *Profits and Politics: Beaverbrook and the Gilded Age of Canadian Finance*. Toronto: University of Toronto Press, 1996.

— ed. *Making Medicare: New Perspectives on the History of Medicare in Canada*. Toronto: University of Toronto Press, 2012.

Marshall, Dominique. *The Social Origins of the Welfare State: Quebec Families, Compulsory Education, and Family Allowances, 1940–1955*. Translated by Nicola Doone Danby. Waterloo, ON: Wilfrid Laurier University Press, 2006.

McKay, Ian. "Tartanism Triumphant: The Construction of Scottishness in Nova Scotia, 1933–1954." *Acadiensis* 21, no. 2 (1992): 5–47.

McKay, Ian, and Jamie Swift. *Warrior Nation: Rebranding Canada in an Age of Anxiety*. Toronto: Between the Lines, 2012.

Miller, Carman. *Painting the Map Red: Canada and the South African War, 1899–1902*. Montreal: McGill-Queen's University Press, 1993.

Morantz, Toby. "Individual Rights versus Collective Rights: The Debate on the Aboriginal Peoples of Canada." In *Tribal Communities and Social Change*, edited by Pariyaram M. Chacko, 64–82. New Delhi: Sage, 2005.

Morton, Desmond. *Fight or Pay: Soldiers' Families in the Great War.* Vancouver: UBC Press, 2004.

Morton, Suzanne. *Wisdom, Justice, and Charity: Canadian Social Welfare through the Life of Jane B. Wisdom 1884–1975.* Toronto: University of Toronto Press, 2014.

Mosby, Ian. *Food Will Win the War: The Politics, Culture, and Science of Food on Canada's Home Front.* Vancouver: UBC Press, 2014.

Murton, James. *Creating a Modern Countryside: Liberalism and Land Resettlement in British Columbia.* Vancouver: UBC Press, 2007.

Nadasdy, Paul. *Hunters and Bureaucrats: Power, Knowledge, and Aboriginal-State Relations in the Southwest Yukon.* Vancouver: UBC Press, 2004.

Nekhaie, M. Reza, and Robert J. Brym. "The Political Attitudes of Canadian Professors." *Canadian Journal of Sociology* 24, no. 3 (1999): 329–53.

Nerbas, Donald. *Dominion of Capital: The Politics of Big Business and the Crisis of the Canadian Bourgeoisie 1914–1947.* Toronto: University of Toronto Press, 2013.

Niezen, Ronald. "Culture and Judiciary: The Meaning of the Culture Concept as a Source of Aboriginal Rights in Canada." *Canadian Journal of Law and Society* 18, no. 2 (2003): 1–26.

O'Connor, Alice. *Poverty Knowledge: Social Science, Social Policy, and the Poor in Twentieth-Century U.S. History.* Princeton: Princeton University Press, 2001.

Owram, Doug. *The Government Generation: Canadian Intellectuals and the State 1900–1945.* Toronto: University of Toronto Press, 1986.

Panitch, Leo, ed. *The Canadian State: Political Economy and Political Power.* Toronto: University of Toronto Press, 1977.

Patten, Steve. "Preston Manning's Populism: Constructing the Common Sense of the Common People." *Studies in Political Economy* 50 (1996): 95–132.

Raboy, Marc. *Missed Opportunities: The Story of Canada's Broadcasting Policy*. Montreal: McGill-Queen's University Press, 1990.

Regehr, T.D. "Serving the Canadian West: Policies and Problems of the Canadian Northern Railway." *Western Historical Quarterly* 3, no. 3 (1972): 283–98.

Robinson, Daniel J. *The Measure of Democracy: Polling, Market Research, and Public Life 1930–1945*. Toronto: University of Toronto Press, 1999.

Sangster, Joan. *Through Feminist Eyes: Essays on Canadian Women's History*. Edmonton: University of Alberta Press, 2011.

Scholtz, Christa. *Negotiating Claims: The Emergence of Indigenous Land Claim Negotiation Policies in Australia, Canada, New Zealand, and the United States*. New York: Routledge, 2006.

Scott, Colin H., ed. *Aboriginal Autonomy and Development in Northern Quebec and Labrador*. Vancouver: UBC Press, 2001.

Scott, James C. *Seeing Like a State: How Certain Schemes to Improve the Human Condition Have Failed*. New Haven: Yale University Press, 1998.

Simeon, Richard. *Federal-Provincial Diplomacy: The Making of Recent Policy in Canada*. Revised ed. Toronto: University of Toronto Press, 2006.

Simpson, Jeffrey. *The Friendly Dictatorship*. Toronto: McClelland and Stewart, 2001.

Sklansky, Jeffrey. *The Soul's Economy: Market Society and Selfhood in American Thought, 1820–1920*. Chapel Hill: University of North Carolina Press, 2002.

Skogstad, Grace. "The Two Faces of Canadian Agriculture in a Post-Staples Economy." *Canadian Political Science Review* 1, no. 1 (2007): 26–41.

Struthers, James. *The Limits of Affluence: Welfare in Ontario, 1920–1970*. Toronto: University of Toronto Press, 1994.

— *No Fault of Their Own: Unemployment and the Canadian Welfare State, 1914–1941*. Toronto: University of Toronto Press, 1983.

Taylor, Charles. "The Politics of Recognition." In *Multiculturalism and the Politics of Recognition*, edited by Amy Gutmann, 25–75. Princeton: Princeton University Press, 1992.

Taylor, Graham D. *The Rise of Canadian Business*. Oxford: Oxford University Press, 2009.

Taylor, Graham D., and Peter A. Baskerville. *A Concise History of Business in Canada*. Toronto: Oxford University Press, 1994.

Thompson, John Herd, with Allan Seager. *Canada 1922–1939: Decades of Discord*. Toronto: McClelland and Stewart, 1985.

Thomson, Dale C. *Jean Lesage and the Quiet Revolution*. Toronto: Macmillan, 1984.

Tillotson, Shirley. *Contributing Citizens: Modern Charitable Fundraising and the Making of the Welfare State, 1920–66*. Vancouver: UBC Press, 2008.

— "The Family as Tax Dodge: Partnership, Individuality, and Gender in the Personal Income Tax Act, 1942 to 1970." *Canadian Historical Review* 90, no. 3 (2009): 391–425.

Titley, Brian. *The Indian Commissioners: Agents of the State and Indian Policy in Canada's Prairie West, 1873–1932*. Edmonton: University of Alberta Press, 2009.

Troper, Harold Martin. "The Creek-Negroes of Oklahoma and Canadian Immigration, 1909–11." *Canadian Historical Review* 53, no. 3 (1972): 272–88.

Tully, James. *Strange Multiplicity: Constitutionalism in an Age of Diversity*. Cambridge: Cambridge University Press, 2006.

Valverde, Mariana. *The Age of Light, Soap, and Water: Moral Reform in English Canada, 1885–1925*. Toronto: McClelland and Stewart, 1991.

Vance, Jonathan F. *A History of Canadian Culture*. Toronto: Oxford University Press, 2009.

Vipond, Mary. *Listening In: The First Decade of Canadian Broadcasting, 1922–1932*. Montreal: McGill-Queen's University Press, 1992.

Walters, Mark D. "'According to the Old Customs of our Nation': Aboriginal Self-Government on the Credit River Mississauga Reserve, 1826–1847." *Ottawa Law Review* 30, no. 1 (1998–9): 1–45.

Watson, William. *Globalization and the Meaning of Canadian Life*. Toronto: University of Toronto Press, 1998.

Whitaker, Reginald, and Gary Marcuse. *Cold War Canada: The Making of an Insecurity State, 1945–1957.* Toronto: University of Toronto Press, 1994.

Whitaker, Reginald, Gregory S. Kealey, and Andrew Parnaby. *Security Service: Political Policing in Canada from the Fenians to Fortress America.* Toronto: University of Toronto Press, 2012.

Wiseman, Nelson. "The Pattern of Prairie Politics." *Queen's Quarterly* 88, no. 2 (1981): 298–315.

— *In Search of Canadian Political Culture.* Vancouver: UBC Press, 2007.

Wright, Miriam. *A Fishery for Modern Times: The State and the Industrialization of the Newfoundland Fishery 1934–1968.* Toronto: Oxford University Press, 2001.

Index

Themes in Canadian History

Editors:
Colin Coates 2003–
Craig Heron 1997–
Franca Iacovetta 1997–1999